# HE WRITES ABOUT US

# HE WRITES ABOUT US

AN AUTOBIOGRAPHY OF A CHICAGO JOURNALIST

## KENAN HEISE

**Foreword by Mary Schmich**

**Marion Street Press**

Portland, Oregon

Published by Marion Street Press
4207 SE Woodstock Blvd # 168
Portland, OR 97206-6267
USA
http://www.marionstreetpress.com/

Orders and review copies: (800) 888-4741

"The Life of Kenan Heise" (p. 178) © 1998 by Gwendolyn Brooks.
"How Bad It Gets" (pp. 138–139), 9 Aug. 1981, © Chicago Tribune.
Reprinted with permission.
Neighbor Dialogue (pp. 143–146), June 4, 1982, © 1982 Chicago Tribune.
Reprinted with permission.

Printed in the United States of America
ISBN 978-1-936863-17-4

Front cover photo, author's portrait in the Franciscan seminary, 1947
Back cover photo by William Harper

Library of Congress Cataloging-in-Publication Data pending

*My friend, I am going to tell you the story of my life, as you wish; and if it were only the story of my life I think I would not tell it; for what is one man that he should make much of his winters, even when they bend him like a heavy snow?*

BLACK ELK, HOLY MAN OF THE OGLALA SIOUX

# ACKNOWLEDGMENTS

To my family, friends, and all of whose help I have received, I thank each of you for enduring me charitably and encouraging me generously—especially those who helped me edit this book: my wife, Carol; my brother, Joris; my son, Dan; and my friends Bob Ford and Chris Thale.

# CONTENTS

# FOREWORD

When I got to know Kenan Heise, he was the obituary writer at the *Chicago Tribune*, where I've worked for many years as a reporter and columnist.

But wait. I shouldn't say I "got to know Kenan" then. The truth is, I didn't get to know him until I read this autobiography of his astonishing life.

Poet. Historian. Dreamer. Seer. Innovator. Idealist. Bookseller. Book author. Chicago lover. Spinner of yarns. Seminarian. Husband, father, grandfather, friend. Kenan Heise—whose original name, it turns out, wasn't Kenan—seems to have had as many lives as the ten thousand he recorded in other people's obituaries.

In the *Tribune* newsroom, Kenan always stood out. He seemed too nice to be a reporter. He was paternal and chatty, helpful to the new kids in the cubicles, and he often had a kind word about other people's work.

But Kenan was far more than a nice guy. He was a nice guy on mission.

As a boy, he wanted nothing more than to be a priest. He spent years in a monastery in that pursuit. Even when epilepsy changed the course of his life and he wound up as a journalist, he never ceased to be a preacher and a minister. He simply conveyed his message via newsprint instead of a pulpit.

Some journalists try to learn their trade in school. Kenan learned it on the go. He infused his unique approach to writing with a naked moral urgency. He wrote about the poor and powerless. He lobbied to have more women represented in the obituaries. He recognized race as perhaps the most important issue of his time.

This book's title comes from something the late Cyrus Colter, an African-American Chicago novelist, told a black friend about Kenan: "He writes about us."

In the course of his busy, humble life, Kenan became friends with some of Chicago's most powerful people. Among them were Mike Royko,

Leon Despres, and Studs Terkel. If you don't know these names, you will by the end of the book.

With deceptively simple, readable prose, Kenan manages to distill his many selves into these pages, a life that has been guided by two questions: What can I do to help? How can I thank those who have helped me? Reading how he has answered those questions may inspire you to answer them for yourself.

—Mary Schmich
Chicago, Illinois

# INTRODUCTION

## Why I Have Written This Book

**A**merican journalism needs to be a door through which we can walk, to hear the voices and read the words of the many, and not just a public relations machine for the wealthy, corporate, and politically connected. Rather, its commitment should be to the poor, the middle class, workers, minorities, women as equals, the disabled, the off-beat, and those left behind—not just to those who we have been taught are "the important people."

It is inherent in the words, "a free press," that the media serve and protect all of us and be inclusive rather than exclusive by considering every person important and possessing the right to life, liberty, and the pursuit of happiness. *He Writes About Us* is the story of the path that I found and then traveled for fifty years in pursuing that conviction.

I started that journey loaded down with limitations, a serious disability, and next to no training. Yet, somehow or other, there always seemed to be someone urgently encouraging me. In retrospect, it feels as though they were legion and that they gave their support more because of the message than the messenger. I hope these facts come through in the following pages.

I was born in 1933, the worst year of the Great Depression. I grew up, nevertheless, with the parentally encouraged hope that "Things will get better," not just for me, but for everyone. In her kind foreword, *Chicago Tribune*'s wonderful columnist Mary Schmich, I believe, acknowledged this when she benevolently called me "a nice guy on mission." I have perceived it looking back far more than I ever did by seeing into the future.

Having entered the seminary to become a Franciscan priest at the age of thirteen, I spent eleven years studying to be one, the last seven in the monastery wearing the religious habit. When I developed a disability, epilepsy, I was excluded under an ancient church law and attitude that classified epileptics with those "possessed by the evil one." In fact, my disability did not actually label me "evil" to the religious community to which I belong but more along the lines of "useless."

Having left the monastery, I took up the door-to-door selling of a Catholic magazine, the *St. Anthony Messenger*. As I continued to have occasional seizures, even doing this began to seem questionable.

Although my writing had produced far more rejections than acceptances, I retained a passionate desire to write. The spur of my wanting to write was an offbeat potential about which I was confused, but which others started to recognize and encourage. Simply put—from the very first article of mine a newspaper ever published about migrant workers—I wanted to write about those whom the press did not. The encouragement I received from others trumped the rejections I had been receiving and encouraged me to persist.

I worked to devise means to help even the poorest of the poor speak for themselves, to share the power of the press with ordinary people through the Action Line column, to start the Neediest Children's Christmas Fund, and to redefine who besides "important" or successful white males should have the opportunity to get an obituary in a major metropolitan newspaper.

In her 1998 poem "The Life of Kenan Heise," Pulitzer Prize-winning poet Gwendolyn Brooks wrote:

> ... To make things go boom in the day-time
> To put forward a hand: to extend your hand that is speech of redemptive Gift
> Isn't that part of what it is like to be you, Mr. Heise?

Her words were flattering and caused me to be deeply appreciative. I have, as she indicated, created my share of "day-time booms." Still, whatever I have done, what hand I did extend or kindness I have shown was a gift given to be given away.

Not one of these, however, did I do by myself. So many people—conservatives as well as liberals, my bosses as well as those who worked under me, those in the broadcast media as well as others connected to the Internet—all were willing to help in these causes in many ways.

I promised myself when I was writing obituaries for the *Chicago Tribune* I would never write my own, much less an autobiography. But then I realized I could not let the message disappear from the printed page along with the messenger.

It has been quite a ride. You are invited to retake it with me.

# 1

# CHILDHOOD

*The author in a wicker chair of the 1930s*

# 1

## The Joy of Being JoJo

*I have overreached in life and failed ever to apologize for it.*

**M**y nickname, when I was a child, was JoJo. It was the dearest possession of my boyhood and it lasted the longest. I smiled often when I heard it and even more when I said it aloud. I still do.

It was the label on my childhood and had, for me, a sweet, innocent, and friendly ring. I think it rang a little bell for some other people also. I remember how my mother said it, more so when she wasn't chiding me. I even recall the exasperated tone my slightly bigger brother Pauly often used in yelling it when he attempted to call me to propriety.

Not everything about my childhood was sweetness and about being cared for; but the many treasured memories I have kept of those times have served me well in being appreciative and, as an adult, in reaching out to others who are as I was then.

At the age of seventeen, when I joined the Franciscan Order, I had to give up being "JoJo" and became "Friar Kenan." I had no other option but to accept this name the Franciscans had given me to symbolize, in their minds and mine, that I had given up my past life and everything personal that I held dear.

Seven years later when I left the religious life, I kept the name Kenan. I had changed and it had become a part of me; but my boyhood nickname continues to remain very special to me. I had also secretly kept memories of my earlier identity as personal treasures. Being a Franciscan or not, I hadn't given them up.

The following few pages are about JoJo, the person who I was, and about my still distinct memories of those who affirmed a little boy who kept running face-first into his limitations.

I talked too much, and some say I still do. I have overreached in life and failed ever to apologize for it. I have been overly proud of the curl of hair at the top of my forehead and it is going, going ... almost gone to the villainy of baldness.

What has been most special about my life is that people in all types of situations have been generous and helpful to me and I have long had a distinct sense that my mission in life is to pass along that which I have received from others.

One of the first outside my family who very early singled me out as an individual did so under circumstances that generated one of the mysteries of my life. The incident was so unusual and disturbing to my mother and to her religious beliefs that she intentionally did not tell me about it until I was an adult.

When my mother finally did, she pulled out an old photograph to help verify the story. The picture showed her standing in the front of the house with a baby. I was that child. "You were so sickly," she told me, "that I did not believe you were going to make it. You were skin and bones, had a hernia and impetigo, a skin disease, beyond belief. You had been sickly for some time and were not getting any better. I was so upset that I had the picture taken to remember you by." This part of the story, I had heard before. The rest—how I got better—would be the new revelation.

"About that time," she continued, "I was sitting in front of the house with you in a baby buggy when a woman, one whom I had never seen before, approached us. The woman identified herself as living a few blocks away." My mother, as she told the story, looked me straight in the eye and continued, "The woman said, 'I hear you have a sick child. I want you to know I have the power of healing.'"

By this point in her narrative, it was clear that my mother was revealing something specific that until then she had intentionally hidden from me. "I told the woman," she said, "'We are Catholics and don't believe in that.' The woman then stroked your forehead, smiled and left." Still, no real revelation. As her statement indicated, my mother was deeply and, in some ways, rigidly Catholic. And this, I knew, had something to do with what she was going to tell me next.

"I don't know what happened or why," she continued, "but within a week you had gained four or five pounds, the impetigo was gone and so was the hernia. I have never understood it."

My mother seemed to feel she had experienced a miracle out of nowhere by somebody who probably was not Catholic. As for me, I view the incident as an instance when a complete stranger cared enough to try to help me in my need. To her, I am thankful, without my judging whether or not she really believed she had the power to cure. The story also gave me a touch of something we all need, the feeling of being unique and special.

If a single event in my childhood helped forge my life in any way, it was an incident when I was perhaps six years old. I was away from our house and playing behind a store. A trunk with travel stickers on the outside attracted my attention and I climbed into it and let the lid close. It latched and I was trapped inside.

My screams, as loud as a child my age could manage, were in vain. No one was anywhere around. It was dark in the trunk and no one came to my rescue. I had no idea what to do. Even breathing started to become hard for me.

Then it happened, not from any knowledge or intent on my part, but from the instinct to do something. I tried to straighten up and my head and shoulders instead of being stopped by the lid of the trunk went through it, taking the rotten wood with them. I was free. I was not forever trapped or smothered to death. I was free.

How can we know for better or worse what impact such an experience has on the thinking and feelings of a growing child? I do not. All I do know is that I found in myself the power to overcome the greatest danger I had ever faced.

I know that I also found in others the spirit to which I was looking to aspire. JoJo's middle name was Harry after my mother's older brother, which led to one of the humorous incidents of my early existence. When in high school, formal names were called out as report cards were distributed, and the whole school assembly broke out into laughter when the first year boy they knew as JoJo was summoned in turn to the stage for his report card under the name, "Joseph Harry Heise." I think they laughed not at my name "Harry" (I had a classmate with that as his first name) but because the three names did not work together and came as a surprising revelation about the youngest Heise brother whom they knew as "JoJo."

The laughter of my schoolmates was one of many revelations that underlined a deep feeling of awkwardness. This sense of missing a beat that others seemed to hear was something I felt about myself more than I did anything that affirmed something special about me.

My uncle Harry—who was also my godfather—was someone who said "yes" to me and remains special in my memories. He lived in Columbus,

Ohio and wrote to my mother, his sister, every few months. Each letter contained the same two lines, "Catherine is doing a little better." And "How is my little JoJo?"

The "Catherine is doing a little better" comment told the story of one of the most extraordinary human relationships I have ever encountered. Aunt Catherine was Uncle Harry's wife. They had no children. In being their godchild, I was the closest they had to an offspring. After they married, my uncle had learned that his wife had contracted syphilis before they met. Within two years of their marriage, she was bedridden and remained so until her death almost sixty years later.

The whole rest of his life, nevertheless, was devoted to his Catherine. His repeated statement that "Catherine is doing a little better" was a symbol of both his fervent devotion to her and his unending optimism.

Personally, I remember how he never forgot my birthday or Christmas. He always called me, "my little JoJo," and would send me a small present such as a top, a jackknife, a toy, or a pair of slippers. The most special item he ever sent was a piece of the Hindenburg, the doomed zeppelin that burned May 6, 1937 in Lakehurst, New Jersey.

It took me a long part of my life to appreciate fully the example he had set and grasp what an inspiration he has been for me. As each of my later years have come and gone I seem to have grown more proud to have had his tender feelings toward me and his interest in my life.

My own father did not talk much about feelings. On the other hand, he certainly knew how every once in a while to express some very upbeat and tender ones. My birthday is just before Christmas and like many individuals with their special day at that time, mine seemed to get trampled anew each year. My mother, who was in charge of such matters, got my birthday wrong year after year without my realizing it. I did not learn the correct date, December 17, until we ordered a copy of my birth certificate to complete my records in order to enter high school. To this day, my brothers and sister tease me by calling me up on the wrong day and singing, "Happy Birthday."

On each occasion as a child, when the day we thought was my birthday (December 18) popped up on the calendar, I had to brace myself for how others would treat it. Some years, for example, I got a "bigger" present for Christmas rather than a separate one for my birthday. If you ever had that experience, you know how very off-putting it can feel.

Finally and decisively, my father ended my feeling sorry for myself as well as my complaints on the subject. His memorable deed occurred when I was studying theology in the seminary in Oldenburg, Indiana. I had given up expecting a birthday cake, when a delivery arrived in my name. My father had stopped off at the local bakery when visiting me three months earlier.

The surprise for me was that it was not an ordinary birthday cake, but rather a massive, tiered wedding cake, with enough pieces to allow one for every cleric in the whole monastery. I later learned it had cost my father, who was far from able to afford such extravagance, twenty-five dollars. That would be the equivalent today of two hundred dollars.

In the complicated and troubled world in which we live, my uncle's love for his bedridden wife and my father's imaginative and generous gift to his son seem but small, isolated acts of concern. Nevertheless, actions such as theirs can and did have a ripple effect that reaches to the ends of the earth. Although my own children were not born in time to have met either my uncle or my father, each of my children has heard these stories. As a result, they have gained the willingness to go an extra yard in responding to one of their unique wants because I had been shaped in part by what my uncle and father had done for me.

My mother was not as imaginative or dramatic in gift giving as my father. She gave in a different way. Despite the hectic life of poverty we faced during the Depression and the brood of seven children in her care, I always thought I was her favorite; but so did each one of my siblings. That is the measure of how good of a mother she was.

I have cherished memories of my family, of a wonderful closeness, of support when I was sick, of special Christmas traditions, of concern and celebration, of jubilant family get-togethers, and of kind acts to one another.

Claude Jr.—now dead—played well the role of oldest brother, protecting me on the playground, and later at the golf course where I caddied, from the spitefulness of others and sometimes even from the just and deserved pique of my parents.

In the monastery, I once roomed with my second oldest brother, Howard, now Father Bert. He ignored my clutter and messiness without becoming a total nag. That was a wow! experience, because he was as tidy as a matriarch. An older brother who picked up the socks you left on the floor instead of snarling at you is extraordinary. Today, having attained his eighty-third birthday, he is in a nursing home in Cincinnati. He is still vibrant and concerned about everyone around him. My brother is a good man and has been a great and noble priest.

My brother Paul—fifteen months older than I—was far more likely to remind me to pick up any socks I had left on the floor, but he has continued to be a dear friend. He is one of the most extraordinary fathers I know. Several of his children have disabilities and he has had their backs. Come to think of it, he frequently had mine when we were kids together.

Charley and I—he is younger by thirteen months—disagree on almost everything from politics to religion. Deep down, I think, we each have a true respect for the other. He has a quick wit and turns to it when the discussion starts to become personal. Thank you, Charley, for that as well as the depth, if not the direction, of your convictions.

Joris—the youngest of the six boys—is an extraordinarily caring person and is every bit as special to me these days, as he was when we were young. He has one of the most curious, inquisitive, and comprehending minds I have ever encountered. He is willing and eager to use it to help me, especially with my writing projects. He has proved over the last decade one of the great supports of my life.

After six boys, there came a girl, Mary Lou. We prayed every night for the baby to be a girl and our mother dared to tease us when we first saw her the day she was born by telling us she was "another boy." We got our prayers answered, but I think my mother did even more. Mary Lou was the one who took care of her for the last twenty-some years of her life. My sister was our "treasure" and may not always realize how much she still is. I like to think that some of the specialness we showed her as a child helped her to be the wonderful single mother she has been and to do the splendid job she did over the years as a highly appreciated first grade teacher in one of the toughest schools in the Washington, DC area.

These are some of the people who made my childhood special. There were many others. My parents' friends often took time to pay attention to us kids, especially the time my father was laid up for months with sciatica.

In 1938, my father was working two days a week at Chevrolet Gear and Axle in Detroit. Other days, he sold a wall-washing compound door to door.

My mother began a cottage industry, making flowers out of crepe and woodfibre, an imported product that looks like and has the intense colors and texture of real flowers. I started selling her hand-made corsages door to door at five years old. The first time I did it was on our block. The flowers were twenty-five cents each, and I came home with three quarters; whereas, my three older brothers altogether sold only two in a more affluent suburb.

I recall one woman who did not have enough money to buy one, but went into another room and brought out a stamp collection and handed it to me as a present. Mainly, I remember people being happy to buy one, some of them digging in the sofa to try to find coins and others who had to say "no" but found at least a smile or a few thoughtful words with which to send me on my way.

My selling lasted five years, until the war in the Pacific cut off the supply of woodfibre. The product was imported from the Philippines, which the Japanese took over as a result of battles we were hearing about at Bataan Peninsula and on the island of Corregidor.

While I do treasure these memories and feel good about the help I provided my family, I am also horrified in retrospect that I started working selling the flowers when I was five years old. Playing with my own grandchildren when they were that age, I realized that I had lost some of my childhood by focusing on earning money rather than enjoying the carefree pleasure of being a child. It created an urgency in me that would have better been tempered by my enjoying more free time and innocent recreation.

My teachers were not always sweet and indulgent, but they were dedicated from my kindergarten teacher at Wilson Public Elementary School in Ferndale, Michigan through the nuns at St. James and St. Michael's grade schools.

Some sixty years later, I still retain sympathy and appreciation for the nuns who taught us. I did not then and I do not now understand the thinking behind the heavy-handed restrictions in those days on women who go into religious life in the Catholic Church. For a sister to travel, even in an emergency such as a death in the family, it was routinely required that another member of the community be found to travel with her. Such regulations did not apply to priests, brothers or seminarians. In in many instances, such inquiries resulted in a flat-out "no" for a nun who request to make such a trip.

I had two wonderful aunts and a cousin who were members of the Sisters of St. Francis headquartered in Joliet, Illinois. Each of them over the years used what freedom they had enjoyed to find ways to be emotionally supportive of our family. I appreciated that a great deal and enjoyed visiting them in their retirements.

Ultimately, I did find a small way to acknowledge all "the good sisters," as my parents called them. Nuns scarcely ever received any public recognition or acknowledgement for their lives, sacrifices, and work.

Seemingly, they had come not to expect it. When I was later writing obituaries at the *Chicago Tribune*, I tried to make a special effort to in clude them, doing it probably more often for nuns and religious brothers (who also received very little recognition of any kind) than priests.

# 2

## A Child's Experience of the Depression

*The Depression was dying. Not for adults, but for children. Or, if it wasn't dying, it was withering on the ground, shot full of the arrows of parents' sacrifices and long-stifled hopes.*

AUNT ELLA STORIES (ACADEMY CHICAGO, 1985)

Years later, I looked back at the year 1939 and wrote the above paragraph as the lead-in for a booklet of nostalgic vignettes set in those years, which I wrote for my friends and family on the occasion of my fiftieth birthday.

The days and years of the 1930s Depression evoked an enormous amount of depressing and discouraging pain for families as poverty and a lack of opportunity always do. Children, parents, and single individuals experienced homelessness and distress beyond belief. They lost their jobs, their homes and, very often, their hope.

Still, the Depression generation—the one into which I was born—managed to hold onto the spark of humanity, the bright light of hope and life-affirming obligation to remain concerned for others as well as family and self. This we can all celebrate and treasure as our inheritance.

The *Aunt Ella Stories,* later published by Academy Chicago, imagined tales that I called up from my childhood spent in the final dire days of the Depression. I looked back at that period of my life and wanted to share the gratitude I felt toward those who had helped us—their children—survive.

While these nostalgic stories portray a positive image of that time, I have never forgotten it was out of genuine heartache that hope was born. Aunt Ella, a distinct but imaginary character, was etched into life among the members of my real family. The background of the stories—Ferndale, Michigan and the Depression—are poignantly real.

Throughout them, Aunt Ella constantly finds ways other than by spending money to survive and to show her sweet side to me. For her

sometimes bizarre but ingenious resourcefulness, she continually encoun-
ters my father's blustering consternation. In 1985, when Academy Chicago published the stories, David Mamet wrote a charming, insightful
introduction, calling them "a compendium of the miraculous, the noteworthy and the commonplace" and "a retelling of our story."

Resourcefulness was a tool, an incredible one that people used to survive hard times, like are dreams, hopes, generosity, and concern. These
themes run through the narrative as they inevitably do the books and
even the movies made about the days of the 1930s Depression. There are
always the arch-villains demanding the rent or shooing the poor off their
homesteads, but there are also the heroes and the friendly neighbors
reaching out to help. And too there is the dreamer, the idealist, envisioning a different future for him or herself and others.

The times were dark, and they were light. They were black, and they
were white. And many, many were gray. None had any splashes of color.
The days, months, and years indeed were tough, but the hearts of the
people were not, at least large numbers of them weren't. Rather, they
remain in my memory mostly generous and concerned.

During the Depression, people did many things to help make life liv-
able for others and themselves, but they also left their marks by rebuilding
the economic infrastructure of this country. They were able to do it in a
way that would help lift millions of American families off the floor and give
them the opportunity to be part of the nation's expanding middle-class.

We as their children did not understand or foresee the future, even as
our parents promised it to us. We wore hand-me-down clothes, ate what
our parents were able to put on the table and frequently heard those sad
words from our parents, "We can't afford it."

And—luckily for us—we had family. We were not Little Orphan Annies.

My Depression Aunt Ella stories attempted to recall the personal support and concern that we as children experienced. Many of us who grew
up in the 1930s have similar stories about the Christmas or birthdays gifts
we were given, the little toy, the book, the article of clothing, the outings
on which our parents took us as well as the sacrifices, which they made
in our behalf.

To me, an even greater gift they gave us was the change, which they
forged, in the economic infrastructure of the country. They worked to
rein in the excesses of the banks, allowed workers to organize, established
Social Security, and welcomed the creation of the Works Progress Administration. These transformations expanded greatly the opportunities for

their offspring to become members of the middle class and remain in it over the next three or four generations.

The poverty of the 1930s is replicated today in many poor and destitute households. It is once again an era when parents are finding it impossible to give their children the decent lifestyle they enjoyed. In some ways, it is worse. Impoverished parents and children now have television to remind them hourly how well off others are. We children of the Depression did not have that to torment us. Furthermore, the present generation is weighed heavily with drugs and the war against drugs with all its consequences.

The great positive thing about the Depression was that its people, using deep-felt hope, built for the future. And that is what today's generation is called to do every bit as much as the Depression era people were.

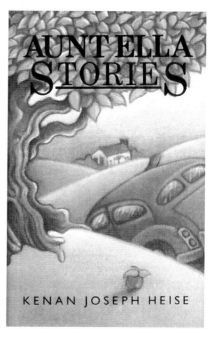

My own entrance into this world occurred at home in Ferndale, Mich., Dec. 17, 1933. Of any year in the decade, 1933 saw the lowest GDP, the Gross Domestic Product, which measures the market value of all final goods and services produced within a country. It was truly the depth of the Depression. Even the 1933 penny, as a consequence of the government minting fewer of them, is uniquely rare.

Ferndale was hit especially hard by the tough financial times because—like Detroit, its giant neighbor immediately to the south—the city's residents were heavily dependent on jobs in the stagnant auto industry. It was not a year of adding to one's "stuff," even those things that ordinary, struggling people aspire to own.

My first dated memory was a radio broadcast in 1937 that I remember hearing a newscaster announce that searchers were giving up the hunt for the missing flier, Amelia Earhart. A child, by nature, is horrified by such news no matter whom it is about. Most children have had fears of being lost in a crowd or even in an unfamiliar building. They tend to think that the idea of people giving up the search for them is the worst thing that can happen in their lives. To this day, I am thankful for the trust my parents instilled in me that they would never do that to me.

I have another memory that has haunted me and deeply affected my life both consciously and perhaps unconsciously. It involved the faces of my mother and the other adult women who were then in my life. Their complexions, when I recall their appearances, were pale; their faces, marked with heavy, dark circles beneath their eyes.

I remember staring at my mother and her friends. Slight, generous smiles were the responses given me when they caught me doing it, with them probably little realizing what I was wondering about. Other women I saw in pictures and downtown when we went there, I came to realize, had less worn, brighter faces with no dark rings beneath their eyes.

Only later and gradually did I realize why my mother and her friends looked the way they did. They were pale because they did not get outside. There was too much work to be done in the home. And their eyes were dark and faces were also colorless because they did not wear make-up. They could not afford it. What little extra money came into their lives went toward making us, their children healthier and happier.

For some reason, I felt it was my fault they looked the way they did. And, to some small, measure I was right. The money saved was for my benefit more than theirs.

The insights I came to have about the willingness of women to sacrifice for children would in later years help me turn into a full-blown supporter of women and their rights.

The Aunt Ella booklet eventually became two published books, *Aunt Ella Stories* (Academy Chicago, 1985) and *More Aunt Ella Stories* (Author-House, 2002). Aunt Ella was not entirely imagined. She represents the adult women of my childhood as well as the single, caring mother, aunt, or grandmother raising children in poverty today.

The historical record has not focused enough on the people of the 1930s and how they fought not only for better lives for themselves, but also for economic and political changes that would make life better for their children in the next generation.

Labor unions, responsible professional organizations and service providing institutions, I feel, helped carry hope up the hill and do so to this day. Legislation such as bank reorganization, the Works Progress Administration, Social Security, the minimum wage, and welfare reform generated a new and broader middle class that made it far easier for us, their children, to join.

Even my father, who was billy clubbed for walking through a picket line, later came to appreciate the benefits that a good union could secure for its members and willingly made use of the entitlement programs initiated in the 1930s.

Three decades later, I was a young newspaper reporter at *Chicago's American*, a *Chicago Tribune*-owned newspaper long since out of existence. It was clear to all of us that our only right as workers was to be employees and that, only for as long as management wanted us to be.

I had a problem. It was one that was on the horizon. A college professor in the seminary, however, had seared my soul with the statement, "A lie is a violation of the intellect."

I heard what he said and agreed on that deep level that you find yourself willing to fight rather than give up your conviction. I believed what he had told me and have tried to live accordingly. To follow his dictum meaningfully, I needed security, more than I felt I had as a reporter. We had a night city editor, Harry Romanoff, who constantly either lied over the phone to get stories or had his reporters do it. And I was scheduled to go on nights and be under his thumb.

Fortunately, I did not get assigned to nights because I was chosen instead to edit the new Action Line column. Still, I felt at the mercy of what an editor told me to do. I was at the bottom of seniority and status. I did not feel I had any leeway to stand up to an editor.

What was I going to do?

Then, relief came in a form I never expected—our union.

Ralph Whitehead—an especially intelligent, outspoken reporter—found himself harassed at *Chicago's American* by an assistant city editor, who all but forced Ralph to quit.

The newspaper had a (non-Newspaper Guild) union, made up of the editorial employees of our paper and the Racing Forum. It was the smallest—and seemingly one of the most ineffective unions—in the AFL-CIO.

Whitehead filed what seemed like a non-winnable grievance against the paper and his tormentor. Taking on and carrying through the grievance cost our weak, little union $5,000, an outrageously high amount, especially since our union's treasury was almost depleted.

The results were completely unexpected. He won. We won.

The win gave me a sense of security and self-confidence in following my conscience. We had won our rights, ones that meant we too could file grievances if we had to do so. Somebody had my back. It was our little, weak union, but it meant we were not slaves, not even remotely so. I still had to duck and dodge once in a while, but I felt incredibly free and independent as a reporter for the rest of my years as a journalist. This was a benefit in my life that came from those who stood up for their rights as members of a union.

There are other benefits I can trace back to the 1930s. Today, my wife and I both receive Social Security and it is making our lives fuller and far happier than if it had not been enacted when I was two years old.

Over the years, I have enjoyed time and again the state and national parks that the WPA built in the 1930s. I collected the WPA state guides, the reading of which gave me some of the most unbiased history of this nation and our states that I have encountered.

I am thankful above all for the memories that stay with me from my childhood in the 1930s.

People seemed to be more friendly and open then, more giving and sharing of what little they had. The one, the greatest treasure they had and knew they did have—was we, their children.

And, yet when the 1940s came and with them a terrible world war, the people of the 1930s offered up to the military and possible death or harm their most precious possessions—the lives, the existence of their children—in behalf of this country and its profound beliefs.

In many ways, we continued to feel the pervasive reverberations of the good will spawned in the 1930s until the "Me Decade" of the 1980s, when safety net programs were slashed, volunteerism dropped to a low of 20 percent, unions declined, and Reaganomics argued that "trickle-down economics" would take care of those on welfare.

Personally, however, I still feel empowered by the 1930s and the people who looked after us during those years.

# 3

## A Courageous Woman

*I can never forget—nor should any of us—either the people who died or the heroes who rose up and fought back against the Nazis with determination and courage from April 19 to May 16, 1943.*

BARBARA STEINER, SURVIVOR, *COURAGE AND RESISTANCE: REMEM-BERING THE WARSAW GHETTO UPRISING* (AUTHORHOUSE, 2006)

**M**y dear friend of later years, Barbara Steiner, and I can look back to September 1939 as a life-changing month in our lives, but for very different reasons. For each of us, living a half a world apart, the impact of that month could not have been more different.

I was six years old, but I remember those days as the ones that nudged our family upward and away from the dreariness of the Depression. Anything white or brightly colored had to be cleaned or repainted and that cost money at a time when there was little of it. As a consequence, people did not expect whiteness or bright colors in clothing, structures, cars, billboards, or even toys.

A dramatic difference came through my eyes and into my conscious-ness. Colors that suddenly and sharply contrasted with the dreary lack of them that had signified our poverty and the harshness of the Depres-sion. Color came into my environment from three sources: the greatest display during the twentieth century of the northern lights; the dramatic explosion of Technicolor in the movie *The Wizard of Oz*; and the exciting, multicolor swatches used for announcing GM's new, no-longer-available-only-in-black car models. So much for the positive in life!

Barbara Steiner is Jewish, a little older than I and was then a pre-teen. In her memoirs—which I helped edit and get published—she recalled September 1939 for an almost complete loss of color in her life. Up until then, her childhood in Warsaw Poland had seemed charmed and was full of a brightly tinged happiness. That life—as she knew it—ended as the Nazis invaded Poland and herded her family and 350,000 other Jews into the confined area of the Jewish ghetto, where almost every one of them would die or be exported to death camps. Barbara was able to participate in the desperate April 1943 uprising, providing medical assistance for those fighting German tanks with hand weapons. Of the more than fifty persons in her extended family, she alone survived.

More than seventy years have gone by. The paths of us two children of 1939—one who found color and the other who lost it—intersected. We worked together, the two to us, to get her sorrow-filled, but brave-souled memories recorded and published in a book: *Courage and Resistance: Remembering the Warsaw Ghetto Uprising* (AuthorHouse, 2006).

I thank Barbara for letting me help her share that experience with the world. She stands increasingly alone today as a witness to the evil thing that happened to her family and fellow Jews in the Warsaw Ghetto during World War II.

Now a resident of Chicago, she has been a hard-charging dynamo in getting that story out to all who will read what she wrote or listen to her tell her story. In the very first sentence of the introduction to her book, she defines who she is today: "I am a survivor. I am a witness. Each of us needs to tell our story to all who will read or listen."

Her account is genuine and crucial in helping us understand what happened and can happen again in the ruthless domination of a people. The introduction to her book includes Barbara's detailed summation of what occurred:

> A fate that I will never understand chose me to survive. Only a handful of us are alive today who were penned up on April 19, 1943 in Warsaw's ghetto. Over the previous two years, the vast majority of the 350,000 Jewish residents—including the members of my immediate family—had died from the terrible conditions there, had been capriciously murdered, or were shipped off to death or concentration camps.
>
> Hitler's birthday was April 20. Heinrich Himmler, organizer of the mass murder of the Jews throughout the Third Reich, had determined to dispose of the perhaps 50,000 or less Jews who were left in the Warsaw Ghetto. It was to be a three-day effort starting April 19 and offered as a birthday present to the Fuehrer.
>
> His Gestapo-led troops met instead a resistance to the death from the residents who had smuggled in weapons and created them out of whatever they could find. I was there as a witness and a participant.

I can never forget—nor should any of us—either the people who died or the heroes who rose up and fought back against the Nazis with determination and courage from April 19 to May 16, 1943. They are all part of the story that a destiny, which I cannot fathom, has determined for me to testify to.

All my close relatives and family friends died in the Shoa in Poland. I alone survived. And yet it was actually a different Barbara who survived. It was neither the sweet, pampered child I had been before the war; nor the sensible woman I was yet to become, but a hounded teenager—wary, cautious, and shrewd.

This is my story and the story of those I knew and loved. My children and my children's children will never get to hear their grandparents' voices, or those of their aunts, uncles, and cousins, or the companions of my childhood. This is the story of all three Barbaras—pampered child, hounded teenager, and sensible woman–as well as our families and the communities in which we lived.

It is clear we are called to make commitments proportionate to our awareness of the realities of our times. I feel myself, as a result, bound to all Jews through the Holocaust.

I found Barbara because I went looking for her. I had just finished editing *Candles Burned in Chicago*, the story of the Chicago-based Midwest Jewish Council's annual programs commemorating the Warsaw Ghetto Uprising. Having done so, I wanted to meet someone who could personalize for me what had happened to the people trapped in the Warsaw Ghetto. And that is what Barbara did.

Some years before, she had dictated the manuscript based on her experiences, but it had not been edited nor could she get it published. At first, I tried my own agent, who happens to be Jewish. He felt, however, there was no longer a market for a book about the Holocaust. I argued in vain that while the story of Warsaw Ghetto Uprising indeed was a significant part of the Holocaust story, it also stood as a unique event in itself. I had also tried a university press, where I had a contact and from which published materials written by Holocaust survivors. Again, the answer was a "No."

Finally, my promise to get it published took me to a print-on-demand publisher and paying for it myself. It is a story, the likes of which I have never encountered in my life. It is her story, Barbara's, a wonderful human being, who kept the divine spark alive in the greatest darkness imaginable.

Here is a passage from the book that I think tells us how she managed it:

> The woman who once worked for our family when I was nine years old hit her baby. When the child cried, I did also, almost uncontrollably. One day when a man called me ugly names in the street, I ran home sobbing. My father told me, "This man says things to those around him. You can get angry, but do not go to that man's level and let it hurt you."
>
> That was the Barbara Zyskind (her maiden name), who at the age of 14 was living in Warsaw Poland when the Germans invaded and ruthlessly moved forward in their plans to degrade and destroy all of us, adult and child alike, who were Jews.
>
> . . . .
>
> It is about those whose lives I shared and to whose deaths I can attest.
>
> It is about the Jewish Warsaw Ghetto and the uprising in which we—men, women and children—fought the Nazis with every means we could.
>
> . . . .
>
> And most profoundly, it is about an unshakable sadness that I carry with me, because it really did happen.

Barbara is now in her eighties and her health is not what it was, but she still speaks wherever she can and sells copies of *Courage and Resistance*. A resilient human spirit, Barbara has joyously rediscovered hope and color through her love of life, her family, her faith, and her world.

# 4

## Thank You to the Boy Next Door,
## Who Died for Democracy

*Eddie never became the person he might have been, and yet he did…He
preserved an extraordinary heritage—democracy—that causes each of
us to rely on the other, to trust in the people of our nation.*

**M**y next-door neighbor, Eddie Goff, when I was ten years old, died for democracy. He was a real person to me. His sister was my childhood playmate. And he was her older brother and a little bit mine.

It was World War II. We were fighting the Nazis and their fascist belief that the state was God. We had something better, more ennobling of the individual—democracy. And Eddie died for it. The war was almost over. I had been cutting the headlines out of the newspapers and they told me that. Soon, our troops were going to cross the Rhine River and then we would be fighting in Germany itself and the Allies would end this scary war. Eddie did not make it across the Rhine and into Germany. He died in the battle to take it.

The preservation of democracy was his gift to me and to the nation. It is the greatest of gifts. It makes us the equivalent of kings, human beings empowered with inalienable rights, among which are those that protect and extend our lives, our liberty, and our pursuit of happiness.

Eddie Goff's body is buried in one of those massive fields of white crosses that testify to the enormous number of Allied soldiers who gave their everything to oppose tyranny and preserve democracy. Somehow what he had done stuck with me, as did Eddie's name. He personalized the cause of a war that I had thought of as us against them, good guys versus the bad. Lincoln's Gettysburg Address helped etch that feeling into the most reflective of words:

Four score and seven years ago our fathers brought forth on this continent, a new nation, conceived in Liberty, and dedicated to the proposition that all men are created equal.

Now we are engaged in a great civil war, testing whether that nation, or any nation so conceived and so dedicated, can long endure. We are met on a great battlefield of that war. We have come to dedicate a portion of that field, as a final resting place for those who here gave their lives that that nation might live. It is altogether fitting and proper that we should do this.

But, in a larger sense, we cannot dedicate—we cannot consecrate—we cannot hallow—this ground. The brave men, living and dead, who struggled here, have consecrated it, far above our poor power to add or detract.

Abraham Lincoln was talking about soldiers like Eddie, who had given their lives for a nation that in its Declaration of Independence stated all men are created equal. And next Lincoln helped us conclude, "We here highly resolve that these dead shall not have died in vain—that this nation, under God, shall have a new birth of freedom."

The Rhine was in front of me and would be all my life. I had to find the means and the courage to cross it no matter what the cost. Eddie helped. He left behind an extraordinary heritage—democracy—that causes each of us to rely on the other, to trust in the people of our nation (not always or in every way) but for the rock-bottom assurance of our rights and freedom. And, if I didn't, the thought of Eddie Goff would haunt me all my life.

During World War II, even we children found ways to express our commitment to the cause for which Eddie died: We made balls out of tinfoil, saved old newspapers and bound them, collected rubber and steel, hesitated to complain about the things we had to do without because they were rationed and we purchased ten-cent savings stamps that helped finance the war effort. We didn't do all these things all the time, but we saw ourselves as child patriots when we did.

The war was not a game of cops and robbers or cowboys and Indians. After the war was over, Eddie and others who gave their lives were still dead and the new task lay before us. Instead of preserving democracy, the new cause was to extend it to the many people in this country who did not enjoy the equal rights for which Eddie and so many others had died.

In his January 20, 1949 State of the Union Address to Congress, President Truman expressed this challenge another way: "If we succeed it will not be because of what we have but because of what we are; not because of what we own but because of what we believe."

As I grew up, I continually heard and participated in loose talk about how stupid people are, that they do not care, and how they are out only for themselves. I no longer believe that. Somewhere along the line, it dawned on me that each judgment or statement that puts down people diminishes the reality of democracy, the tactileness of it.

We shudder at the following antidemocratic words that Alexander Hamilton expressed during the debates over the framing of the United States Constitution in the 1780s:

> Take mankind in general, they are vicious, their passions may be operated upon. ... There may be in every government a few choice spirits, who may act from more worthy motives. One great error is that we suppose mankind more honest than they are. Our prevailing passions are ambition and interest; and it will ever be the duty of a wise government to avail itself of the passions, in order to make them subservient to the public good.

Many Americans, even today, idolize Hamilton, for any number of reasons, especially for promoting the United State Constitution and establishing the first government-owned bank. Yes, according to his biographer, Ron Chernow, Hamilton so strongly supported the wealthy of this country that he not only disdained "mankind in general," but deeply believed "the rich could put their own interests above the national interest."

In contrast, in his book-long 1936 poem, "The People, Yes," Carl Sandburg presented a fascinating contrast to such thinking when he wrote:

> The learning and blundering people will live on.
> They will be tricked and sold and again sold
> And go back to the nourishing earth for rootholds,
> The people so peculiar in renewal and comeback,
> You can't laugh off their capacity to take it.
> The mammoth rests between his cyclonic dramas.

If we do not believe to some degree in the goodness of the people, how do we ask a soldier, a police officer, an astronaut, or someone serving in a contagious ward to risk their lives daily for them? I think we do believe in the people with the caveat Sandburg and other great writers have expressed.

I am mindful of the great sacrifices people in the past made in behalf of us, unknown or even yet to be born. My great-grandfather, Jonas Bigelow, was a soldier in the Civil War and his diary tells of him twice being taken prisoner. My father and three of my brothers served as millions of other Americans have done. They put themselves in harm's way for democracy. My oldest brother, Claude, was severely disabled at the Shreveport, Louisiana Air Force base in a 1951 crash of the same B-29 Bomber in which he had flown missions during the Korean War.

The memory of what Eddie Goff sacrificed has kept him alive in my heart and mind and continues to connect me to him 65 years later. His is the name I remember from when I lived in that block. When I wrote a novel, *The Sin of Obedience*, I needed to find a name for a character, who acted in the stead of a big brother for the protagonist and then disappeared. I gave that caring person the name of Eddie Goff.

Eddie never became the person he might have been, and yet he did. On the fiftieth anniversary of the peace treaty that ended World War II, I was able to pay homage to the memory of those who died in the war by suggesting to the editors of the *Chicago Tribune* that they publish a special section with all the names of those soldiers and sailors from Illinois who died in the war. On September 2, 1995, the fiftieth anniversary of the signing of the terms of surrender by the Japanese aboard the U.S.S. Missouri, the newspaper responded to my suggestion. It honored the soldiers and sailors from Illinois who had perished in the war by listing the names of all 22,283 of them.

I was asked to write an introduction and out of respect for the occasion, made it brief. In addition to thanking those from the Illinois State Historical Society who provided us with the names, I wrote: "In the spirit of "Lest we forget," in the name of those who died and with a thought to family members who survived, the Chicago Tribune offers this list of those who died in World War II."

# 5

---

## June 22, 1946:
## A Fatal Automobile Accident Affects the Future

*I was twelve years old and had no idea then that there was a word*
*"surreal," much less what it meant, but I certainly was*
*experiencing it.*

In life, as in the most edgy of dramas, a single, seminal event can stop the tide and forcefully turn it in a different direction. And this is what on June 22, 1946 happened to me and to the family of a man who was doing my brothers and myself a small favor.

It was a car accident, a totally out-of-nowhere, metal-twisting, and death-dealing crash. It put two of my brothers and me in the hospital and caused the death of the driver. I had been sitting next to him and my face went through the passenger-side windshield.

I was working as a caddy at Birmingham Country Club just west of 14 Mile and Southfield Roads in Birmingham, Michigan. My brothers and I were very young for being caddies. World War II had been an occasion for boys only eight or nine years old, including myself, to be hired as caddies. The driver of the car was a member at the golf course. My brother Paul had caddied that day for a different golfer in the same foursome as the man who gave us the ride. Perhaps, this fact was why, when he saw us hitchhiking at the entrance to the club, he was more than willing to give my brothers and me a ride the three and half miles home.

The accident happened at the then rural intersection of 11 Mile and Southfield Roads. A driver heading west on 11 Mile had ignored the stop sign at the intersection and hit us broadside. Even recalling the startling impact today brings up in my chest a tangible, unpleasant fright. That moment ended the abandon, the let-happen-what-may attitude of my childhood. I was not in control and, out of the corner of my eye, saw the car coming and realized in a second that it would not stop. No longer would I be the carefree child who could run freely across streets whenever I wanted.

Three of my brothers—Howard (now, Father Bert), Paul, and Charley—were in the back seat. I was in the front. "Hitching a ride" was the usual way we and other caddies got to and from the golf course. In those days, no bus lines served our suburban Southfield world.

The car in which we were riding rolled over three times, hit a deep ditch, and then flipped back over front. It was before shatterproof glass. My face went not only into but also through the windshield. Charley broke his leg in three places and Paul suffered a long gash in his forehead. Howard was unhurt. It was in an era before seatbelts and the driver of our car was thrown out of it and subsequently died. His last name was Buckingham and he had a family. That is all I was ever to learn of him.

The attention of those who started to crowd around the damaged car focused on the blood spurting from my face. Out of a sense that combined responsibility with irresponsibility, the somewhat intoxicated driver of the car that hit us borrowed someone else's car and rushed me to Mount Carmel Hospital seven miles away. He let me off at the front steps to walk up the stairs leading to the reception desk in the lobby, which was then especially crowded because it was the beginning of visiting hours. "Where should I go?" I asked. "I'm hurt."

By this time, my clothes were covered with blood and my face was continuing to spurt more of it. The receptionist's mouth was agape and her speech, stuttering. Not certain as to whether to lead me to the right or the left of the large, semicircular desk, she reached over, picked me up and carried me off to the emergency room. There, pressure was applied and the bleeding stopped. My brothers were brought in and put on gurneys next to mine.

Howard got to a payphone and, with concern about shocking my parents, informed them that we had been in a "minor accident" and we had been taken to Mount Carmel Hospital. They arrived as soon as my father's well-known heavy foot on the gas pedal could get them there. My brother Paul was groaning and my mother attempted to calm him by assuring him he was not as bad off as the boy on the next gurney (meaning me, whom she did not recognize because of the blood that covered my face.)

At this point, the accident—the unbelievable—had happened and my fate was in the talented hands of the resident physician (in training to be a plastic surgeon). He did a superb job of repairing the damage. I would not die or even be horribly scarred, but the turn into the forceful winds of the future had begun.

To this day, of course, I still bear some traces of the scars of the accident on my face. Never once have I had occasion to regret they are there. They are not easy for others to notice. The physician has my gratitude. I would, from a 1964 accident, acquire more scars from sixty more stitches. I have always accepted them as one of the more normal aspects of my appearance as well as a reminder of past near-tragedies.

Over the years, I have probably told one hundred people—maybe many more—the story of what happened the moment that followed the stitching up of my forehead, eyelids and lip. I was twelve years old and had no idea then that there was a word "surreal," much less what it meant, but I certainly was experiencing it.

In a strange, murky vision, I could see the future, however unclearly. I was alone. My parents did not count. Nor did my brothers or the doctors. I knew I could have died. I realized I would not. But what was to come? Someday I would die. I knew my vulnerability as a human being living in an all-too-mortal body. I became aware that on the outside, I would continue to be the same, but never again on the inside. I would not continue to be as carefree as I had been all my days.

The moment passed. The impact of it did not. When I was released two weeks later with thirty some stitches up and down and across my face, I got into the car with the bandages finally removed. I was glad to be heading home; at least until we came to an intersection and I saw a car on a side street heading toward us. I was certain it was not going to stop. It did, but the same fear hit me at the very next intersection and would for decades afterwards.

In my inner self, I was overwhelmed by a fear of riding in a car, a fear that would last thirty years and then transpose into a fear of flying that is with me still. It was and actually is more than a fear. It is a terror and my efforts to shoo it away with hypnotism and psychological therapy have been in vain.

And I had most likely suffered some brain damage, a likely cause of my epilepsy later in life. I was still myself. I was still JoJo. But I was also a squirrel that wanted to build my nest as high as possible in a tree, where the cold and the frost could never snatch my life away from me.

Sixty-seven years have passed and I am still that squirrel.

# Part II

# THE SEMINARY AND MONASTERY

# 6

## The Seminary:
## Exultation Wrapped Up in a Paradox

*When I hear or read about some other child being sexually abused, the painful memory of being in someone else's emotionally powerful grip threatens to cut off my breathing. Fortunately, something happened in my situation that kept the grip from tightening on me.*

In September 1947, I took a Greyhound bus to the Franciscan seminary in Mount Healthy, Ohio, three hundred miles away from my home in Southfield, Michigan. It was the beginning of a front-seated journey that engendered far more anticipation and thrill than any around-the-world trip or imaginable vacation trip to an exotic location could have.

In my case, I had experienced an unusual added incentive for going off to the seminary. Two of my older brothers had started on the journey before me and assured me it was better than great.

I was thirteen years old and God was calling me to be a priest. Despite my age, I had tied myself to a deeply purposeful mast and was hearing not the siren call of teenage female charmers, but rather the life-directing words of Matthew 22:14: "Many are called, but few are chosen." These were the words of Jesus at the wedding feast. The priests at the seminary applied them to those of us who they felt had vocations to become priests. And we, with proud self-satisfaction, accepted them. What a path they laid out for us!

Skiing can really look great, especially from the start of the run and I was on the top of the mountain. Becoming a priest—from everything I was hearing about it—would be an incredible experience in itself. And, in truth, it was a stunning, if aborted, run. When people in my world learned I was going to the seminary, they—for the most part—started distinguishing me as never before in my life. Some of them, I believe, did so because they were considerate people and respectful of the priesthood; others, I think, because I was in a spotlight that might almost be called a halo. I learned a lot, became a more reflective person and struggled with profound issues that I think all human beings are deeply challenged to explore on some terms or other.

For all this I am deeply thankful, especially to those who insightfully steered me away from absorption with my own needs and turn my focus toward others. The seminary itself was a cake with icing on it. I more than enjoyed it; I gobbled it up. I choose to go into a seminary, commit myself to becoming a priest, and remain celibate, willing to give up forever having sex, a wife, and children. Why? If my father loved my mother—and I believed he did so in a very special way—why would I give up ever having that kind of love or that personal of a companionship?

I was on a high, a spiritual and self-fulfillment euphoria that diminished things that were off to the side. And, if they were not off to the side, I put them there.

I was on a mission; one that I felt God had given me through his church and the priests who ran the seminary.

I was at an age when sheltered children begin to feel the world getting bigger around them and competition with their peers causes them to seek the high ground as a distinct way to stand out and become special.

All this can be overwhelming to someone seeking direction in his or her life at that age. Later, these drives and little-understood commitments would give way in my later teens to new ones, equally little understood. Difficulties, I would very slowly discover. They do so arise when deep-rooted change is not total and the individual is left with contradictory goals. This happened to me, but I did not get a whiff of it for many years.

I was encouraged to have "a personal relationship with God." I tried very hard to do so. I worked on it with such fervor that it felt as though I did have it.

I prayed hard, read the Bible all the way through, resisted various minor temptations assiduously and took the sacraments of the church seriously. And I loved sports, everything from hiking to ledgeball. I also loved softball and volleyball. Most of all, I loved that the seminary had an outdoor swimming pool. And I tried to be good and say the right things. While I was not always successful, I seemed to be getting better at it. There was a route determined for us, and I tried to stay in the middle of it. The message we received at each and every stage was that the seminary led to the priesthood.

My hormones were not an in-my-face issue, but I did work out a timid compromise that I could read something that might "accidentally" arouse me if it were a "good" book. Not many such tempting books were available in our seminary library, however. The seminary was a thrill also because I was being given the opportunity—poor kid that I was—to attend a very exclusive boarding school, get a classical education and become a priest, one of the noblest professions I could then imagine; no, the noblest.

It was about me, because being chosen as a candidate for the priesthood made me special. It put me in a category separate from all women (including my mother, my little sister, the girls in my grade school class, and even the nuns who taught me). It also put me an enormous step beyond my father and the other ushers at church, because they were married and consequently not called to be a priest, nor eligible to be one.

Then there were the Franciscan priests. Any number of these men "chosen" by God truly seemed to embody the ideals and aspirations I wanted to share. Most of those who were my teachers in the seminary were good men and, for the most part, excellent teachers. They certainly were better trained and therefore more qualified than the nuns who had taught me in grade school. I thank those nuns and those priests for everything they gave me from their hearts and from the training they did have.

Father Vincent Kroger, who formerly headed up our Cincinnati-based province as its Provincial, taught us both freshman English and Latin. He sped us through the textbooks and then spent the last third of the school year helping us study the subjects in context. It was the most brilliant way of teaching I was ever to encounter.

Father Ralph Ohlman, who taught history and civics, was an offbeat character with a brilliant and rebellious mind. He had been studying for a doctorate in Germany in the late 1930s, but had been kicked out by the Nazis. He wrote a concentration camp play that the school body staged while I was at the seminary.

His offbeat mentality showed up distinctly in a joke he told us in class that touched the funny bone of thirteen- and fourteen-year-old boys in a seminary:

Question: "Do you know what the bellybutton is for?"
Answer: "For putting salt in when you eat celery in bed at night."

I thank in particular "Uncle Joe" (the late Father Ermin Schneider) for flunking me in German on my first six weeks report card. It proved a good life lesson. Even more, I thank Father Leonard Foley, also now deceased. He taught me to reach down the ladder to help whoever was there and needed it. For want of any better way of expressing it, his example led me to grasp the meaning of empathy. It was a key that would open many doors for me. He altered what I had felt was my mission, making it not only about God, but mankind also. Father Leonard gave me new, more complex goals that were more tangible and which allowed me to have my own faults.

How did he teach me this key to a good life, human empathy? By having it himself. In a preparatory high school, whether a seminary or an exclusive Ivy League one, concern for those on the fringe—I have been assured—is not often taught by word or example. He showed me to reach out with kindness toward those whom the group did not embrace. What he taught me was, I feel, the great lesson of my life.

Through all the attention he paid to and kind things he did for my marginalized classmates—the kids who were outsiders—Father Leonard set quite an example. He embodied the principle of including rather excluding those in need of friendship. As a result, I saw it so clearly that I was constantly conscious of how far I was from reaching his level of understanding the simple role of being a good human being. We had, for example, a classmate whom we called "Messy Jessie" in our meaner moments. Father Leonard made a point of calling him not simply by his last name or more familiar "Billy," but the more respectful "William."

Father Randolph Thompson embodied the opposite—sexual abuse. Even though he is long dead, his memory is still a thorn in my heart. It is framed with his infamy and buried there beneath a mountain of sadness. When I was fourteen years old and a seminarian at St. Francis Seminary, he tried to molest me.

This sophisticated, debonair second-year priest, smelling of Old Spice aftershave lotion, had wooed me. Previously, before becoming a Franciscan and being ordained, he had been a member of the Christian Brothers religious congregation. Father Randolph was mentally sharp and aloof, but he could be extraordinarily friendly. I, on my part, was in my second year in the seminary and excelling in geometry, the subject that he taught. I was one of the youngest in my class and, for reasons that had much to do with the strictness of my family's moral upbringing, one of the most innocent.

Father Randolph always seemed to be around when I least expected him to be, especially when few if any other people were. He came close up to me when we talked, often complimenting me and, with his friendly smiles, making me feel special in a personal way that no one else ever had before. He was my teacher and treated me as though I were his pet student.

I reacted to his wooing by nibbling at it. Then, in a situation I did not anticipate, he talked me into leaving a church service and meeting him alone in one of the curtained door guest parlors. He was already there when I arrived. He gave me one of his big smiles and then embraced me, pressing his full body against mine. My body warmly tingled; my mind went blank.

Probably only a minute passed. I had no sense of time. I felt confused about what was going on and why I was there. The smell of Old Spice wafted up my nose and it, too, tingled. It was for only a couple of seconds, but I have never in my life felt less in control. It was like having a baseball thrown up at the plate and not knowing whether to swing. It was like being in an accident and realizing the other car was going to hit me whatever I did. When I hear or read about some other child being sexually abused, the painful memory of being in someone else's emotionally powerful, confusing grip threatens to cut off my breathing.

Fortunately, something happened in my situation that kept the grip from tightening on me. For me, it was in the form of a question that came from the priest who was hugging me. He asked, "Do you like this?" Somehow, my brain managed to register what he was saying. He was making a strategic mistake. He was letting me know I had a choice. I shouted "No!," squirmed out of his embrace, and ran from the room. Fear mixed with anger had helped thrust the word out from my throat. I did not return to chapel. Instead, I went to the bottom of a stairwell, stood there, and shook. I had been on a brink and had teetered precariously.

In retrospect, I think "abuse" is nowhere near strong enough of a word for what he had done. I lost a lot in that encounter, and he tried to take more. Someone had reached out and put a chokehold on my budding sexuality and much-treasured innocence. Since then, whenever I smell Old Spice shaving lotion, the odor of it recreates his presence. It also brings back to my mind the horrible brink to which he had led me.

If I had mumbled, "Yes," I know my whole life would have been different. I would have crossed a line, over which it would have been impossible for me to return. I told a friend in the class ahead of me, but he simply shrugged, looked confused, and told me, "Just forget it." Father Randolph meanwhile was transferred at the end of the year, and I said nothing.

Three years later, when I was in the Franciscan novitiate, Father Randolph was recalled to teach at the minor seminary, from which I had by then graduated. Because my younger brother, Johnny, was there at the time and I could not stand that the priest might try the same thing with him, I reported what had happened to me to Father Benno Heidlage, the assistant novice master and a classmate of Father Randolph's.

Within a few weeks, I learned that Father Randolph had again been removed from the seminary. Unfortunately, another encounter with him awaited me.

Just recently, I located online an obituary of Father Randolph as part of a necrology for the Cincinnati province of the Franciscans. My reporting him, the necrology indicated, did not seem to have much effect. After leaving his teaching position at the seminary, the province assigned him to a series of parishes and then appointed him assistant to the provincial (the head of the province) and confessor for priests at the provincial motherhouse. He died in 1991 at the age of eighty-one.

(In 1958, he would reappear in my life. I will write more about that in another chapter.)

On the day on which I found myself writing this account, an article in *The New York Times* quoted Cardinal William Levada on sexual abuse by priests. He was head of the Congregation of the Faith and Doctrine in Rome and former archbishop of San Francisco. In an interview, the Cardinal attempted to explain the Catholic Church's highly criticized policies in handling pedophile priests by stating, "It took a lot of time to understand how much damage is done to victims, to children, by this kind of behavior."

When I read his words, my eyes moistened. I looked up Cardinal Levada on the Internet. Who was he? What was he saying? Why did it take a long time for the Church to understand how much damage is done to victims, to children?

The minor seminary, whatever its virtues (so many of which I enjoyed) and shortcomings (which I also experienced), was about to disappear. The numbers of boys applying to them started to decline. Church officials would ultimately close the vast majority of them. The Catholic Church apparently had come to question whether the tradition of recruiting prepubescent boys and placing them in an exclusive and isolated preparatory high school might be ideal for creating an elitist cadre of priests, but not a formula for turning out a considerate, caring, empathetic, and deeply moral clergy.

Deep down, the seminary and the Church itself presented me with an enormous paradox. I believed the authority of the Catholic Church was divine in origin, and I wanted to accept it completely. And yet, within me, was a strong, motivating conviction and belief in individual, personal freedom, which at times seemed to be in conflict with that authority.

Today, I have begun to understand the source of the personal dichotomy that I found within me. My mother represented a commitment to Catholicism and all of its rules. Her unquestioning adherence to the church and respect for its clergy ultimately led four of her sons to enter the seminary and take its highest demands and commitments very seriously.

My father, on the other hand, embodied an open-ended sense of personal freedom. He told each of us on multiple occasions that there was always a bed waiting for us at home if we decided to leave the seminary. He meant we did not have to do what we were doing. My father was proud of us and quite capable of bragging that his sons were studying to be priests, but he would have been willingly to give that up if we chose to find happiness elsewhere. My mother, on her part, would never have expressed such a thought explicitly or implicitly. To her, we were the offering she had willingly made to God in place, I believe, of herself.

When my brothers and I were Franciscan friars at Duns Scotus College, my parents—who lived four blocks away—were allowed to visit with us once a month. Afterwards, even though we had not gone off the grounds, we had to check in at the end of the visit with the "Master of Clerics," Father Raphael Clouse. His title said everything. He was, even in little matters of obedience, our "master." We were required to seek him out and get his verbal *benedicite* ("Bless you!") to return back to our less-worldly life inside the monastery. My father, on his part, resented this requirement and grinned broadly on those occasions when we told him Father Raphael was not in and therefore we would not be required to get his blessing. With such an attitude, my father was sowing within me the seeds of the idea that my life with its monastic rules and intricate requirements did not make the sense I thought it did.

My parents' conflicting messages of respect for authority and a sense of freedom confused me. I liked rules, and I did not. When I crafted articles or term papers, I tried to squeeze the two contradictory ideas into whatever I wrote without realizing what I was doing. As a result, much of my writing came across as a confused mishmash. I was slavish in my respect for the church and yet almost radical in my ideas about freedom. One paragraph would extol the church and its authority and the next, would raise human problems and the need to have the freedom to resolve them. How does an individual bridge the two?

"True freedom," I said years later, "means that Catholics should be free to leave the Church if that is what their consciences tell them." My Catholic friends were aghast. Leaving the church to them was apostasy, "the unforgivable sin against the Holy Ghost."My confusion was that at the time, although I said it, I more than half agreed with them and less than half with what I had said.

When I read the life of Charles Darwin, I was reminded of a parallel to my parents' relationship in learning that Darwin's wife believed evolution contradicted her religious beliefs. My mother nagged my father against going too far in complaining about the Church. My father, on his part, once scandalized me by saying publicly, "One religion is as good as another," but he never would have repeated that in front of my mother.

My father, ever on the verge of rebellion, led a vocal but unsuccessful campaign against Father Bart Ohr, the Franciscan pastor of our parish, St. Michael's in Southfield, Michigan. In one of life's ironic twists, some forty years later, my father's son (and my brother) Father Bert, held for six years the same position as pastor of St. Michael's Parish as Father Bart had.

Father Bart and my father were both dead by then. My mother was alive and proud of her son, the pastor.

# 7

## 1950: A New Year and
## My Classmate Archie Is Missing

*We were not only his classmates. We were also his friends.*

(An imaginary letter projected into the past and answered in the present.)

January 7, 1950

Dear Whoever I Will Become,

This is about Archie Harris, all about Archie. Sometimes, in the seminary, you look around and you wonder who is going to make it and who isn't going to graduate alongside you, enter the Franciscan Order with your class, and be there in 1960 to be ordained a priest. Archie Harris is not going to make it, and I do not know why.

The rest of us came back from Christmas vacation. He did not. In a way, I should not be surprised. Less than 10 percent of those who started with us will be ordained. That statistic holds up in class after class. It is our third year here. More than half of my class has left. But Archie?

Because we are next to each other in the alphabet, the two of us always sat beside one another both in class and study hall. When I could not think what else to write home about to my parents, I would look over at him and think of something to tell them about Archie—such as his favorite expression, "By golly," and how he says it every time he gets excited. I would report how he would in other ways express himself distinctly, directly, and quaintly.

Archie is from Lafayette, Indiana and, to hear him tell it, there is no better town in all of the United States than Lafayette nor any state more worthy than Indiana. I have repeatedly told him that he was mistaken. The best state is Michigan and the best town, Detroit. He would then outright contradict me by saying, "By golly, you are wrong."

*Ralph "Archie" Harris*

At the beginning of each year, the seminary students are given a sheet of rules. These deal with where and when we can talk, go off the premises, address the priests, take care of school property, or dress on different occasions (such as wearing a suit and tie to Sunday High Mass). If we break any of these rules such as talking after "lights out," one of the faculty members (especially the disciplinarian) can require us to write out all of the rules five, ten or even twenty times. Needless to say, my brother, Howard—who regularly gets 100s in conduct—has not been given the punishment of having to write the rules even once; but Pauly and I have often been required to do so. Pauly, I think, even more than me.

I was sitting in study hall in my free time doing so yet another time when Archie came up to me and said, "By golly, JoJo, you should not have to do that. It's not fair."

"For once you are right, Archie," I said. "I didn't deserve this. Decote pushed me, and I said, 'Stop it.' And yet I was the guy who got punished!"

"No, that is not what I meant," he said. "They should have made you wash windows, rake leaves, or something like that. Writing the rules over and over doesn't help anything."

"You got a funny idea about what's fair," I said. "But I'm glad you at least seem to care."

Still, Christmas vacation came and went this year and then Archie did not come back to the seminary and I don't know why.

January 10, 2014

Dear JoJo,

Time after time for over more than a half century, I tried to get in touch with Archie Harris, but I had his real first name mixed up. Then, it happened. I got his phone number through an organization of former students at St. Francis Seminary.

I called. A woman answered, "You want Archie Harris? You mean Ralph Harris? No one calls him 'Archie' anymore."

She put him on the phone.

"Archie," I said, "this is JoJo Heise from almost sixty years ago. My name is Kenan, now."

"By golly," he said.

I had the right kid, even if he was sixty years older.

He then told me why he left the seminary and about his life after leaving. His father had been killed in a car accident and he had to go home to help support his mother.

I cannot believe that no one at the seminary told us about his father dying. We were not only his classmates. We were also his friends.

Archie told me a dear story about his bashfulness in first meeting the woman who would become his wife and an equally dear one about a grandchild.

Interspersed in his stories were "by golly" after "by golly."

And fairness? It turns out he had spent his whole life being fair. After graduating from high school, he had become a union electrician, later ran for secretary treasurer of his local union, handled a lot of grievances, and helped negotiate a contract that retained a great number of factory jobs in his beloved Lafayette.

"When people complain about unions," he told me, "I tell them that unions are what created the middle class in this country."

Yes, by golly, Archie, and you helped.

*(Note: I sent this piece to Archie and he was able to read it just before he died in 2009. His family called me to share with me that they had read it aloud at his funeral.)*

# 8

Being a Franciscan Novice:
"No One Will Understand."
Right!

*For a year, we were asked to stand still and let life pass us by.*

At seventeen years of age, I entered the novitiate in St. Anthony Monastery in Mount Airy, Ohio and became a Franciscan friar. JoJo Heise received a new name: "Friar Kenan." He was also given the brown robe, cowl, and white, knotted rope belt like those of Friar Tuck in a Robin Hood movie. Of the nearly one hundred that had begun in our class four years before, sixteen were clothed as Franciscans on August 15, 1951.

As we went through the ancient religious ceremony of investiture, conducted in Latin, the new clothes and new names we were given reminded us how different our lives had become. Deep down, I didn't think any of those participating in it could believe what a change was really happening to each of us. It was a new life, which we were entering. One of the first things the novice master, Father Cornelius Grein, told us was not to tell people that our new life was like in the novitiate. This prohibition specifically included telling any member of the senior class still at St. Francis Seminary, who themselves would be entering the novitiate the next year. "No one would understand," he warned us.

One of the key aspects of religious life was obedience, and this was probably the first clear command of what we were to do or not to do.

No longer bound by obedience to the man as my religious "superior," I will now attempt to tell what life was like for us as novices. In some ways, my year in the novitiate was intense and focused on living a life devoted to religion and to God. In others it was simply freakish.

I recall once sitting outside in the novitiate's bush-and-fence-enclosed garden with a group of other novices. Through the bushes several had noticed a new model car whiz by on the road outside the enclosure. The glimpse we had lasted for only a second and, at best, was a partial view. Nevertheless, two of my fellow novices engaged in a heated debate over what year and make the car had been, even though there was absolutely no way of ever retrieving the car as evidence.

It was a metaphor about life that year. The days were speeding by and we had not a single inkling about was happening not only in our neighborhood, but also in the world. Still, we were not averse to attempting to form opinions or argue about present reality from what had happened in the past. Throughout this year, we were asked to stand still and let life pass us by.

In high school, I had been a great fan of the Detroit Tigers and the assistant novice master told me near the end of the year the fate of my favorite team. The Tigers were on course to finish last for the first time in their history. And I had not been thrilled by a single one of their victories nor grown dejected as their losses had piled up. Life in the novitiate was not about new model cars or professional baseball teams but about getting closer to God by other means, many of them self-depreciating. It was a step—for many of us, the most difficult one yet—into the Franciscan religious order and up the ladder toward the priesthood.

*Friar Kenan Heise O. F. M.*

I entered the year of novitiate and took on my new name (Friar Kenan) in order to generate a new persona under the guidance of full-fledged Franciscans. Living in a cloistered monastery and dressed in a brown robe, I accepted a life set aside from the world and circumscribed by vows of poverty, chastity, and obedience. In retrospect, it was very bizarre. Here are a few examples:

We were self-caged. I remember feeling startled, if not shocked over any classmate who rebelled in the least against the strange rules and customs we were obliged to follow and accept.

We were not allowed to smoke. At the minor seminary, when we were seniors; we were allowed to do so, but only pipes and solely in the recreation room or out of doors. In the summer, I was a heavy smoker, but once we started the novitiate, had to quit cold turkey.

The novice master himself did smoke. Only one novice that I know of did not quit smoking as ordered. His room stunk of cigarette smoke and we could smell it when we passed by. We had no idea where he ever got the cigarettes. The novice master, being a smoker, could not detect the odor. Also, my classmate grew a plant from a sweet potato to help absorb the odor. It was inconceivable to me that anyone would "cheat" as he did.

Similarly, we could not drink alcoholic beverages and had no access to them. On the Feast of St. Francis, the monastery had a fund-raising party in a hall. It was on property away from the cloistered area of the monastery. We could not attend this, but were charged with cleaning up afterwards. The novitiate was in Mount Airy, a suburb of Cincinnati. That city had a reputation for liking its beer. The sponsors of the event had managed to sell quite a few bottles of it. Consequently, our helping to dispose of hundreds of empty beer bottles was a major part of the clean up. We stood in awe as one of our fellow novices rather than emptying the left over contents in the sink poured it bottle after bottle down his throat.

Once a week in the novice master's office, we individually had "a chapter of faults," which consisted of us reporting to him any minor infractions of the rules we had committed. I am confident that neither the smoker nor the beer drinker mentioned his infractions. I recall reporting that a glass broke while I was shaving and being chided for not acknowledging, "I broke a glass."

Father Cornelius was a laid back individual. He had been a missionary in China. Around the holidays, however, he would become a yeller, getting very uptight about the preparations that had to be made for the occasion. Members of the prior novitiate class had warned us about his proclivity to scream at his charges on such occasions.

I found myself terrified when another classmate and I were told to string up Christmas lights on the front of the church, having to put nails into the mortar between the bricks to hold string of lights. We had to use high ladders and brave an icy rain to do it. We stretched the string of lights along a rarely used driveway just before putting them up. A car drove up and ran right over all of them. We both felt our novitiate would end there and then, but Father Cornelius surprisingly took it calmly and the event did not put an end to our days as Franciscans.

Others were thrown out of the novitiate as a result of being literally blackballed by the priests in the monastery, who voted on each of us four separate times during the year. They used black or white beans rather

than balls and put one or the other into a bag with a novice's name at-
tached as it was passed around the table. If you got enough black beans,
you had been voted out.

We did not even know when the votes were taking place. We lost five
members of our class. Whether they left voluntarily or received too many
black beans, we never knew. Two of those who left were the smoker and
the drinker.

The novitiate was so cut off from the outside world that the class of
novices in the summer of 1945 figured out that World War II was over
upon hearing the guns and fireworks being shot or set off in nearby Cincinnati. The war ended, in fact, while they were in a retreat preparing for
their big day of investiture.

The priests' recreation room had a television set. Ours did not. We
did not even have a radio. The only time we got to be in their recreation
room to see any television during the entire year was for a one-time
showing of "The Bishop Sheen Hour." Some of what the easy-speaking
bishop said went over our heads because he referred to current events,
incidents about which we had no way of understanding what he was
talking about. Having no radios, phones, or any of the electronic devices
developed since then, we had no means to keep up with the news of the
day. We did not even hear rumors of the Korean War, which was being
fought and in which, if we had not been in the seminary, some of us
might have been fighting.

During Advent and Lent, the novice master withheld letters from
home and distributed them to us only on Sundays. This practice caused
one of the more freakish experiences of my life. I had been expecting a
visit from my brother, Claude, who was returning from a tour in the air
force that was fighting in the skies over Korea. Because of the special circumstances and because my religious superiors knew my brother, who as
a young man had spent a short time there as a brother, they had made a
special exception to allow him to visit me on his way back home. His had
been a precarious existence in the Korean War. The one day he did not
fly a specific mission with his crew, the plane crashed and all his fellow
crewmembers were killed.

He did not show up at the novitiate as expected and I did not know
why. When Sunday came five days later, a pile of letters awaited me. I
opened one. A newspaper clipping fell out with a picture of my future
sister-in-law. A cutline read, "Her fiancé injured in deadly air force plane
crash." My brother Claude's B-29 bomber had crashed on landing at the

United States Air Force base in Shreveport, Louisiana. Everyone in the cockpit of the bomber had been killed. My brother was sitting in the back section of the plane. Both of Claude's legs had been smashed. After a long therapy, he would be able to walk with a cane. We did not get to see each other until the next year.

One of the other odd facts of novitiate life was that our heads were shaved bald (four times throughout the year). Also, our knees developed such ugly calluses from praying on them in chapel for hours at a time. It was a good thing that we did not own or ever wear short pants.

Unlike the Trappist monks, we could talk, but only during certain hours of the day and often not during meals and never after *magnum silentium* (the "Great Silence"). This began at eight o'clock at night. We received no newspapers, heard no radio, and received no phone calls. Our immediate family could visit only once during the year at Christmastime.

Life in a Franciscan seminary, especially in the novitiate, was a strange wall of rules and practices meant to separate us from "the world," to change whom we were and to train us in the observance of the Franciscan Rule. The emphasis of this were the vows of poverty, chastity, and obedience.

The monastery was in many ways a bare and oftentimes intense environment. It was a personality-erasing effort to get us to accept obedience to our religious superiors over our own inclinations. It was similar to the thorough breaking of some already tame young stallions. Dangled in front of us was membership in the Franciscan Order and ultimately ordination to priesthood in the Catholic Church.

Still, if I shake out the ashes from early adulthood, I can yet appreciate much of it. Though it distorted and confused me in any number of ways, I owe a great big thank you to the Franciscans for giving me an otherwise mind-expanding education, a unique awareness of the spiritual dimension of life, a heightened concern for others, and a penchant for at least trying to being kind to others.

While the Franciscan life itself was all these things; in the long run, it also attempted to take something crucial away from me—my personal freedom. First and foremost, life in the novitiate taught us obedience while leaving us fundamentally confused because less stress was put on poverty and chastity than on how, why, and whom to obey. Perhaps the novice master was right. No one would or could understand the novitiate, not even those of us who went through it.

*Friar Kenan (in the middle row on the right) with classmates*

If the transition to the one-year of being a novice in the isolated monastery in Mount Airy, Ohio was tough and confusing; the change into the four-year stint at Duns Scotus College, in Southfield, Michigan—four shorts blocks from my home—was easier and somewhat more natural.

I was cloistered. My parents were not. Their house and their lives were part of the world. Everything about my life, except once-a-month, one-hour visits with them took place in a different universe than everything they did. We saw each other occasionally, because my mother helped the nuns cook some of the meals and my father did the electrical maintenance work for Duns Scotus. I was like a puppy with an invisible electric fence. I did not bark at it.

After Duns Scotus College, there would be another four-year course of studies, theology, in Oldenburg, Ind. And then would follow to ordination to the priesthood and an assignment to further studies, a parish, a teaching position or even, possibly missionary work—whatever plans God and the Franciscans might have in mind for me.

# 9

## Three Individuals in My Life
## on Their Way to Canonization

*We reacted sharply to the accusation that when it came to private morality the Catholics shone but when it came to social and political morality, they were often conscienceless.*

DOROTHY DAY

**W**hither my life?

Before I went to the seminary to become a priest, I had wanted to attain the impossible—become a saint of the Catholic Church. Maybe, I had begun to think I should go back to trying to be that. It was, I half knew, an immature and impossible goal.

Well, if the truth be known, that thought did not last very long. Life, even in the monastery, offered far too many bobbles and temptations extending in too many directions to think I could measure up to that. It would take an enormous amount of self-sacrifice and I had only so much to give. Maybe, just maybe I could become hermit-like, but not a saint. If nothing else, my curiosity about life and what it had to offer stopped me from ever continuing to think about becoming in any way a saint, much less a hermit.

Still, three individuals—two men and a woman—who had a profound influence on my life are today on the road to just that, canonization in the Catholic Church.

Two of them, Father Solanus Casey and Dorothy Day, were individuals whom I personally met. The third, I did not encounter face to face, but I assiduously studied his writings and speeches and met his death with tears. He was Eugenio Pacelli, born an Italian aristocrat, made a cardinal, and then Vatican secretary of state before becoming enthroned in 1939 as Pope Pius XII. He died October 9, 1958, just months after I had left the Franciscan Order.

Each of the three has now passed the first stages of the Catholic Church's canonization process with flying colors and can now officially be called "venerable." Eventually, I traveled in a much different direction than they did. Nevertheless, I owe something to all three, but to the first two far more than to Pope Pius XII. For him, my gratitude has congealed under the frost of profound disappointment, the kind of sadness you feel toward a friend who has deeply betrayed your trust. Revelations about his lack of courage and conscience during World War II make me wish I could somehow stare him in the eye and ask, "How could you have followed the course you did?"

Father Solanus Casey O.F.M. Capuchin, whom I had met in Detroit when I was 11 years old, had the longest beard of anyone I ever saw and was one of the sweetest, simplest of men I could imagine. He looked like a picture in my grade school catechism of a father of the church. The truth was that his superiors did not consider him smart enough to be an ordained a priest with all the powers of the priesthood. He was thus ordained what is called "a simplex priest." This restricted him from confessions or preaching from the pulpit on things that pertained to dogma.

I found Father Solanus to be friendlier and more jovial than I could ever possibly have imagined anyone to be who looked like him. My sister, Mary Lou, also met him years later while she was still a little girl. She later told me of the incident, recalling that, when he realized that there was no chair left for her to sit on, he reached in a drawer of his desk, pulled out a sucker and added a smile to make up for her inconvenience.

I had met him earlier in 1944, and no one then was thinking of him ever being canonized a saint, at least my brothers and I weren't. His reputation would grow and the people of Detroit would come to know him as the priest who served as "the doorkeeper" at St. Bonaventure Monastery on Mount Elliot Street—a sweet, concerned, good, and holy man willing to see and listen to them any time day or night.

He was a Capuchin, a branch of the Franciscans, one that had the reputation of being even less connected from the world than were the branch of regular Franciscans, which I would join. The easiest way to distinguish them at that time was that they wore beards and members of my branch did not. More basically, they attempted to observe the Rule of St. Francis more literally than other Franciscans do, especially in regards to poverty.

My parents had not gone to see him to confess their sins or have him preach on theological issues. Their financial situation was tough and, while hoping that things would get better, they had been arguing a lot.

Somehow—I never leaned the details—they got his help. They did not seem to argue as much after that, at least for a while, and their marriage and friendship lasted the rest of their lives.

We kids who went along with them and waited while they spoke with Father Solanus got something too. I remember him saying to us that he came from an even larger family than our six boys and one girl. When he learned how many there were in our family, he said, "Six boys and each one has a sister. That makes twelve, doesn't it?" We tried to correct him on the number, but he just smiled. Each of us probably repeated his little joke more than one hundred times whenever people asked how many kids were in our family.

My parents had taken three of us kids (Howard was already in the seminary at the time) who later entered the Franciscans, a different branch of the same religious order to which he belonged. I would like to believe that the endearing image we got of him had some supporting impact on that.

Over the years, when I have repeated his jest about the number of children in our family, his face and manner have inevitably come to mind. And he certainly helped teach us that a person did not have to be smart in school to be special.

The concept of spirituality, however, became more confusing to me the more I tried to attain it. Some feel the way to a closer personal relationship with God is devotion and asceticism at the highest level of self-denial one can attain. To others, the route to sanctity is through imitation of the saints. And, for not a few, it is a focus on sacred scripture, the sacraments of the church, and participation in its liturgy. I tried them all: devotion, prayer, asceticism, self-denial, spiritual reading, studying scripture, and participating in the church's liturgy.

This belief drew me to the highest authority in the church, the Pope in Rome, his encyclical letters, and his speeches. The then reigning pontiff, Pius XII, fit the bill just fine for me. He was an ascetic, a brilliant and eloquent speaker, whose august words seemed directed personally to me. His spirituality focused on the church's devotions as simple as praying the rosary or participating in the Church's liturgy. The very thought of this austere man as my ultimate religious superior provided me with the soothing assurance I felt I needed. I looked to his encyclical letters and pronouncements as my spiritual guides. Pius XII himself directed me there in his 1950 encyclical letter *Humani Generis*.

After quoting "He who hears you, hears Me" (Luke 10:16), he added a directive that pertained to himself:

> If the Supreme Pontiffs in their acts, after due consideration, express an opinion on a hitherto controversial matter, it is clear to all that this matter, according to the mind and will of the same Pontiffs, cannot any longer be considered a question of free discussion among theologians.

His encyclicals were mostly about such religious subjects as devotion to the Sacred Heart, "The Queenship of Mary," and the Rosary as well as on sacred music, the Church's liturgy and praying for peace. These words, I felt, met my deepest needs. I shed tears when he died in 1958. I had lost the guiding star to the far-out heavens.

Today, I think and feel differently. I learned very little through Catholic channels about the distance my spiritual hero maintained from those who suffered the most during World War II. With an incredible intelligence network, the Church had to have known from the beginning what was happening not only to the Jews in Germany but also to the mentally ill, the homosexuals, the gypsies, the socialists, and any who opposed or criticized Hitler. The Nazis knew Pius XII knew, and they paraded the Italian Jews being taken to German concentrations camps past the Pope's Lateran Palace.

How did they and we know he knew? Pius XII was the former Vatican ambassador to Germany and had the almost unlimited resources of the Church in Germany, Italy, and around the world to learn exactly what was happening. Each of us, the Church taught me, has a moral obligation to find some way to stand up and defy evil, especially when it takes the form of slavery, discrimination, genocide, ethnic cleansing, concentration camps, anti-Semitism, mass torture, or other crimes against humanity. Pius XII later spoke out strongly against communism, but backed away from so many opportunities to do so about Hitler and the Nazis. He had been my hero, and I always presumed that he and the Catholic Church had protested vehemently against the Holocaust, but I found no ready way to check it out until after his death. Pius XII had chosen to protect the institutions of the church over those outside of it including the six million Jews who suffered and died in the Holocaust.

I have come to believe that Pope Pius's actions helped, in part, set the stage for the enormous church scandal of priests molesting of children. In 1955, while he was the pope, the Vatican issued an instruction to seminaries that specifically forbade the psychological testing of seminarians in determining their suitability for the priesthood. It took away a barrier that might have kept some seminarians with a penchant for abuse from being ordained. The instruction, I believe, led away from any psychological understanding of the men being trained for the priesthood. I spoke to a priest-theologian who had participated in the vetting of young candidates for the priesthood years later. "We were well aware," he said, "of the church's ruling against using psychological testing of candidates to weed out those who were unfit. We felt frustrated we could not make use of it. And some questionable people got by as a result."

When Pope Pius XII died in 1958, I did not grasp any of this. Instead, I missed his existence. I did not know then Pope Pius XII—whom I had once considered a saintly and vigilant father—had gotten it all very much very wrong.

Dorothy Day, on the other hand, was like a mother and she got a lot very right. From my first contact with her through her works and writings, I felt redirected from spiritual devotions alone to kindness and fairness toward people. Years later, when we shared a lunch, everything I came to feel about her through her writings would be reinforced by her smile, acceptance of my awkwardness, and my over-eager earnestness.

It was in the early 1950s that I first read her book *The Long Loneliness.* I was at the time a Franciscan seminarian just turned twenty years old. Up until then, my path ahead had seemed unobstructed as I searched for the road to spirituality through the course of the Pope's encyclicals, the lives of the traditional saints and the writings of the more conservative religious thinkers. Besides St. Francis (the founder of my religious order) and Pius XII, two of my spiritual champions were Thomas a Kempis, who wrote *The Imitation of Christ,* and Pope Pius X, who was against every form of modernism.

I had also reads dozens of lives of the saints, at least eight volumes of *The Lives of the Pope,* and the sermons of the fifteenth century Franciscan missionary, St. Bernardine of Siena, in Latin. As a cloistered Franciscan seminarian, I was not involved in or even in contact with politics or political issues. Still—from what trickled down—I heartily supported the fight against communism led by a prominent Catholic senator from Wisconsin, Joe McCarthy. I was at first horrified by Dorothy Day as I read of her accounts of picketing and demonstrating alongside communists.

Then, I read her explanation. She quoted St. Thomas Aquinas to the effect that, "The truth is the truth and comes from the Holy Ghost; no matter from whose lips it comes." Then, she wrote something that really struck me:

> Many times we were asked why we so named the paper, *The Catholic Worker*. Of course it was not only because we who were in charge of the work, who edited the paper, were all Catholics, but also because we wanted to influence Catholics. They were our own, and we reacted sharply to the accusation that when it came to private morality the Catholics shone but when it came to social and political morality, they were often conscienceless.

For years, I have had in my house a photo that embodied her spirit even more clearly than her words did. It was taken in 1973, when she had traveled to California's San Joaquin Valley, grape country, to support the right of the United Farm Workers to strike. In the photo, she is seventy-five years old, seated on a portable stool with a wide-brimmed straw hat and a serenely defiant look. Armed policemen, ready and willing to take her into custody, frame her.

Hers was the kind of social and political conscience I felt I had to acquire to become holy and to respond to Jesus' words in the form of the beatitudes. My attention shifted from traditional and conservative principles and saints to ordinary down-to-earth people, especially those in need.

I wanted to learn more about Dorothy Day and the Catholic Worker Movement. Her books and the stories in her paper talked of injustice, poverty, soup kitchens, labor unions, and pacifism. It was a Catholic newspaper but it talked about non-Catholic heroes Mahatma Gandhi and Leo Tolstoy as much as it did about Catholic saints.

In the 1930s and 1940s, a Franciscan priest stationed at Duns Scotus College, Father Sebastian Ercbacher, served as the chaplain for the Catholic Worker House of Hospitality in Detroit. As a result, the college's library contained a file of all the issues of the *Catholic Worker* newspaper back to 1933, when it was founded.

I read many, if not all, of them. They spoke of poverty, racial discrimination, the horrors of war, social justice, and an incredible idealism. First and foremost, they focused on individuals and a philosophy of life that Dorothy Day and the Catholic Worker's co-founder, Peter Maurin, called "personalism." The latter thinking is that the more personal our approach to the world and its problems, the more real it is.

For a writer, as I would later learn, that personalism—emphasizing the significance, uniqueness, and inviolability of individuals—is a powerful way to view the world and extraordinarily effective means of communication. People want to read about people. They understand issues and events better if the writer outlines them in terms of people. Never in my life did I encounter better examples of this personalist approach than in the speeches of Dr. Martin Luther King and writings and actions of Dorothy Day.

When I retired, I looked back at my own career and saw that every assignment I had or position I held as a journalist was about people and owed a salute of acknowledgement to the personalism that Dorothy Day and others had taught me.

In college, however, I was finding little or no opportunity to actually do anything about what I was learning. I looked to wider reading, initiating small study groups at the seminary on race relations, labor unions, and what are called the papal "social" encyclicals. I felt as though up until then I had been in a speedboat anchored to the bottom. When I pulled back on the throttle, all it ever did was go faster and faster in circles. Now, I had a compass, pulled up the anchor, and was able to travel to places where I could reach other people and help them.

Years later, and in a new life, I would become close to Lou and Justine Murphy of the *Detroit Catholic Worker* and, through them, have the unique privilege of sharing lunch with Dorothy Day. I remember her presence, her smile, and her grace more decidedly than any words she spoke. It was her complete acceptance of me—as clumsy as I was—that impressed and delighted me the most.

I still recall Father Solanus and his simplicity with fondness. Dorothy Day's words, books, and photo to this day hold a place of honor in my heart and home. And although Pius XII expressed many brilliant and deeply spiritual thoughts, what I learned most decisively from him was the high cost of walking away from one's responsibility.

If the Catholic Church does canonize the man, I am certain I will cry, but for a very different reason than I had in 1958. Pope Francis has said Pope Pius' canonization process has "stalled."

# 10

## Once My Talents Were Called into Question, I Had to Write

*It was as though someone had encouraged me to quit trying to imitate others and write in my own personal language. I started doing just that. I started by spinning a real life story in my own voice. It helped immediately as I used my talking voice to weave the fabric of a true experience into narrative form.*

First, I first wanted to write; and, then, starting in the eighth grade, I had to.

The change in me came as the result of an unkind response that my teacher, Sister Abundantia, heaped on my entry in a citywide poetry contest for eighth graders. I had worked assiduously at writing a poem and proudly handed it in to her to submit in my behalf. A month passed. I heard nothing. Finally, I asked Sister Abundantia if the results had been announced yet. "Oh yours," she chided. "I never submitted it."

Her words and put-down placed a burr in my saddle that's there still. I do not understand why her disdainful comment had such a lasting impact on me, but it did. It has helped drive me to write, write, and write for more than six decades now. It also has encouraged me to be generous in willingly critiquing the efforts of others, but never ever to put them down in the process of doing so.

In high school, the school newspaper refused the first six articles I wrote for it. So, I submitted a seventh. It was published. In looking at them years later, I discovered the pieces were interesting, at least to me, but awkward, even to me.

In college, my English teacher formed a remedial writing group with three students. I was one of the three. I had three articles published, two in a newspaper and one in a magazine before I graduated. Something changed. People started helping me. My writing got better.

The first to help was my older brother, Paul. He was on the staff of *The Brown and White,* the monthly school paper for our high school,

St. Francis Seminary. I might have given up. I was thinking about it. He, however, talked the editor into publishing that seventh attempt on my part.

Then in college, my English professor, Father Leander Blumlein, put me in the remedial writing group. There, I learned an important key that ultimately unlocked the path to writing, which would serve as my full-time profession for more than fifty years. "Write about what you know and use your experience to do it," he said. And then he repeated it, catching my attention with the second time he said it.

It was as though someone had encouraged me to write in my own personal language and quit trying to imitate others. I started doing just that. I began by spinning a real life story in my own voice. It helped immediately as I used my talking voice to weave the fabric of an actual experience into narrative form. The story, which I wrote as my assignment in the remedial group, flowed right out of me, and got me out of any further remedial writing sessions.

Sixty years later that same story would serve me in great stead when I spoke at a grade school career day in one of the poorest suburbs of Chicago. The point that I tried to make to the students was while the other speakers were talking about what the students could become after they graduated I was offering them something they could become starting that day—a writer.

The story was about my brother Pauly and me when we were in grade school. It happened as I was going into the eighth grade and he was about to go away to the seminary. My oldest brother, Claude, kept a loaded .22 pistol hidden away in the attic. Pauly knew where it was. He got it out to show me and David Sackett, a friend of ours. Pauly knew the gun was loaded and put his finger behind the trigger so it would not go off. But it did! And the bullet tore a noticeable three-inch slit in our living room ceiling. It went off because a mechanism *behind* the trigger caused the gun to shoot. David Sackett and I fled as quick as our legs could take us, leaving Pauly to explain the slit in the ceiling to my parents when they got home. When I returned several hours later, my mother was standing on the front porch, wagging her finger threateningly and saying, "Don't any of you kids ever, ever swing a golf club in the living room again!"

Three months later, after he got home from the seminary for Christmas vacation, his guilt forced him to face up to his deed and his lie. "It wasn't a golf club," he blurted out. Our mother was mystified. When Pauly told her what his cryptic confession pertained to, she was far more forgiving than she would have been three months earlier. He obviously had spent those months weighed down with guilt for what he had done and the lie he had told.

When I told this story to the grade school assembly, one kid raised his hand to ask, "Did he get a whupping?"

"No," I said.

Another boy shouted out, "My father doesn't whup us either!" His words made me especially glad I had told the story.

I have diverted.

Back sixty years ago at Duns Scotus College, I was studying scholastic philosophy in the form of *ontologia*, *epistemologia*, and rational *psychologia rationalis*—all in Latin. Using that language to study such subjects was not doing much to help me learn to write. Fortunately, very fortunately, I got away from the cloistered monastery in summer to take four courses at the Jesuit-run, open-to-the-general-public University of Detroit. During the last two summers at Duns Scotus, my classmates and I were permitted for the first time in our school's history to go to summer school away from our confines.

I took four courses there over the two summers. I believe that without the impact of all four of these courses I could never have made it as a professional writer. They yanked me good and hard away from the thirteen and fourteenth century scholastic philosophy that had been up until then the mainstream of my college education. They were also the first optional courses I had ever taken in my life. The first course I chose was Storytelling. In a husky, off-putting voice, the president of Dun Scotus, Father Philibert Ramstetter, challenged me on my choice. "Friar Kenan, I know I said that students could take any course they might choose, but Storytelling?"

"I don't have any approach to small children," I answered in as simple of a tone as I could state it. He liked my answer, I could tell, and it became the beginning of a profound relationship, in which I would encounter his powerful support any number of times. Even after I left the Franciscans, we kept in touch.

Time and again throughout my career, I would be unusually fortunate in finding support at such high levels when I did or at least tried to do things differently. These individuals were not so much complimentary as they were supportive. They said little but allowed me room to break the rules of which it was their jobs to serve as guardian. Their support more than my courage helped me make my mark.

The storytelling course was designed for lower grade-school teachers. The class consisted of thirty-five women and myself (wearing my Franciscan habit). For four years, I had not even spoken to any women, except my family and the nuns who cooked for the seminarians. Now ...

On the first day of class, I sat in the front row and blushed my way through it. I eventually got past my awkwardness and learned the art of storytelling not only to children but also to others. I have continued to use it ever since.

The other course that summer was Social Problems. The ancient Jesuit professor, Father John E. Coogan S.J., was ahead of the crowd on the issue of race; but behind it, far behind it in his anti-Semitic and anti-labor positions. In class, he attempted to use the Socratic method of teaching, which involves dialogue, questions, and answers. These lead to other questions and, hopefully, better answers. It worked well until he attempted to push his anti-Semitism onto his students with a narrow and biased "definition" of a Jew. For his class, I wrote a paper about migrant workers. It would become the first article I would ever get published outside the seminary.

The next summer, I took a course in theater appreciation, which Richard J. Bergwin gave. He had perhaps the broadest understanding of the humanities of any teacher I ever encountered. With logic and clarity, he helped his students see how each of the arts is intertwined with the others. He led us to appreciate what art is and to comprehend how theater can meld with art. Professor Bergwin instilled in us a broad sense of culture, and taught how the art, theater, poetry, literature, and culture can entertain and, at the same time, awake people to universal truth.

Some forty years later, I would become part of a local play-writing group that would encourage us to experiment with dramatic writing as a craft. It would be composed of talented and helpful people enjoying what they are doing. They are good at it and my pleasure arose not only writing plays myself, but also in helping to critique my fellow-writers' works at the same time. In writing plays, I have gone to hell with Clarence Darrow, to prison with Joe Hill, into madness with Al Capone, and to the early days of Christianity with St. Peter's wife as well as to all the places my fellow playwrights have taken me.

In Professor Bergwin's class, I was a child being taught how to stretch my arms and swim about in a sea almost entirely new to me. I have long owed him a big, big thank you. I recently looked him up on line to see if I could do so. My effort resulted, alas, in finding his obituary rather than his phone number.

His inspiration and later a friendship with playwright David Mamet encouraged me to write for the theater. As a result, my dialogue and sense of the dramatic needed and received loads of help from others in my efforts such as *Clarence Darrow in Hell*, *Alphonse: A One-Man Play in the Words of Al Capone*, and *Holy Mother of God*. But, because of the teaching and example I encountered, not one of them fell short in aspiring to reach beneath the truth of the facts involved.

The fourth course I took was titled, The Papal Encyclicals. The teacher was one of the most highly respected Jesuits in the country. I did not know this when I signed up for it. From 1948 to 1955, my teacher, Father Robert C. Hartnett, had served as the editor of the prestigious Jesuit magazine, *America*. The class I took must have been the first one he taught after stepping down from the editor's job. In the magazine, he had thumped hard against the then high-flying searcher for communists under everybody's beds, Senator Joseph McCarthy.

Between the covers of *America*, Father Hartnett provided extraordinary coverage of the Army-McCarthy hearings that ultimately precipitated the senator's fall from grace in the eyes of the nation. Many in the Catholic Church, including some of Father Hartnett's fellow Jesuits, defended the controversial Jesuit-educated senator from Wisconsin. Though the magazine denied it, historians have tended to agree that Father Hartnett was relieved of his position as editor of *America* as a result of his criticism of Senator McCarthy.

While I was in awe of Father Hartnett's level of intellectual brilliance and moral fortitude, it was his ability to challenge each student to reach one or more rungs up the ladder that impressed me the most. He got me to try to do this and then ratified my efforts, if not my accomplishments, with a hard-worked-for A in his course.

I was not yet a writer, but the work being done to make me one was beginning to show. While I had a clearer focus for my writing, I was far from out of the woods. It was while I was a sophomore student at Duns Scotus that I overheard a conversation that has had an impact on my life and writing. Two members of the senior class were talking about me. One said with a measure of annoyance, "You know Kenan, he will try anything. I mean it. Anything!"

The other, though not particularly close to me, came to my defense, "Yes, you are right. But you know what, Kenan follows through on what he tries." Believe me, I was not used to people coming to my defense.

My defender was Friar Norman Perry. He was the editor of our school publication, *The Assisian*, and was in the midst, as I recall, of considering three pieces, which I had submitted.

In the end, he published a poem and an article I had written. Father Norman Perry would go on to become the editor of the very popular *St Anthony Messenger* and be named the Catholic Press's Journalist of the Year in 1997. The citation read: "In an era of polarization and name-calling among Catholics, Father Norman has been a powerful voice for thoughtfulness, fairness, and reason."

Father Norman died two years later. My brother, Father Bert, was his religious superior and personally took care of him as he was dying. My brother also helped work it out with the Catholic Press Association that Father Norman, although in very poor health, could be surprised by and receive the honor in person.

Friar Jeremy Harrington, Friar Norman's successor as editor of *The Assisian*, helped encourage me by publishing three of my poems in one issue.

My efforts in college to learn how to write were not—for me—geared to my ever becoming a success as a writer. That would have been a leap beyond my imagination. I wanted to write. I wanted to be published. I had convictions and I wanted to put them into words that would be read. Life to me was a paper bag that surrounded me, and I felt desperately in need of proving to myself that I could box my way out of it. I felt my pen could help.

The next step I took would punch through. The paper, which I wrote for my University of Detroit Social Problems class, was published outside the seminary system—and its publication would have far-reaching conse-quences for me. Duns Scotus College was located in Southfield, a suburb just north of Detroit. It received a copy every month of *The Wage Earner*, a labor paper published by the Detroit Catholic Labor Conference and sold in the backs of Catholic churches.

I got hold of a copy of the small monthly tabloid and sent my mi-grant workers class paper off to the editor, William A. Ryan. Once again, a month passed and I heard not a word about it, not even a rejection! Seminarians at Duns Scotus were not permitted to read the newspapers. The priests were, however. As matter of fact, when I was eleven years old, I had a newspaper route that included Duns Scotus, and I delivered all three Detroit papers—*The Detroit Times*, *The Detroit News*, and *The Detroit Free Press*—to them.

Now, as a seminarian there, I did not have permission to read the papers. Still, because I was in charge of collecting the trash, including newspapers from the priests' recreation room, I was able to do so anyway. As far as I know, I was the only seminarian who ever got the chance. I was perusing them one day, when—to my complete surprise—my article on migrant workers was on the front page of a discarded copy of *The Wage Earner*. I was a published writer. I had to reread my published article several times before my heart would calm down.

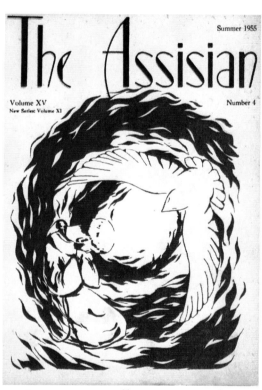

It was a fated moment for me. If I had not encountered it in the strange way I had, I most probably would never have known my piece was published. I believe that had I not seen it, my life would have been far different from what it has been. The publication of that article turned out to be my wormhole into another universe— and an exciting one it would be.

*Duns Scotus College magazine that published my articles and poetry*

My writing improved while I was in college for yet another reason. I started writing more and more poetry. Each verse I etched or rewrote helped give me an appreciation for choosing the right word and using a figure of speech as well as trying to improve everything I penned. Poetry was and continues to be my friend, as it has been over the years for so very many prose writers.

## 11

## Music, Architecture, and Me

*Then, things changed. I progressed from a lack of interest to curiosity,*
*appreciation and finally deep-rooted convictions.*
*It was a wondrous journey.*

For many people, a life-long appreciation of music and architecture comes easily and naturally. For me, it did not. I felt the loss; but, in truth, not enough to do much about it.

Still, a dormant passion for such deeply human interests was there, even if dammed up. As my writing started to touch on these areas, a new curiosity and unexpected feelings started to flood into my life. I began to see connections and through them reasons to care and care a lot. The pursuit of these new interests in my life was attended initially with surprise and then with a wonder and joy I had not experienced before. Was something missing in me that I didn't arrive at such interests more naturally, more directly? Then, things changed. I progressed from a lack of interest to curiosity, appreciation and finally deep-rooted convictions. It was a wondrous journey.

Music, which I had neglected, became a companion. Architecture could be awesome, but was a, "So what?" To me, a nice building was a nice building, especially if it was big, white, and reminiscent of Rome, Athens or Florence. Then, I read Louis Sullivan's writings and looked at buildings he had designed as well as about the ideas and works of John Wellborn Root and Frank Lloyd Wright. Investigating them changed my perspective on the beauty of architecture. The fruits of each of these new discoveries filled my plate, soothed my spirit and enriched my life in ways I had no reason to think they could.

Music for me stood as the greatest challenge. Since childhood, it had marked a deep and embarrassing failure in my life. There was in me no talent. When I was in grade school, the bullies in my class tried to get me to sing just so they and others could laugh at me.

In preparing for the priesthood, I was submerged in church and religious holiday music such as Christmas carols. Without any memory of ever having been challenged for it, I can report that I was considered the worst singer in the seminary. My music teachers tried to improve my singing, if only a little; because some day I would be singing the Gregorian Chant music of Solemn High Masses as well as the various priestly parts of the Church's liturgy. It would be a sad distraction for any member of the congregation with a decent ear for music.

Over the years, three priests—Fathers John de Deo Oldegeering, Venance Zink, and Aubert Grieser—each used his PhD in music training in vain to have a go at my musicality and singing.

Father Aubert told me, "You have a range of four notes and you have trouble finding them." All three flat out stated at the beginning of working with me, "Anyone can learn how to sing." They took me through vocal training that varied from singing hymns to attempting to learn the scale, humming and, finally, doing mouth and throat exercises. Each individually acknowledged he had been wrong in what he had told me about anyone being able to learn how to sing.

It was one sad experience after another for me because I worked hard at it, and I sincerely wanted to improve.

I thanked them for the effort they put into me, especially because I must have been a profound frustration to those who loved music the way each of them did.

While attending Duns Scotus College, I "belonged" to (as all the students there automatically did) the choir what was often referred to as "the second best" Gregorian chant choir in the country. To keep it so, some of my less vocally endowed classmates were encouraged to sing softly. I was urged to read a book.

I have never learned how to sing, but I have developed a far deeper appreciation of music than I had in the past. Music now appeals much more to me, especially anything my young grandchildren play on the violin, guitar, fiddle, piano, or sing. In addition, I have also come to enjoy the notes, energy, and melodies of a wide variety of music that ranges from Mozart to rowdy jazz, exuberant Gospel and, most of all, authentic folk music.

My curiosity would eventually help me to discover that the octave and a perfect fifth (although I am not certain my ear can recognize either) are at the core of both the indigenous as well as the sophisticated music of the world.

An interest in the down-to-earth lyrics of folk music led me to script a two-person folk-musical in 2001 around the words of the song "I dreamed I saw Joe Hill last night" and the ones which he composed for the Industrial Workers of the World (I.W.W.). The title of the musical was *The Songbird of the Wobblies,* with folksingers Kristen Lems and Mark Dvorak singing and doing a reading performance in the Theater Building in Chicago.

I had, about the same time, built a collection of forty to fifty books on the history of jazz in Chicago. When Penny Tyler, who had for years had chaired the Chicago Jazz Festival, lost her complete jazz library in Hurricane Katrina, I gave her my collection.

Even though my vocal chords cannot generate music even acceptable to me these days, my ears have attained some ability to distinguish and enjoy melodies and music passages they had not over the years.

A lack of appreciation for architecture gave me the same kind of opportunity for growth. My first peek at the pleasure, which great and imaginative buildings can engender happened on an incidental bike ride almost sixty years ago. In Birmingham, Michigan, five miles north of Duns Scotus College, lies one of the most serene settings that I have ever encountered, Cranbrook. It is environmentally a staged community built around the fine arts.

A classmate and I at Duns Scotus took a bike ride north and discovered it by accident. The buildings, sculpture, and landscaping come together to provide a visual experience, the likes of which I never imagined I might experience on this earth. It was a total surprise so pleasant to the eye, such a complete discovery, and so incomprehensible perfected that I felt it a bit of heaven. It was as though I saw around me a reflection of the divine. Critics have called Cranbrook "the most enchanted and enchanting setting in America," and I heartily agree. It was not just the architecture but also the sculpture and the integration of nature that had crafted it into such a place of beauty.

It would be years before I would read Louis Sullivan's *The Autobiography of an Idea* and *Kindergarten Chats* and learn that the enchantment I experienced at Cranbrook could be experienced over and over again in beautiful buildings. As a result, I would learn that not awesomeness but exquisite taste and purposeful meaning give a structure inner character and beauty.

Sullivan synthesized the means for determining good architecture in the formula, "Form follows function." He said sarcastically but incisively that it mattered little if someone designed a bank after a Roman temple as long as its employees all wore togas.

More to the point, no one should model a library after the Acropolis or a Roman bath and expect that youngsters would feel it inviting to visit. Similarly, a courthouse with a large dome and judge's benches raised high above the floor contributes little to concept of a level field for plaintiff or defendant. Again, larger and loftier churches might seem to honor God, but they also take away from the person praying there. Architecture, I discovered, is not a fine art in the sense it is for the sensitive, educated connoisseur. It is rather a living art that deeply touches all of us and helps shape our lives.

Chicago architects, almost from the beginning, stressed the window as a key factor in their work. The window of Chicago architects' buildings tend to have surprising visibility—making it so people outside have an interesting frame to view what is inside and those inside are gifted with a clear and distinct view of the outside. A window that pioneered this in the late 1800s became known as "The Chicago window."

Great architecture can turn the world into an enchanted Cranbrook.

I have one word for great architects: Thanks.

# 12

## Out of Frustration, I Write
## My Own Moral Theology Book

*I did not have a complete vision, but there were things I wanted to learn. I knew the theology that they were teaching me in the class-room would not help inspire people to be kinder and more spiritual. I wanted the Catholic Church's morality to be a Holy Grail. I wanted it to be jeweled with love, justice, and charity rather than with abstract and remote moral choices decided by scholastic theologians writing in the very different world of 13th and 14th century feudalism. I felt the language of Jesus could be, but the moral distinctions in my textbooks were not only unfeeling and unmoving, but also failed that test.*

Oldenburg, Indiana is a small, charming little town in the hilly southeastern part of the state. The Franciscan theological seminary was in a large, one-hundred-year-old wood frame monastery there. As a Franciscan friar, I studied theology there in 1956 and 1957. With a population of seven hundred, and multiple church spires, this quaint, off-the-beaten-track hamlet bespoke otherworldliness. It seemed to me more a Brigadoon—a mythic village, which reappears every hundred years—than a part of the real world. I enjoyed the setting, but, at the same time, I found its isolation disturbing.

If Oldenburg seemed out of this world to me, the theology courses and textbooks (in Latin) that formed the bases of my studies did even more so. The closest they came to being up-to-date was a reference (the only words in English) in Father Thomas Iorio's *Theologica Moralis* that offered a condemnation of the "Black Bottom," a raunchy, boisterous dance popular in the 1920s.

Some fifty-five years later, I still have my copy of the Iorio text with its agonizing, legalistic details of moral theology. For years it had served as *the* guide for Franciscan seminarians around the world about what is "sin" and, incidentally, what pleases or displeases God.

The other available text was Adolphe Tanquerey's *Theologiae Moralis et Pastoralis*, which had been updated in 1930 from its first edition of 1904. It was unfortunately little different in presentation or relevance from Iorio's textbook.

We had all been somewhat prepared for this. Our courses in philosophy were in Latin and used the same memorize-the-lengthy-syllogism approach, but I had ignored a lot of that. I learned Latin well enough, but otherwise I memorized material and forgot it the next day if I did not find it relevant. But this was different. This was meant to mold me into a Catholic priest in four years. I could not play the same trick I had in philosophy.

The book started off with the statement that its material is offered for the purpose of the sanctification of souls for which Christ the Lord underwent torture and gave his life. But only vaguely does this purpose underlie the actual moral assertions that follow. What we hear instead of the voice of a loving God is the hammer of authority along with an ever-present screaming threat of eternal damnation.

The deeper into the moral theology text and course I found myself, the more uncomfortable I became. I memorized the facts, but I could not get hold of how they pertained to goodness and fairness. Lacking were a noble idealism, an enthusiasm for how morality can uplift a person and any sense of Christ's words urging, "What you do to the least of these, my brothers, you do to Me."

My scrambling reaction was to write a book for myself. It would be my first. It was not in my mind an effort at protest, but a release valve for my half-developed thoughts. No one, except myself, would ever read it, not even in the fifty-some years since I wrote it. I titled it, *Catholic Social Enthusiasm.*

In retrospect (I still have the manuscript), it was an enthusiastic belief in my faith and religion. I based it more on confronting moral lapses and needs of the world as I saw them than on the traditional Catholic distinction-making moral theology text we were studying. Today, as I look back, writing that book helped take me in a reasonably sane direction. It also revealed in me a deep conviction that I had then that good intentions, hope, and moral will power could be enough to change the worst of situations.

I did not have a complete vision, but there were things I wanted to learn, holes to fill in. I realized that the theology that they were teaching me in the classroom would not help inspire people to treat each other better or to be more spiritual. I wanted the Catholic Church's morality to be a Holy Grail. I wanted it to be jeweled with love, justice, and charity rather than with abstract and remote moral choices decided by scholastic theologians writing in the very different world of thirteenth and fourteen century feudalism. It wanted it to be based on truths that were absolute, immutable, and eternal. I felt the language of Jesus could be, but the moral distinctions in my textbooks were not only unfeeling and unmoving, but also failed that test. This was my dream. It still is.

So, in my isolated world, I wrote my own moral textbook but kept it there. In retrospect, it marked a mini-milestone on my life's journey. My thinking, feeling, and writing caused me to doubt many of the legalisms of the Church's moral theology and to look elsewhere to find the moral revolution the world seemed to need.

It was, as I recall, a time of angst and loneliness. I still had to study the texts, take exams in which I gave the answers, which were asked for. And I was aware I never dare talk to anyone about my book. Not surprisingly, I developed an ulcer, which further cut me off from the rest of the community. I was forced to eat at a special table, where softer, more digestible foods were made available. The Oldenburg library was less relevant than it had been at Duns Scotus College. Consequently, I could not even escape there.

Stomach distress plagued me throughout my first year of theology. I had a number of tests to determine whether I had an ulcer, and none were conclusive. Years later an endoscopic examination showed scars verifying the fact I had had several. My health problems, I found, were more annoying than threatening.

My studies grew far more bothersome. I was not living in an environment in which a student felt or had opportunity or permission to question the principles behind, much less the direction of Catholic theology. I could not even dare to think of attempting it.

I did not challenge Catholic dogma or basic morality, but I believed that it had to start including the church's teachings on social justice and people's rights, especially those of the poor. My fellow cleric at Duns Scotus who had said with a measure of annoyance, "You know that Kenan, he will try anything. I mean it. Anything!" He was proving dead-on right—at a level and a direction that neither of us could have imagined.

Looking back, I can see it was in part the spirit of my father—with his sense of freedom—overriding in me my mother's rigid belief in the authority of the Catholic Church. The struggle I felt was especially awkward and painful, because I couldn't win it! The only tangible result of that struggle was my first book-child and I never, to this day, have shown it to anyone.

The content of the moral theology textbook I studied confused me. It was written in Latin by a Franciscan priest, a moral theologian in Naples. It was a formulaic textbook, far more dependent on antiquated theologians than on the Gospels, on hackneyed Latin phraseology rather than on insightful thoughts (much less experience), on the details of sin rather than the inspiring and living examples of other people.

The book, for example, provided a long list of varying times with which to determine when to begin or end a fast day. It also let us seminarians know at which hour on Friday we could choose to stop or resume eating meat. These specifications went so far as to include the option of using standard time, daylight savings time, real time, estimated time as well as several times I no longer remember. Yet, the timing of one's act could determine whether or not a person in ending or starting a fast or eating meat you were committing a mortal sin that could condemn you to the eternal fires of hell. This was neither an author I was reading nor a random lecture. It was the unchallengeable moral teaching of the Catholic Church, which I had to learn and to accept.

The moral textbook also clearly and decisively stated, *Omne mendacium est peccatum*—"Every lie is a sin." Then followed five to ten pages carefully describing when and how deception is or is not a sin.

The simplest and most profound moral statement I ever encountered in the monastery had come at Duns Scotus, when Father Philibert Ramstetter told us in an ancient voice totally filled with conviction and emotion, "A lie is a violation of the intellect." The words still resound in my head and lean me strongly in the direction of truth no matter what. I got no such moral conviction out of anything taught me in moral theology.

One part of theology I did not reach, because of the order in which it was taught in our house of theology concerned—sins involving sex. That part of theology was offered in the final year of study and therefore reserved for the twenty-six- and twenty-seven-year-old seminarians ready to be ordained and to hear confessions. Whenever the course was being taught, the classroom transoms were shut so the rest of us (all in our mid-twenties) could not overhear the lectures or discussions. The worst error of the moral theology textbook, I felt, was not in what it said but in the omission of all it did not say. I fervently wanted that corrected, but knew it would not be—not in my age and not by my hand.

As I have considered what I feel missed in my studies at Oldenburg, I have arrived at a list of what I would liked for us to have learned there in those years meant to teach us theology.

I wanted something from my religion that was based in the beatitudes that Jesus had given the world in Matthew 5:3–12:

> *Blessed are the poor in spirit for theirs is the kingdom of heaven.*
> *Blessed are they who mourn for they shall be comforted.*
> *Blessed are the meek, for they shall possess the earth.*
> *Blessed are they who hunger and thirst for justice, for they shall be satisfied.*
> *Blessed are the merciful, for they shall obtain mercy.*
> *Blessed are the pure of heart, for they shall see God.*
> *Blessed are the peacemakers, for they shall be called sons of God.*
> *Blessed are they who suffer persecution for justice sake, for theirs is the kingdom of heaven.*

I wanted a moral theology that said, "Love one another as I have loved you."

I wanted a moral theology that God was the center and man, the object.

I wanted a moral theology that preached social and economic justice.

I wanted a moral statement that any form of bigotry is unequivocally wrong.

I wanted to study the morality of the social teachings in Pope Leo XIII's encyclical *Rerum Novarum* on the rights of workers to organize into unions and Pius XI's encyclical *Quadragesimo Anno* on a worker's right to a family and a living wage.

I wanted something to show me that sexism and the sexual and physical abuse of children and women were against the very heart of the teachings of my religion.

I wanted a clear statement on empathy for victims of sexual abuse as well as of war, sexism, racism, tyranny, and economic injustice.

I wanted it clear and emphatic that as a society and as individuals, we have an obligation to help those who are disabled—and especially for their basic rights to be recognized.

I wanted my church to say as clearly and decisively as the Declaration of Independence declares that we are all created equal and endowed by our creator with unalienable rights, among which are the right to life, liberty, and the pursuit of happiness.

I wanted it to be said of Catholics, "They have consciences, even social consciences, and they act on them."

My book *Catholic Social Enthusiasm* was specific in its scope and deeply sincere in its emotional tone. At the same time, its weaknesses were that it was filled deep with naiveté and marked by over-enthusiasm. I realized no bishop or religious superior would ever consider putting a "*nihil obstat*," a stamp of censorship approval that "nothing stands in its way."

But, so what? Well, for one thing, it helped keep alive in me a conscience-driven spark, which I longed for the communicative ability to share it with others. The opportunity would come and I would find joy in it. But, first, there would be mountains and deserts for me to cross and there still are.

# 13

## I Become as Unordainable
## as If "Possessed by the Evil One"

*A news story dated March 10, 2010 by the Times Online news service reported that Father Gabriele Amorth, eighty-five, "the Vatican's chief exorcist for 25 years," stated that he had dealt with seventy-thousand cases of demonic possession. How many of these "possessed" individuals might in actuality simply have suffered, as I had, from undiagnosed gran mal epileptic seizures?*

June 10, 1957 was the morning on which my older brother and roommate was ordained a priest. It was one of the most anticipated days of my life and turned out also to be the one on which I first came to realize that, although I had already spent ten years working toward it, I would probably never be allowed to attain that goal myself.

An hour before the ceremony marking his ordination, I suffered a *gran mal* epileptic seizure. It was eleven months after I had had an earlier one. At the time of the previous one, my religious superior at Duns Scotus College had decided there was no reason to have the cause of the episode diagnosed. The repeat attack now engendered a strong suspicion that I suffered from epilepsy.

I returned home to attend the celebration of my brother's First Mass and indicated to my mother what might be the effect of my seizures by telling her, "Don't necessarily expect for this to happen for me." I did not know the specifics of how church law dealt with epilepsy, but I had my fears.

A thorough three-day checkup in a Catholic hospital in Cincinnati two weeks later confirmed that I did have epilepsy. During my hospital stay, I learned something else that perplexed me. Black patients, even though it was a Catholic-run hospital, were confined to a segregated ward. It apparently was something that routinely happened to African-Americans out in the world. And, in this case, a church-run institution was doing it. I spent time visiting on that ward and came quickly to the conclusion that segregation therefore perplexed me to the point of almost hopeless confusion.

What did God think about it? This was not how I thought He wanted Catholic institutions to conduct themselves. I had served Mass in an African-American parish when I was in grade school, eaten meals in the parishioners' homes, and had a black classmate in the seminary. I felt both the chain of obedience and the weakness of my being a mere seminarian and now, an epileptic constrained me from speaking out against such a policy on the part of the hospital. Or, was I just finding excuses? I left the hospital a very discouraged Franciscan friar. The results that defined my epilepsy were very bad news and God's own hospital segregated blacks from whites only added to it.

The horizon was about to grow darker. On the issue of epilepsy, the Catholic Church's canon law, it turned out, was as cold and bizarre as though it had been taken out of storage from a Dark Ages crypt. Although its canon law had supposedly been updated when it was codified in 1917, its terminology and language in addressing epilepsy as a barrier to the priesthood still echoed the poignant past, the prejudices of a thousand years earlier.

Canon law banned all candidates for the priesthood from being "ordained or exercising orders already received if they *are or were epileptics either not quite in their right mind or possessed by the Evil One.*"

That law pressed its thumb squarely down on the likes of me. Ouch!

I still shudder as I read those words and realize they applied to me. The phrasing of the canon law statute was directed at epileptics and, in application, combined the categories of mental illness and satanic possession with epilepsy. The three hurdles in the canon law prohibition were not even separated with commas. It was as though a real, live, fire-breathing dragon had come from the dark and distant past to get me.

Epilepsy was a switch in my life that turned some lights off and others on, making day out of night and night out of day. Almost as soon as I came out of the seizure, I realized what had happened. It would take the rest of my life to deal with it.

Even now I am still coming to terms with the enormity of having gone from thinking of myself as a person called and chosen by God to one rejected as a candidate for the priesthood by the untempered prejudice of Catholic Church law.

From when I was thirteen years old until I was twenty-three, I had focused simply on being a Franciscan and then to become in three more years a Catholic priest. Only the hope of some day going to heaven surpassed my long-held aspiration to become a priest.

For four years in the minor seminary and then six in the religious habit, I had remained on track, been mostly steadfast and met the specific requirements of being a male, enjoying good health, displaying adequate moral character, showing sufficient scholarship, and demonstrating a "calling" to achieve the goal of the priesthood. Until then, I had accepted it as right and good for the Catholic Church to exclude from the priesthood a long list of people, including women, the disabled, and those who do not personally disavow marriage. In being chosen, in meeting these and other stringent requirements, I could not help but feel spiritually select in contrast to those on whom a vocation to the priesthood had not been bestowed. What a personal come down! Suddenly, "the few are chosen" part of the equation was working against, instead of for me. Had I taken a prideful path toward the priesthood and the tripped on it?

"Possessed by the Evil One!"

Was something twisted in my thinking or theirs? Were the church officials possibly doing God's will in putting and maintaining those three categories in the same sentence? They must have believed so. Demonic possession long has been and still is a serious matter in the innermost workings of the Catholic Church. A news story dated March 10, 2010 by the *Times Online News Service* reported that Father Gabriele Amorth, eighty-five, "the Vatican's chief exorcist for 25 years," stated that he had dealt with seventy thousand cases of demonic possession. How many, I wondered, of these 'possessed' individuals might in actuality have suffered, as I did, from undiagnosed *gran mal* epileptic seizures?

This 1917 canon law provision was still in effect and would remain so—I would later learn—until 1983, when a revision dropped it and went silent on the subject. That change would occur twenty-three years after I would have been ordained.

I take it personally—very personally—that I was excluded from the priesthood because I had epilepsy. It is not because of who I am or that I was in any way particularly deserving of being ordained a priest. Rather, it is because when any of us is excluded, stigmatized, or shunned as a member of group of people those who do it depersonalize not just the individual but also all who are excluded.

Was the mentality that shorted me from the priesthood the same that confined black patients to a segregated ward, denied women and the disabled equal opportunity, including the priesthood? I had questions, but I was in a hierarchical church where the answers did not come from the individual but from the teachings of the church itself. I could commit a sin of disobedience by thinking otherwise.

There was a whole church structure between me and the clear-cut message of Jesus of Nazareth when He spoke the words, "Whatever you do to the least of my brothers you do to Me."

I had taken a vow of obedience that, in effect, forced me to respect that structure and preserve the teachings and rulings of the Catholic Church as they were handed down to me. I might sidestep them in little ways, but could not allow myself to do so in anything as big as this.

I had spent ten years studying for the priesthood and not once in a single class had a student stood up and challenged anything in any way was presented as the teachings of the Church.

I had questions, but they were all penned in my upbringing, training, and mother's commitment to the letter of the law, which the Catholic Church taught. I treasured the wall that was around me, even if it left me with questions I could not answer without the possibility of consequences I did not want to face.

# Part III

# OFF THE PEDESTAL

# 14

## Off the Pedestal
## and
## Out the Door

*I was, in God's eyes, no longer chosen, no longer special.*

**W**hat had happened to the inner me in the midst of the tumultuous life change that epilepsy had brought with it? My chart was gone; my course had become uncertain. I was like the marathon runner or Kentucky Derby horse about to win the race and suddenly being disqualified on a bizarre technicality. I was no longer in the race and I never would again be.

God and his Church had withdrawn the call. I had signed up to attend what, in effect, was an officers' training school in the army of Christ, but I had been dismissed and would have to serve out my enrollment as a private. I was off the pedestal. I was with the "others." I was, in God's eyes, no longer chosen, no longer someone super special. I did not, would not ever share in the magisterial power of the church as only those who are ordained can and do.

I first started to feel my lack of position and power in my last days in the Franciscans. I felt it, but I did not understand it. I could see this fully only when I was long off of the pedestal, feeling what for many years seemed to me as an unimaginable come down. It was not just a canon law provision from the Dark Ages that came down on my head, but it was living the rest of my life without the mantra, "Many are called, but few are chosen." Only slowly, very slowly, would realization come to me of being freed from the prideful yoke of being teamed with God.

Believing what I had learned about human dignity, I felt that it should have been my theology books rather than Thomas Jefferson who first told the world we are all "created equal and are endowed by our creator with unalienable rights, among which are the right to life, liberty, and the pursuit of happiness." But it was not.

I began to realize I—we—were considering women at best second-level members of the Church. Not one of them had a right under church law to the power and position I had sought. I could not figure out why or a single thing to do about it. In my monastic life, I did not even have contact with any of them other than my mother and even that was extraordinarily limited. Later, Pope John Paul II would not only defend the issue of excluding women from the magisterium of the Church, but also insisted with all his authority that it was not even open to debate. His argument was that Jesus, himself a male, choose only men as his apostles, and this action was "a free choice by a sovereign Christ."

I had always thought, "Of course women are not called as boys and men are." It was not just on the surface, but also deep down a part of my pride in the great promise that stood before me. It was only later that I personally felt free to question, much less think of challenging church authorities on such matters. I realized that it helped that I had been excluded as they have been.

If some pope at some time in the future is open to eliminating such prejudice and discrimination in the Catholic Church and needs a theological argument to do it, I came up with one—in Latin, no less. I suggest the logic and appropriateness of a scholastic syllogism: *Potuit, decuit, ergo faciebit* (*"God could. It is fitting. Therefore, He would do it"*).

This simple perception, to me, gave us a whole new way of thinking about religion. It looked to a God who is in the present rather than as a being preserved from the past. It uses what we know of goodness, kindness, and fairness to help us conjure up the divine.

It is heresy, of course, because heresy is about looking for new ways to express reality and truth versus accepting the *status quo*. I dared not, could not, would not have thought this way if I still stood on the pedestal. The threat would have been real of my being taken off of it for such open-minded thinking.

But I was off of it, and I had a new companion, epilepsy. And it was very real, and scary. While I mostly put off any normal fear of it, sporadic attacks reminded me it was real. My first two *gran mal* seizures had not carried with them—as later ones would—the precarious sense that I might not survive the next one. Furthermore, it only vaguely occurred to me that such attacks would cause others to see me as a person who could at any moment upset and frighten them with an attack. A disability— and that is what I had, but no longer do—does something to the inner gyroscope that carries us forward. You fight. You can even seem to win.

But those around you are telling you that you are not whole and that you alone will have to anticipate whatever might happen next.

What did happen next in my life after my attack the morning my brother was ordained was that I was sent to the minor seminary in Mount Healthy, Ohio to teach algebra to first-year seminarians. I kept my cleric status, which neither listed me as neither a brother nor a priest. I was uniquely alone. Still, I liked teaching and the excellent teachers I had had while I was a student at St. Francis Seminary inspired me to try hard to be like them.

Then I had another seizure and another. The distance between the rest of the community and me grew ever wider—and I felt it. Nevertheless, I was stunned when the provincial board—without anyone bothering to discuss it with me—transferred me at the end of the semester of teaching to the Franciscan provincial motherhouse at 1615 Vine Street in Cincinnati. The large, ancient church and friary was not so much a vital, community-serving religious institution as a warehouse for members of the community who had problems.

The huge building itself dates to just before the Civil War (1859). It has dozens of individual bedrooms called "cells." Three floors of high-ceilinged, ill-lit corridors made it out-dated, cold, and somewhat macabre. You could almost expect to see ghosts slinking along their walls. Instead you saw crucifixes and antiquated religious pictures hanging on them.

What I saw in those corridors was not a ghost but a phantasm of sadness that reminded me of the chained figure of Marley from Charles Dickens's *Christmas Carol.* It was a Franciscan priest, Father Randolph Thompson, the same man who had attempted to molest me at the seminary and whom I had reported. Nine years had passed and I found myself stationed with him in the same residence, the warehouse for Franciscans who did not fit anywhere else. Father Randolph avoided me and I, him. We never spoke a word nor in any way acknowledged each other's existence. The sadness, which I projected that he carried with him, however, seemed contagious, and I caught some of it just from seeing him. I accepted my assignment there. I had no other choice. I had taken a vow of obedience, and I was now complying with it.

The priest who was the provincial, the head of the province, assigned me three perplexing jobs. One was to translate a book on religious vocations from French into English. I had had only one quarter of a semester of French, offered when the priest who taught us Spanish at Duns Scotus College was ill for a brief time. I was handed a French-English dictionary but, of course, it did not make me adequate to the task. Out of obedience, I did struggle to get the words and sentences to try to make some kind of sense, but the results as I put them on paper did not do that.

The second job was an appointment as a part-time assistant to the director of vocations for the province, even though he had just been given a new full-time assistant. The third was a project to write a history of St. Francis Seminary, but they gave me only a small box of documents and photographs with which to work. I accepted all three assignments in the spirit of the vow of obedience, which I had made.

I had no desire to get out of my vows or leave the Franciscans. I did not even once think seriously about it. Three months passed. Then, seemingly out of nowhere, the priest whom I had chosen as my spiritual director brought up the issue of my leaving. Through all of the now eleven years since I had entered the seminary, I considered the idea of separating myself from the Franciscans comparable to sailing off the end of the earth. It was inconceivable.

We were sitting there in the priest's office. He had been looking away. He turned around in his chair, focused his eyes on me and then asked, "Have you considered leaving?"

I felt as though I were someone else than I had ever been in my life. I answered, "No. I have never considered it."

Still, I knew my world had turned inside out. His words created a tremendous change in the direction of my thinking. He had not just asked a question. He had given me a seemingly independent assessment of my situation and spiritual permission to end my pursuit to nowhere and to know that, in doing it, I was not offending the Franciscans or God himself. That which I had not considered now stared me in the face. The thousand questions I needed to ask myself at this point were about "why," "how," "when," and "what if"; but they seemed at the moment, irrelevant. I felt rejection and at the same time, freedom. I knew in that moment that I was not wanted and staying would never work as long as that was true.

I am not certain whether he had raised the question in consultation with the provincial. I tend to believe he very much had and that a number of priests if not almost every one of them who led the province were involved in the call. He certainly had available all the answers about what I needed to do next in order to get a papal dispensation from my vows and leave. All the Franciscan Order's actions toward me, I now realize, said one thing: "Sorry, but you are useless here. Maybe, you can fit better somewhere else."

Once the person on whom I relied for spiritual guidance and some measure of my own sanity questioned my vocation to be a Franciscan, quitting the order was the only option that made any sense to me. I did not for a second take into account my disability and my questionable employability. Nor did I consider my ignorance about life in a world, which I had for all practical purposes left at the age of thirteen. Nevertheless, I applied that day to the Vatican authorities for a dispensation from my vows. It was granted, and my years and aspirations as a Franciscan were over.

I did not wait for the papers to go through. Instead, I left for that bed at home that my father had said would always be available should I decide to leave.

# 15

## From Selling Door-to-Door
## to Becoming a Newspaper Reporter

*The first story I would write as a staff member of The Wage Earner
was about the "slave market" along Eight Mile Road in the heart of an
impoverished African-American community. To do the story, I walked
along Eight Mile and interviewed men who each day would rush
almost every car that stopped at a red light to ask the driver if he had
any work to offer.*

. . . .

*I had, without realizing it, found something that utilized my limited
talents. With my notepad and a place to publish the facts, I was able to
transform a social problem into a personal one for readers by individualizing the people in the picture.*

U pon arriving home, I was more confused than hurt or angry. I
was adrift. My hull was cracked, and I was separated from my
mooring. I was intimidated by illness and my drastic life change.
I felt I had to find a way to stay near the shore and eventually let happen what may. Little did I know at this point in my life that the winds
eventually would come into my sails more fulsome than I could ever hope
they would.

Up until I left my studies, my compass had pointed in only one direction—toward the priesthood. It no longer did. Worst of all, now, I could
no longer trust that the nearby shore was as friendly as I thought it to be.
The Franciscans—the people whom I so much admired—had, in the end,
been insensitive to me. They had found me useless and warehoused me
at the motherhouse like a piece of broken-down furniture or a pedophile
named Father Randolph Thompson. The law of the Church, the origin
and authority of which I believed to be divine, had excluded me from the
priesthood. This was done because of a handicap, one that I now carried
with me into a world that struck fear in me.

My epilepsy remained a problem. I would continue over the next eight years to have sporadic seizures. Each attack would figuratively hurl me against the rocks. While I have not had another in the last forty-eight years, the almost primal fear of having one still lurks in the back of my thoughts.

Like an animal that has been shot at, I wanted to run, but all I could do at this time was stay close to familiar territory. And this was my family, the Catholic Church, and the Franciscans. I lived at home, went to Mass every day, and took on a job selling door to door the Franciscan Province's magazine, the *St. Anthony Messenger*. The sales pitch, which I was given and used for selling the magazine, told people how the profits went to help young boys become Franciscan priests.

At the time, I was very glad to have the job selling the Catholic magazine. For all I knew, the limitations caused by how people viewed epilepsy might prove selling Catholic magazines door to door the only job ever available to me. Part of the irony came from the fact that I had been a successful door-to-door salesman at the age of five. Since then, I had put in eighteen years learning to be more than that. But my drive was still there, and I did well enough.

Still, selling the magazine was a mere job, one for which I had traded a life-long mission. My unhappiness grew, and the light at the far end of the tunnel seemed to be getting smaller rather than larger. I worked for several months at the job. And suddenly, without any alert as to what was going to happen next, I took a giant leap in life. It came about because someone was willing to believe in me. That has been the case in virtually every move forward I would ever make.

Writing—the limited talent with which I had struggled so hard and for so long—was about to come to my aid. I was to go from selling a Catholic magazine door to door to being hired full time by a newspaper as a reporter. The man who believed in me in this case was Bill Ryan, who was a United Auto Workers local union president, a Michigan state legislator and, fortunately for me, editor of *The Wage Earner* newspaper.

Several years before, *The Wage Earner* had published two articles I had written while I was a student at Duns Scotus College. We had not been in touch since then. Then one day, I decided to call him up to say hello and share with him that I was no longer a Franciscan.

"Want a job?" he asked.

"What?"

"I asked if you care to work for *The Wage Earner*," he said. "We need someone."

I had mentioned my epilepsy, and he was aware of my gross inexperience. It was as though an untrained and disabled man was offered a horse and a chance to ride it into battle. I was stunned. "Yes," I said, little realizing what a step it would be in my life.

Bill Ryan—a slender, self-depreciating but keenly assertive and brilliant man was a Robert E. Lee when it came to strategizing. He was a focused thinker as well as a profoundly experienced negotiator. His understanding and appreciation of friendship and loyalty, I would find, to be very much on my side. On my part, I was a very raw recruit and saw labor unions, race relations, and politics only from having been in study groups in a monastery. On his part, Bill was a tough, battle-tested, and very determined veteran on such issues. His enormous patience helped me work my way through many mine fields both in my thinking and writing.

He genuinely cared about people and that is what ultimately bonded us—that and our mutual agreement that our Catholicism and humanity carried with them a responsibility to be concerned with the basic needs of others. Later, Bill's integrity and brilliance would win him the highly respected position of speaker of the House of Representatives for the State of Michigan.

What we faced as a newspaper in the Motor City that wanted to take on the city's challenges and problems was formidable, far more than I could ever realize. Detroit in 1958 was a scarred battlefield, one where the vicious poverty, racism, and growing unemployment were winning the battle over day-to-day survival.

My mother had something to do with how I would confront these issues. Whenever any of the children in our family complained or even spoke about a social issue, she inevitably challenged, "Why don't you do something about it? At least try." Such words can be a real push into the fight if they come from your mother and are repeated often enough. I did not know it, but I was about to take on or at least to try to some of the major issues facing Detroit.

A large billboard along the Ford Expressway told a grim story. It gave the tally of how many cars Detroit had manufactured so far that year. In the late 1950s, the numbers it was posting were dropping significantly from year to year as foreign competition was making ever increasing inroads into the American market. The decline translated in 1959 into three hundred thousand people in the Detroit area being out of work.

The first story I would write as a staff member for *The Wage Earner* was not about the inner city, but Detroit's north border, Eight Mile Road. A two-mile stretch of it was a 'slave market' in the heart of an impoverished African-American community. To do the story, I walked along Eight Mile and interviewed men who each day would rush almost every car that stopped at a red light to ask the driver if he had any work to offer. Some, a very few, found work as Eight Mile Road had become a day labor market. Here, contractors could come to find someone to dig a ditch, carry something heavy, or clean up a mess.

The pay was whatever the two parties would agree to, and the actual work opportunity might last only an hour or two. No regulatory agency or rules in any way supervised or controlled the conditions under which the men worked or the pay they received.

The investigation and ensuing story became a forerunner of others, which I would write for *The Wage Earner* and the *Chicago Tribune*. I had, without realizing it, found something that used my limited talents. With my notepad and a place to publish the facts, I was able to transform a social problem into a personal one by individualizing the people in the picture. *The Wage Earner* story made some mark in the city. The local public television station invited me to come into the station and give an on-camera interview about my reporting.

I moved from my parents' home in the suburbs to the near-downtown Briggs Stadium neighborhood. Next to the house in which I now lived, men were working in a car wash for a one dollar a day plus tips. Not many cars could ever be seen making use of it, and consequently the tips were few. To keep themselves warm on the cold winter days, the men gathered wood from wherever they could find it and used discarded oil from a nearby service station to keep a fire going in a corner of the building. Finding kindling wood was getting harder and harder, they told me. Despite the desperation of their daily lives, I heard a young man who was out of work say, "At least they have jobs."

The local parish owned the house in which I lived and which I was encouraged to make a boarding house for young men. The pastor, who remained remote, was pleased it was no longer vacant. Still, he proved more a suspicious than a generous man. I felt that I had to use a ruse to turn the house's rickety fence into firewood for the men at the car wash. I complained to the pastor about the condition of the fence next to the house and asked him to take it down. "You take it down," he said.

I went to the men at the carwash and told them, "You can have the fence for kindling." It disappeared in five minutes.

I wrote their story up in *The Wage Earner* (without mentioning the fence). The paper got a response from the car wash association, acknowledging the conditions and expressing the hope things would get better. The letter also mentioned an innovation that was about to take place in the car wash industry—automation. *The Worker* (a Communist Party newspaper that had by then dropped the word Daily from its name) rehashed my car wash article without attribution, changed a few facts, giving the story a slant of its own.

I also took photos for *The Wage Earner* of devastated areas of the city. One picture said everything. It was a street sign that read "Third Avenue One Way." The background in the photograph showed how bleak and barren of houses and commercial buildings the area was. It had been leveled after thousands of area residents had fled Detroit in the hope of finding job opportunities, following the one way sign as far as California or Alaska.

I was not proposing solutions as much as I was trying to put a personal face on the city's problems. Through a variety of contacts and an openness to engaging people in conversation, I came to know dozens of individuals without jobs as well as others who labored for the minimum wage or less. My parents, living in the suburbs, knew no one out of work. This lack of personal knowledge on the part of many and negligible coverage in the city's newspapers minimized any pressure on those to provide additional job training or other services that might have benefited the unemployed.

Bill Ryan taught me the basic facts of journalism and edited whatever I had written. A veteran employee of the *Michigan Catholic* newspaper worked with me every month to put the paper to bed at the printers. Virginia Ryan, Bill's wife, helped me almost as much as he did, handling the secretarial work and serving as the "managing" part of my job title of managing editor.

The narrative exposes I wrote continued. One told of a bus that came and parked twice a week on the skid row section of Michigan Avenue. It was there to recruit the unemployed to go to Mississippi and Arkansas to pick cotton at just above slave wages. Another was about Hank, a friend of mine who was a young unemployed steelworker. One day he would say confidently, "Anybody can find a job." The next morning he might weep because he could not find work himself. He had been unemployed for almost two years. It was the kind of illogic that so often grips the unemployed and disenfranchised.

I interviewed a man pushing a handcart around the city to collect salvageable junk and sell it. A year earlier he had been working in an auto factory. Despite inclement weather and the paltry income he received from his efforts, he pushed on, a symbol of the desperate people, I observed, forced to do whatever they could to survive.

I encountered a vendor outside Briggs Stadium. It was the hottest day of the year. He had an ice cream pushcart, but he was selling peanuts rather than ice cream. I asked him why and he told me he couldn't afford the dry ice needed to keep the ice cream from melting. I gave him twenty dollars to buy some dry ice, believing it would help him many times over. A week later, I met him again and asked him if he had bought the dry ice and, if so, how it had worked out.

"No, I didn't buy any ice," he said. "I used the money to buy food for supper for my family." Probably, most of us would have done the same, I concluded.

We also did a front-page piece that called on all four candidates for Governor of Michigan to state ways in which, if elected, they intended to battle unemployment. We ran each of their answers in one of four parallel columns.

I went as a reporter in 1959 on the United Auto Workers-sponsored Unemployment March on Washington. I boarded their train to the capitol and wrote about it. I felt that such efforts help personalize the unemployed and their needs. The Eisenhower Administration Secretary of Labor James Mitchell greeted us on the stairs of the United States Capitol and promised that if the national unemployment did not dip by the end of the year below a certain percentage he would eat his hat. His optimistic prediction proved wrong and months later he ate a cake made in the symbolic form of a hat as a form of public recognition of the fact. To Mitchell and the administration, joblessness was something statistical. I wrote about it to make it personal.

In my own life, I had only once been unable to find work. It was right after high school and just for the two months of my summer vacation before entering the novitiate. But even under those circumstances it was as though my fragile-for-the-moment ego was wearing a badge that said "worthless." In *The Wage Earner*, I had a tool that—even if it could not solve the problem of joblessness or even reach many readers—it could help focus on the issue. The paper was a means to call attention to some of the more hopelessly unemployed and I used it.

It was difficult for me to comprehend that less than a year before I had been wearing a religious habit and trying to perform useless tasks. My focus was now on the world around me, but it was still in my mind very Catholic. I wrote about the Catholic Interracial Council and its work with a coalition of other groups to break the civil rights logjam that marked the late 1950s. I did story after story about the many different imaginative

*1961 issue of paper that gave me my start*

attempts of Father Clement Kern at Most Holy Trinity Parish to aid people in need and I wrote about the efforts of the Murphy family at the Catholic Worker to help the homeless and hungry of Detroit.

We were a labor paper, and I was able to cover the founding in Detroit of the Negro Labor Alliance by A. Philip Randolph, head of the Brotherhood of Sleeping Car Porters. He was a logjam breaker and consequently a government agency had once labeled him "the most dangerous Negro in the United States."

A spokesperson for the Capuchin's St Bonaventure Monastery on the East Side of Detroit called to complain that the people in their soup kitchen lines were stealing copies of *The Wage Earner* from the back of their church. "It is the only thing they are taking," he said.

"Then, we will double the number you receive," I told him, "and charge you nothing for any of them." I very much wanted those men to get the paper.

I also developed a form of resume for the jobless, including even the so-called unemployables. On the resume, I listed as a reference almost any friend or relative who had a phone, probed for any work experience whatsoever, and listed schools they attended rather than ignore them because they had not graduated. Perhaps the most effective parts of the resume were the correct spellings and addresses as well as phone numbers that the applicant might not have had available otherwise. We mimeographed a stack of these for each job applicant and gave them to him or her with the advice to leave a copy even if turned down.

The very first time we tried it, the resume worked. A young inner-city man had been seeking a job as a dishwasher and was turned down any number of times. At the first place, he left a resume, the owner read it, then yelled for him to come back and hired him. "I have used it successfully several times," he told me when I met him some months later. In other words, he did not always manage to keep the job. Just the same, I kept writing resumes for others.

# 16

## Father Clem Kern:
## A Priest Like I Would Have Wanted to Be

**A**fter reentering the world, which I had forsaken eleven years earlier, I felt that I was at times wearing my awkwardness, confusion, and frustrations on my sleeve. I did not have any idea who could or could not see my frequent clumsiness and inappropriateness. In trying to make small talk, I might start talking about the dogmas of the Church or think someone was talking about astronomy when he or she mentioned the rock and roll group of Bill Haley and His Comets.

Even now, I am capable of feeling embarrassed when I think about my disconnect at times back then. One person helped immensely. When I was in the presence of Father Clement Kern, pastor of Most Holy Trinity Parish in the Corktown port-of-entry neighborhood of Detroit, I genuinely felt not only comfortable but also a better person.

Father Clement Kern (none of his friends used his more formal Church title of monsignor) was perhaps the most respected and loved man in the city of Detroit. The heart and soul of Detroit's caring community, he was a priest liked I had hoped I might have become. He was also a character.

Although he was short and well past fifty, you had to step back a second when he started grossly exaggerating his still-retained ability as a basketball player worthy of being on the Detroit Pistons. And this was bizarre, because—other than this—he was also accepted by Detroit as probably its most humble and spiritual citizen.

Clem Kern (Sometimes, his closer friends dropped even the "Father" part of his title) had another quirk. He was perpetually late for almost everything. (No, take out that "almost.") One reason was that he owned an old, beat-up car that was forever breaking down. A more universal explanation was that he would stay as long as he could with anyone whom he felt needed him. He was a good, kind and deeply spiritual man; but in contrast to his overestimation of himself as a basketball player, he greatly underestimated how extraordinary he was.

His twinkled smile spread all across a beleaguered Detroit during the several generations of his ministry. Father Kern was a thoughtful and supportive person, and I was not the only one who felt myself a better person in his presence. Others noteworthy facts about him included

- a long anonymous list of alcoholics, to whom he had been a friend;
- his five hundred Mexican parish families, whom he loved;
- non-Catholics of every variety, who really liked him;
- the grossly underpaid handbill passers of the city, whom he tried to help become organized into a union;
- the homeless men and women, who relied on him to find shelter and a meal for them;
- the organized workers of the city and those who sought to be, who respected him for respecting them and their unions;
- the city's top labor leaders from Walter Reuther to Jimmy Hoffa, who knew he cared for the workers;
- the members of the Henry Ford family, who invited him to their weddings;
- the staff and officers of the American Civil Liberties Union, who appreciated his aggressive and supportive stands on human rights issues;
- the Jewish community of Detroit, which singled him out for honors on several occasions;
- the politicians, whom he helped bring down to earth;
- the lawyers of the city, a number of whom met regularly in his rectory to help find ways to make their profession nobler;
- the Catholic archbishops of Detroit and his own fellow priests, who realized that a great man and noble priest walked among them;
- the Hispanics of Detroit, from the migrant workers to the successful leaders of their community, who knew him as "El Padre" and "compadre";
- Dorothy Day and Lou and Justine Murphy, as well as others in the Catholic Worker Movement, to whom he was friend and hero;
- Charles Wexler, Marie Oresti, the people of the Catholic Interracial Council, and the people of color in the city who could count on him and did;
- And even the thousands of us over the years whom he frustrated by being late for all those events and meetings.

It was his deep, personal, strong convictions and his willingness to serve that uplifted us all.

Father Kern fought in the trenches for social justice. When others rallied to it, he would hold back until the worst assignment or least glorious job was left for someone to do. And, this he would accept. This task was often to talk to whoever was being truculent or to serve as chairman of the fund-raising part of the effort.

The rest of us let him shoulder the responsibility, excusing ourselves by arguing that he was good at it; but we always knew he was the better man for it. We—on our parts—enjoyed the benefits and spoke with pride of the results we were helping him to achieve.

In everything he did, something very simple about him came through. He handed out praise generously but gracefully ducked receiving it. I recall Father Kern chiding me one day. For what, I do not remember, but it caused me to go into a funk until suddenly a lightbulb turned on in my brain, and I felt appreciative for what he had done.

I am proud and grateful to have known Father Kern, but there was a time when I came close to being embarrassed about him. After I had left Detroit, I happened to be in charge of the Young Christian Workers National Convention in Renssalaer, Indiana and asked him to be the major speaker.

He addressed a crowd of three hundred young people who were seeking the kind of commitment his life represented. His presentation to them, however, started out flat and his voice, monotonous. I could not believe this was my genuine hero and true friend Father Clement Kern at the podium. He had probably delivered more speeches and sermons than any other priest in the Detroit area since the Father Charles Coughlin routinely preached sermons at all the Sunday masses at the Shrine of the Little Flower Church. Father Kern, normally an easy going individual, was now showing himself to be out and out nervous and letting his timidity kill his talk.

Then, something happened, as though by magic. The half of the audience that was still trying to listen laughed at something he said. The response must have helped him realize he had an audience of real people in front of him. A spark lit up in his eyes, determination flushed his cheeks and passion arose in his voice. As he continued his comments, a sizeable part of the audience sat straight up in their seats, while the rest either half-rose out of them or simply stood up. By the end, every person in the auditorium was standing and banging his or her retractable seat in a rousing and loud recognition and approval of the man and the message they had just heard. As I recall the scene, my skin tingles, just as it did then.

That was then that I realized his secret. He could not talk to the air. Rather, he spoke to you and he needed to know that you were there and hearing him. In other words, he did not talk to an audience but with them.

His speeches were simple. He talked about God, love, and neighbor. In the end, it was his honesty and decency that came through.

And what he did was often more important than what he said. He believed in the labor movement and when he came to realize that the young priests of Detroit were not in touch with the unions or their members, he brought a dozen of these priests to the offices of the United Auto Workers for a sit-down discussion with UAW President Leonard Woodcock.

In the late 1950s, the auto industry slumped and Detroit was started on its way to become a shadow of what it had been during World War II and the years following. Unemployment rose phenomenally high. The unions were losing their hold. Homes were being abandoned and whole areas of the inner core of the city were being flattened. African-Americans and Hispanics suffered the worst and had to watch as violent crime committed out of desperation increased in their areas of the city.

In his first meeting with a new Catholic archbishop of Detroit, Father Kern called for the Detroit Catholic Archdiocese to form a black caucus that could help deal with the needs and problems of the city's African-Americans.

His work among Hispanics, who had come from Mexico and Texas in search for work, saw him go to the roots of their culture and needs by his spending a month every year working with the poor in Mexico. His special concern was for the Puerto Ricans and Mexican migrants working the beet fields and orchards of Michigan. He was active in behalf of migrant workers at every level and on any number of occasions raised money and public consciousness on their behalf. Many times he found jobs and housing (sometime on the third floor of his rectory) for those who came to Detroit. He spoke out for them through The Migrant Workers Defense League, an organization he created. He brought Caesar Chavez to Detroit to call attention to the lettuce and grape boycotts and visited him often in California to help picket and demonstrate along with the members of the United Farm Workers. Commentators have readily credited Father Kern with playing a major role in the improvement of conditions and pay for migrant workers across the country.

In his own parish, he had helped set up a dozen organizations, which the laity ran and which served the needs of the poor and outcasts. These included legal, medical, and dental clinics. Two Catholic Worker houses, located in his parish, provided food and housing for the homeless. Other organizations which he helped found in the parish included Casa Maria (a community center), a parish organization for homosexuals founded in the 1950s called Dignity, at least four or five Hispanic organizations, a credit union, youth organizations, and a weekly dinner once a week in the rectory for activists willing to do even more.

He humbly garnered awards and honors from Jewish organizations, labor organizations, the March of Dimes, the National Council of Alcoholism, the Catholic Interracial Council, the Detroit City Council, and the President of the United States. He accepted the awards because they bonded him to those who honored him.

When the *Michigan Catholic* wanted to do a catch-up piece on Father Kern, an editor there asked to borrow *The Wage Earner* file on him. It included sixteen articles, which I had written about him or in which I elaborated on the various projects he had initiated.

Once when he was the announced speaker for a local Young Christian Workers' program, he showed up too late to give the speech because his ramshackle car had broken down on the way. When he did arrive, he insisted on taking up a broom and helping to finish cleaning the hall. That action was a speech in itself.

He was the strongest voice in Detroit for organized labor outside the union movement, yet each year when he would come to the downtown Detroit Labor Day rally, he would stand in the audience rather than sit, as he was invited to do, with the dignitaries.

For a long time, he and Teamster President Jimmy Hoffa were close, but Hoffa cut off the relationship when Father spoke out strongly in support of Cesar Chavez and the United Farm Workers, who were in a jurisdictional dispute with the Teamsters. Father Kern had a prayer service for Hoffa when he went to prison and later another after the former Teamster president had disappeared. Someone him asked how he could do that. "Do you know of anyone who needs it more?" Father Kern asked.

Father Kern died August 17, 1983.

In his eulogy, Monsignor George Higgins referred to an effort that was of extraordinary importance to Father Kern: "In particular, he recognized the need for a strong trade union movement in a highly industrialized city like Detroit, and he did as much as anyone outside the movement to help Detroit workers get organized. The autoworkers and their union never had a better friend."

Those of us who knew him believed he deserved the latter title, "Father," in the fullest and richest sense it could be interpreted.

# 17

## The Catholic Worker's Hospitality: It Brought Me Out of Myself

*After I reentered the world, I was horrified to learn how very many people fervently believe that the poor, "the lower classes," by a combination of their lifestyles and misfortune have surrendered the rights to the pursuit of happiness and to be treated equally.*

I have given my memory the luxury of it nostalgically reminiscing about Lou and Justine Murphy of the *Detroit Catholic Worker*—two of the most giving friends I have ever had.

Dorothy Day—the cofounder with Peter Maurin of the Catholic Worker Movement—was more the saint. Her virtue and *persona* worked miracles in the hearts of ten thousands of people, including mine.

The Murphys and their children were down to earth. How they lived and treated others showed me that I could be myself and still be inspired by the radical sanctity of Dorothy Day and the Catholic Worker.

Dorothy Day had turned me around. The Murphys—with their five children—sent me on my way. They did it as a family and as my friends, casually being there for me and for everyone around them, especially for the neediest of the needy.

After I reentered the world, I was horrified to learn how very many people seem to believe fervently that the poor, "the lower classes," have by a combination of their lifestyles and misfortune surrendered their rights to the pursuit of happiness and to be treated equally.

We can argue that these naysayers and their mentality go against the deepest of religious and American values and still not move them from any of their position one iota. But, if they had sat in the living room of the Murphy family as I often did in the late 1950s, they might have begun to see things differently.

I came to the Murphy household fresh from dropping out of the monastery, a wounded bird, afflicted with epilepsy, and confused as to who

I was and what I could do in this strange and distancing world to which I had returned.

I was full of ideals, but they were rooted in the monastic way of life. They presumed good intentions, based on the premise that if people only knew better. I, on my part, had deep convictions about wanting to be good and do things for others; but my powers seemed to fail when I tried to plug them into real world sockets. From the Murphys I learned that kindness can be the universal connection between all that is good. If it is true, it can—in effect—work miracles.

*My brother, Father Bert, serving a meal at the Catholic Worker house in the 1950s*

These two parents and their children were considerate at a level I had not encountered before. It was not about being overly nice. It was more that looking to the needs of others was automatically their fallback position.

In Lou Murphy, I found rock-solid strength. It was the unique kind that was willing to accept those more righteous people felt justified in disdaining. As a conscientious objector during World War II, Lou had served on the extremely dangerous front lines in Italy as an unarmed, unprotected, and unpaid combat ambulance driver.

He returned to Detroit to operate the Catholic Worker House of Hospitality and to marry Justine L'Esperance. He set a tone of respect and helpfulness for the men who lived in the various rooms of the house at 1432 Bagley or who ate free in its large, bare dining room. His was a tone that resounded with acceptance, respect, and dignity for the lonely, often lost men in the house. These were required to be civil, but there were no sermons and never a put down of any kind from Lou.

Here, from a 1946 letter written by Father Kern, are descriptions of the St. Francis Catholic Worker House of Hospitality for men as well as the Martha House of Hospitality for women and children, a block away. The latter ten-room house became the home for the Murphy family as well.

The full letter appears in Genevieve Casey's biography, *Father Clement Kern: Conscience of Detroit* (Marygrove College, 1989).

### St. Francis House of Hospitality:

Tonight there are 27 men staying there. These men get up at 7:30 a.m., roll up their mattresses, fold up their cots, and set the table for the soup line. The truck picks up each morning the soup left over from the concessionaire at Ford Motor Company, from 35-50 gallons, and this is the main item served to perhaps 415 men from 8-12 daily. The lines run to perhaps 500 sometimes on Sundays because the Capuchins do not serve the men on Sundays. Bread is picked up the day before from the bakeries and institutions, coffee from wholesale grocers, other things from like contacts through the years.

. . . .

It takes 10 of the 27 to run the soup line, about two on the truck that does pickups, three to keep the house clean, etc. The rest are old men and cripples who can do nothing or just came or may be pretty sick for a couple of days.

. . . .

They take anyone for any length of time, regardless of anything, and no questions are asked or records kept. No color line is drawn and as long as a man is not drinking too much and as long as there is room he can stay as long as he likes.

### Martha House:

Given by the Diocese, no rent, shelters women and children who come with mothers. Originally intended for women in need of a place to stay who no one else would take in, but now has grown to be a place where Travelers Aid, the Welfare Department, and like agencies place people until they can find a place for them. Every couple of weeks they get calls and pick up families in bus stations, etc. Ordinary house, perhaps 10 rooms. One week last month there were 11 children, 8 adults staying there. Miss L'Esperance slept on the floor gladly. While this is the cleanest and nicest looking house, its problems are heaviest by far. Neighbors object to colored. Children who are poorly trained. Mothers are wont to waltz off and leave three or four. Social workers are wont to forget where their charges are. Some agencies think it is an awful place, Catholic agencies too, of course, but poor mothers and little kids and the meanest of the mean who are turned out by everybody and have no place to go think it is wonderful.

Father Damian DeVeuster, who spent years serving the lepers on the Hawaiian Island of Molokai, one day announced to them, "Today, I too am a leper," Lou ultimately shared with the men served by the Detroit Catholic Worker House that he too shared with many of them tuberculosis (not mentioning that he presumably caught it from one of them).

Lou had a chiseled face, a cocked Irish smile, and red hair along with eyes that were bright, observant and determined. Beneath everything—while he was not soft—he was fatherly, witty, and, most of all, open to the wants and needs of others.

He gave me a very special gift: lunch with him and Dorothy Day.

Justine had the same toughness as her husband, but she effused more. She would try to make you comfortable, offering a pillow, a special seat, a blind pulled down, something to eat, a willingness to listen, an empathetic response, and a needed touch or hug. Justine Murphy was such an individual.

She had all of these tools and readily used them, but she had more. She had perspective and the ability to inch you upward toward her insights. If a child would come in the room, he or she had the same rights with her as a prominent visitor did, even if her guest were the most interesting or important person in the world.

It was as though the Murphys knew a secret about hospitality and you wanted to learn it from them. Her house—not so much because of ownership or title, but because of the role and responsibility she accepted—included not only the seven members of the Murphy family but also any number of otherwise homeless women and their children, whom she and her family were currently taking in.

Lou and Justine died more than a quarter of a century ago. They had hosted the two houses of hospitality for more than twenty years. I deeply wish they had left behind written memoirs. I would like to have had an even greater insight into what they achieved through their deeply personalist, day-by-day beliefs and actions. Their five children—Sheila, Christina, Brian, Kevin, and Maureen—were an integral part of the Catholic Worker House and are, to those who came to know them, their parents' memoir.

# 18

## The YCW:
## Eight Dollars a Week Plus Room and Board

*Although few of us were truly charismatic, we who were in the YCW (Young Christian Workers) were believers, young and willing to give up much and create change. In my experience the sacrifice and idealism often got through. We were asking much of ordinary young people. Thousands of heretofore-sheltered Catholics got involved and made significant contributions to the developing the social conscience of the Catholic Church in this country.*

**W**ithin a year of leaving the monastery, I had moved from my parents' home in the suburbs to a house in the impoverished Briggs (later, Tiger) Stadium neighborhood of Detroit. I rented it from a Catholic parish. It would serve as a headquarters for a Catholic youth organization, the Young Christian Workers (YCW) that I was working with an organizer from Chicago to try to get going in Detroit. It had three floors and enough rooms for us to turn it also into an inexpensive rooming house for single young men

The house was a challenge. It forced me to find fellow boarders, stoke the coal furnace on cold winter mornings, and to decide whether to accept as a boarder a young man fresh out of prison. Fortunately, he made the decision by moving in with a girlfriend instead.

As the YCW spread to parish after parish in the city, I served as its president and the house became a hub of activity. The organization in Detroit grew from a very tentative group hanging on to its existence in one parish to fifteen sections throughout the city.

A 1959 *Detroit Free Press* article cited the local YCW's work trying to help friends who are unemployed, to promote a civil rights agenda in the city, and to support young people in their attempts to deal with problems that ranged from dating to making political choices.

Best of all, the Detroit YCW was attracting special young people willing to perform incredible sacrifices to help attain its aims. Over those years, several members of the organization's full-time staff came to Detroit as organizers. They and some very driven members helped do the recruiting. These included YCW chaplain Father Jerome Fraser, Harvey Kuehn, Ted Zelewsky, Joe Kelly, Patti Ryan, Helene Mrokowski Evans, Kae Williams Cox, Bob Saenz, Bob Trautman, Grace Farr, Mary Swain, Jerry Curtis, Hank Vasquez, Jim McCormick, and Dan Shay, to name a few of the Detroit members who proved good and supportive friends to each other and to me.

I then did a kind thing for the Detroit YCW and its fifteen parish sections—I left the city for Chicago. Other, more natural leaders took my place.

My move to Chicago in 1961 began as a result of the Young Christian Workers's national chaplain, Monsignor Reynold Hillenbrand, saying at a national board meeting, "What this organization needs is for the young man at the other end of this table to join the national team."

It took me a moment to realize he was talking about me. Once again, having lost my calling to the priest, I felt myself summoned. It was not the best paying job in the country. Actually, it was one of the worst: eight dollars a week, plus room and board. It offered absolutely no fringe benefits.

Still, Monsignor Hillenbrand was someone very special in the history of the Catholic Church in America. Almost single-handedly among the clergy, he had attempted to swing the whole body of the American Catholic Church toward forming for itself a collective social conscience and a love for the church's liturgy.

He was from the beginning the guide, the inspiration, and the national chaplain for the Young Christian Workers (YCW), the Young Christian Students (YCS), and Christian Family Movement (CFM). Through the lay members and chaplains of these organizations, he launched an incredible effort to educate and form students, young workers, and families in the social ideals of the great encyclicals of the popes as well as the social implications he saw in the church's liturgy.

For two years, starting in 1961, I worked full time for the YCW at its national headquarters located at Adams and Paulina in Chicago. I had next to no savings and I had to live as best I could on my eight dollars a week pay. Good things happened—some very good things—and I had the opportunity to work with genuine and hopeful young people. Still, poverty grinds individuals down. Even voluntarily chosen poverty does. And it did me.

By the summer of 1963, my bank account was at zero; my socks could no longer be darned using thread and a light bulb, the cuffs of my pants were frazzled and the seat of them, shiny. It was time to find a new job. Though I had not fulfilled Monsignor Hillenbrand's dream of rescuing the YCW, I had no regrets about accepting the responsibility of telling its members' stories or earning the low pay of a YCW full-timer.

What I did for the Young Christian Workers was to help write its weekly observe-judge-act parish section programs, organize sections, including one in a Chicago South Side poor black parish, and to publish a national newsletter telling about what individual members were doing as part of the "act" resolutions formed at meetings.

I was beginning to write articles for a number of publications including *New City*, the *National Catholic Reporter*, and *Apostolate Magazine*. I had two job offers. They could not have come from more disparate sources. One had been as managing editor of the *National Informer*, a grocery counter tabloid that at the same time wanted to demonstrate a social conscience along with its sex ad section. The other was from St. Meinrad Abbey, which offered me the editorship of its *Marriage Magazine*. I rejected both.

Monsignor Hillenbrand and the movements he helped develop such as the YCW, YCS, and the CFM attempted to recruit and train lay people to be progressive, responsible followers of Christ. In the 1930s and '40s, the main issue that separated American Catholicism had been the support of labor unions; in the 1950s, it was how to respond to communism; in the 1960s, civil rights and the War in Vietnam; in the 1970s, the rights of women; in the 1980s, the poor and social welfare programs; and in the 1990s and 2000s, opposition to abortion as the litmus test for being a true Catholic.

In 2010, Fox News radio and television commentator Glenn Beck helped make the divide between the two sides even more decisive. He urged Christians to leave churches that used terms such as "social justice" and "economic justice" because they were simply "code words for communism and Nazism."

Monsignor Hillenbrand was the person in the history of the Catholic Church who was the most successful in getting these words accepted as part of the thinking and language of the Catholic laity in this country. To him, they were indeed code words, not for Nazism and communism; but against these ideologies. He saw them as a call to fight greed, selfishness, and reactionary politics.

Monsignor Hillenbrand and the members of the three organizations that he chaplained worked to train ordinary people to carry out the principles behind social justice, civil rights, and human rights to fight for any and all who were denied their basic human rights. From the late 1930s, when Monsignor Hillenbrand first stepped up until the 1970s, each of these organizations sputtered and oftentimes prospered in scattered parishes and cities across the nation. The key to the success they had attained was in their being able to train people to be leaders in their communities through social concern and stand-up action.

In his early 1930s, when Cardinal George Mundelein had appointed him the rector of the Chicago Diocese's major seminary, he introduced Monsignor Hillenbrand to the seminarians by saying, "I've brought you a man with imagination." If God did not call me to be a priest; Monsignor Hillenbrand did to be a member of the YCW national team. My poorly outlined job was to be a combination organizer, writer, and communications director.

Although few of us were truly charismatic, we who were in the YCW were believers, young and willing to give up much and create change. In my experience the sacrifice and idealism often got through. We were asking much of ordinary young people. Thousands of heretofore-sheltered Catholics got involved and made significant contributions to developing the social conscience of the Catholic Church in this country.

Sometimes what they did was dramatic. A young woman in Cincinnati made use of TV coverage in helping to integrate the most prestigious (but hitherto segregated) restaurant in Covington, Kentucky. I considered it a privilege to have been one of the other three people she recruited to do it. A YCW leader, Tom Trost, went to jail for a year in Michigan for throwing blood on documents in the offices of Dow Chemical to protest its contribution to the army's chemical warfare in Vietnam. Mary and Bill Goode—YCW and YCS staff members—became man and wife and went to Selma, Alabama to help the civil rights movement, staying there for more than five years.

According to Mary Irene Zotti's book on the YCW between 1938 and 1970, *A Time of Awakening* (Loyola University Press, 1991), Parish YCW groups in Detroit and Chicago not only recruited blacks as members but also several times accepted gang and past gang members.

Members in Ramsey, New Jersey observed the lives of migrant workers on the small farms outside their town. After doing a survey and compiling the facts, they helped to form a community council to deal with the problems they uncovered.

A YCW member in Chicago, Len Boksa, was asked to take a young Canadian student out on the town who had to drop out of Devries Tech and return home for lack of funds. Part of the tour turned out to be a stop at the YCW member's home, where he picked up the funds to loan the student enough money so he could complete his studies. The young man did and was able later to pay back the loan in full.

Members got active in their unions because of the YCW and won election as officers. John Czarnecki became an alderman in Milwaukee and Joseph Ferris, a member of the New York State Legislature.

Many enlisted in the Peace Corps, VISTA, and PAVLA, while others served in the Great Society's 1960s poverty programs as well as on Human Relations Commissions and boards. Any number, when they got married, adopted children, including ones with major disabilities. In a doctoral survey that located thirty-four Catholic young women who reported becoming involved in social justice issues, thirty-one were former members of the YCW. I felt my own most meaningful contribution to the movement was in compiling such stories and sending them out in the Young Christian Workers monthly newsletter.

The YCW weekly parish meetings used the unique training formula that Cardinal Joseph Cardijn of Belgium had developed with young workers there in the 1920s, long before he was made a cardinal. It was to train YCW members to "observe, judge, and act." The groups looked at problems, considered what was the right thing to do, and personally assumed responsibility for doing it.

John F. Kennedy's call to Americans to "Ask not what your country can do for you, but ask what you can do for your country" was the challenge of the time. Whereas the Catholic Youth Organization (CYO) focused on leisure and church activities, the YCW groups, on their part, were better prepared to respond to Kennedy's call.

Catholic high schools and colleges, if they had community involvement programs, were not attempting to inspire the young to change society and its institutions through observation, envisioning what could be done and doing it.

The early 1960s represented the beginnings of the Second Vatican Council, the civil rights movement, and the initial protests against the Vietnam War. The Catholic young people who became involved in these social revolutions were to a large extent those who had come into contact with or had been trained in the Young Christian Workers and Young Christian Students. Monsignor Hillenbrand did have an imagination and it was taking root, even if not in the great numbers it needed to.

My special heroes were the young people in the YCW group organized in a very poor parish in the ghetto neighborhood of Englewood in Chicago. I was never in a group that listened to each other better. They shared their experiences with me and helped inspire me to compile the book, *They Speak for Themselves: Interviews with the Destitute of Chicago.*

Abner Mikva wrote the introduction and the YCW published it in 1965. More than sixteen other publications asked permission to reprint material from it and a tutoring program in Chicago did their own run of the book so they could pass it out to all their tutors.

At the end of my two years full time on the national organization's staff, I did find another job, one as a reporter with a Chicago newspaper. A YCW chaplain recommended me and my background in the movement was certainly helpful in my getting hired.

Some forty years later, a strange and wonderful coincidence turned up in my own family. My daughter-in-law, Jill Schwendeman, published a book based on her experiences working with teen members of the White Bear Unitarian Universalist Church in Mahtomedi, Minnesota. The title is *When the Young Lead: A Guide to Intergenerational Social Justice Ministry* (The Unitarian Univeralist Association, 2007).

I seriously doubt that a single member of the Unitarian Universalist Church anywhere in the country took the advice of gruff, archconservative TV pundit, Glenn Beck, when he suggested people run away from any church that uses the term, "social justice."

She had no association with the YCW, but one line in her book sums up the underlying principles common to both the YCW and her youth ministry: "This is how the change begins: one person who is cherished, one respectful human connection, one communal alliance at a time."

# 19

## The 1963 Civil Rights March on Washington: A Stand-Up Bookend in My Life

*I heard the rest of Dr. King's "I have a dream" speech in that*
*frozen stance as though I were at Gettysburg and*
*Abraham Lincoln were speaking.*
*I was ready for a new life. I had a dream.*

As I closed the book on the Young Christian Workers and on my two years working as a member of the national staff, I found a perfect bookend for the varied discussions, experiences, and protests in which I had been involved up until then. It was the August 28, 1963 civil rights March on Washington.

A bookend, yes, but it would be in the middle of the shelf rather than at the end. The future would be full of opportunity to stay in the struggle in which so many of us were beginning to see progress and hope.

The trip to DC was a reunion with members of my family, a number of whom lived in the Washington area: but it was also a chance to see and talk with people whom I had worked with in Detroit in what we had called race relations and now was becoming known as civil rights.

I could even chalk up a decided accomplishment. I invited my brother Paul to march along with me and he accepted. He was working for the Federal Trade Commission at the time, but would later prove his progressive credentials, working in the Carter White House under U.S. Trade Representative Robert Strauss. After garnering masters degrees from Georgetown and Harvard, he would earn a PhD from the New School In New York, one of the more liberal schools of economics in the country.

The people with whom we wound up marching included Roy and Victor Reuther, the activist brothers of Walter Reuther, the brilliant and innovative president of the United Auto Workers International Union who was in the front row of the stage that day. Paul and I had brought lunches. The Reuthers did not and, in the spirit of the day, we shared ours.

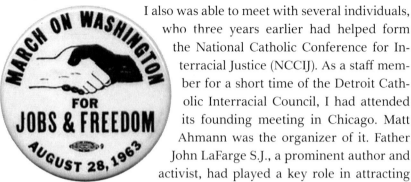

*Badge of Honor*

I also was able to meet with several individuals, who three years earlier had helped form the National Catholic Conference for Interracial Justice (NCCIJ). As a staff member for a short time of the Detroit Catholic Interracial Council, I had attended its founding meeting in Chicago. Matt Ahmann was the organizer of it. Father John LaFarge S.J., a prominent author and activist, had played a key role in attracting other noted Catholic progressives from around the country.

The early 1960s in civil rights, whatever your connection, were no longer about organization as much as they were about protest, demonstration, and action. I was an activist more often than not, providing one more body who someone else called in to make a demonstration larger.

I had protested in front of Catholic churches that discriminated against blacks in Detroit, helped break the racial barrier of a prominent Covington, Kentucky restaurant, demonstrated in the streets in Chicago, been blocked in my efforts and been chided by the Catholic archdiocese of Detroit for issuing a statement in cooperation with the Detroit Catholic Interracial Council questioning the racial policies of the city's police chief.

The March on Washington came at a time of transition in my life. I was leaving the YCW and the whole professional Catholic scene. I saw softness in the Catholic will to fight for civil rights. It was as though we who represented it felt we had to look back over our shoulders to see if there was Catholic support for what we were doing. The Catholic Bishops Statement of 1958 was decidedly firm and assertive on racial equality, but the bishops and their immediate subordinates seemed not to be. Often, they wanted us to meet, discuss, and pray rather than protest or demonstrate. This was especially true of a number of people whom I had relied on to be more out front than they were willing to be.

These issues and the questions that swirled around me may have been the reason my heart and soul was not fully into how I at first saw the March. Meeting and discussing may have been all right in the monastery, but they were no longer credentials that had any bearing on the civil rights movement that had been born and was coming of age on this day.

The crowd in the Washington Mall was beyond enormous. I had become separated from my brother and anyone else I knew. I considered the public transportation problems in getting to his house, so I started to leave early to find room on a bus.

I did not succeed. The loud speaker system was incredible. Over it, I heard a voice roar, "I am happy to join with you today in what will go down in history as the greatest demonstration for freedom in the history of our nation." My skin tingled. My hands froze in front of me. My feet stopped beneath me. I was mesmerized.

I heard the rest of Dr. King's "I have a dream" speech in a frozen stance as though I were at Gettysburg and Abraham Lincoln were speaking. My doubts left me. They were replaced by a dream, one that was somebody else's but that had become mine. I was ready for a new life. I had a dream.

# Part IV

# JOURNALIST

# 20

## Jack Mabley and I
## Go on a Two-Year Adventure

*"Do you consider yourself a conservative or a liberal?"*
*I blurted out: "If I don't know the facts, I tend to be conservative. If I*
*have them, I am a liberal. If I understand the whole situation, I can be*
*a radical."*

In 1963, in leaving the Young Christian Workers and looking for a job, I potentially had to face the following daunting questions:

Who would be interested in giving a meaningful job to a person with *gran mal* epilepsy? (Certainly, the Franciscans had not been.)

What value did a degree afford if it were in scholastic philosophy (taught in Latin) from a non-accredited college?

What practical experience could a person carry over from eleven years in the seminary, seven of them in a monastery?

Oh, yes, and why did I leave? ("I wasn't wanted," sounded terrible.) And what was the pay scale in your most recent job? ("Eight dollars a week.")

Would you have any trouble passing a physical? (Ouch!)

Fortunately, none of these questions were asked or had to be answered.

What I needed was that which every unemployed man or woman needs—a chance. I was also aware that I now needed what would amount to an apprenticeship of some kind as well as an employer with patience to cover over my lack of experience and journalistic training. Jack Mabley, the highly popular news columnist for *Chicago's American*, interviewed me for that chance, an opportunity to be his assistant or "legman."

Over the years, that slot had provided a number of aspiring Chicago journalists with an excellent measure of training and proved their stepping-stone into the newspaper business. The pay would not be a problem for me. I could survive on the less than $3,000 a year the newspaper job

paid. It was, after all, far above the eight dollars a week I had been earning from the YCW. First, though, I had to survive his interview.

I was in luck. Jack's previous legman had been very conservative and
had thus contributed to slanting his image as a journalist far more to the
right than Jack saw himself to be. He had determined to hire someone
who could help shift the material he used in the column to the center
if not a little to the left. He asked one of Chicago's more liberal priests,
Father Robert Reichert, if he knew someone who might fit the bill. The
priest, knowing of my writings and that I was looking for a job, recommended me.

I showed Jack copies of *The Wage Earner* articles that I had written,
and he was impressed. Then he popped the question that was central to
his search for someone to serve his needs: "Do you consider yourself a
conservative or a liberal?"

I blurted out: "If I don't know the facts, I tend to be conservative. If
I have them, I am a liberal. If I understand the whole situation, I can be
a radical." Despite that answer and its open-endedness, he hired me and
we set out on a two-year adventure together.

Jack had entered the field of journalism in the late 1930s as a reporter
for the *Chicago Daily News*. Newspaper journalism had been much less
sophisticated then, but arguably more in touch with its reader than today.
By the early 1960s, it still had limitations as to the depth of its coverage,
but it remained the main source of news. Television had entered the field
and was beginning to some degree to show viewers visuals of who, what,
why, and where; but newspapers were needed for background, investigation, scope, and details.

Jack was out on the proverbial limb. He had hired me as a reporter
and legman although I had never taken a course in journalism or worked
for the City News Bureau, the training ground for almost every good
reporter in the city. I was incredibly unsophisticated about the world that
newspapers covered. My references rested squarely on my Catholic faith
and training. On the other hand, I was curious, well meaning, and committed to being honest.

Another limitation was that I could not even type. The seminary had
introduced typing to the class after mine. As a beginning reporter for a
major metropolitan newspaper, I was a hunt and peck typist. I still am
after a more than an almost fifty-year career as a writer.

Jack appreciated my talents, but he also enjoyed not-so-subtlety tweak-
ing me about my naiveté and straightness. Among the assignments he

gave me throughout my two years with him were to check out the city's strip shows, visit a nudist colony (I turned that one down), and conduct an investigation of crime and vice on the city's colorful North Side nightlife area. He liked my growing investigative skills and the unique stories I brought him, but my writing style with its sometimes clumsy and awkward sentences caused his head to shake fairly often.

There was considerably more depth to Jack Mabley than his sometimes peculiar assignments indicated. He was conscientious. He could also be profound. He cared deeply about the most easily forgotten of human beings, those individuals institutionalized because they were severely physically or mentally disabled.

And I am honored to have worked for him. Jack was an excellent newsman and mentor. Together, over the two years, we did solid investigative reporting that resulted in upwards of a dozen front-page headline stories.

The first was an exposure of a south suburban justice of the peace who was substituting dime-store receipts for lesser amounts than the courtroom fines he had collected. My contribution was finding his records in a different place than they were supposed to be and locating the defendants, without having their addresses. I kept asking where receipts from his courtroom could be. After finding them, I dug through the records for unusual names. I selected a dozen or so of them and called. I discovered they had received receipts like those sold in ten-cent stores. These were for higher amounts than those listed on the official UARCO receipts the justice of the peace had handed in. He had been pocketing the difference.

He gave us three explanations for his malfeasance:

"I am not very smart."

"My wife, who helped me, is not very smart."

"The press is persecuting me."

He later made a retraction. After consulting with his lawyer, he took back the third explanation. In the end, he went to jail.

Acting on a tip, Jack sent me to the capitol in Springfield to investigate state use of an envelope-printing company supposedly owned by the newly elected Governor Otto Kerner and his state finance director, Ted Isaacs.

I felt the answers and proof could be found in examining the records. Two *Chicago Daily News* reporters believed they could get the story by interviewing the state's purchasing agent. I turned out to be right, and their method took them nowhere. The documents I researched showed

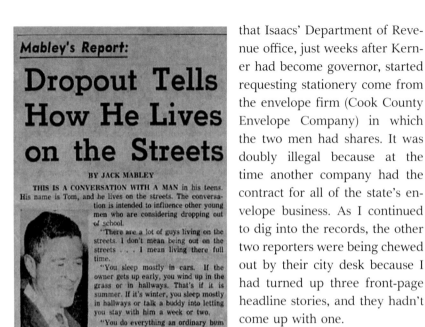

**Mabley's Report:**

# Dropout Tells How He Lives on the Streets

BY JACK MABLEY

THIS IS A CONVERSATION WITH A MAN in his teens. His name is Tom, and he lives on the streets. The conversation is intended to influence other young men who are considering dropping out of school.

"There are a lot of guys living on the streets. I don't mean being out on the streets . . . I mean living there full time.

"You sleep mostly in cars. If the owner gets up early, you wind up in the grass or in hallways. That's if it is summer. If it's winter, you sleep mostly in hallways or talk a buddy into letting you stay with him a week or two.

"You do everything an ordinary bum would do. You wait early for the milkman and for the bakery man behind the store, and you even steal the newspaper.

JACK MABLEY

"The thing is not to take all the cakes the bakery man leaves. If just four or five are missing, the people figure he made a mistake.

"You run into a little job every once in a while. A guy will know you are on the streets and he'll let you wash his car or move some furniture for a couple of bucks.

"When you're on the streets, a girl don't trust you. She's scared of you. She tries to act nice, but you absolutely cannot get near her. You cannot touch her. That's one thing that gets me mad because before I was on the streets eight girls used to hang around me.

*Jack's column from May 4, 1964*

that Isaacs' Department of Revenue office, just weeks after Kerner had become governor, started requesting stationery come from the envelope firm (Cook County Envelope Company) in which the two men had shares. It was doubly illegal because at the time another company had the contract for all of the state's envelope business. As I continued to dig into the records, the other two reporters were being chewed out by their city desk because I had turned up three front-page headline stories, and they hadn't come up with one.

In a bizarre twist, the Sangamon County states attorney next had me going through Governer Kerner's bank account records at the very time the states attorney himself was holding a press conference in his outer office for reporters attempting to catch up on the story. Jack received a national Sigma Delta Chi journalism award for breaking the story originally and acknowledged my contribution. How Kerner survived the scandal, I have no idea. Years later, he was convicted of bribery as part of a racetrack stock scandal.

In another situation, I was sent to interview the Cook County treasurer about the annual sale of tax delinquent properties. He misunderstood what I was asking him and nearly jumped out of his seat to question me, "How did you know about that?" I quickly realized he was holding back information from me about something interesting. Acting as though I knew what he meant, I was able to land for our newspaper an exclusive story that the county was going to hold its first "scavenger tax sale" in almost twenty years. Such a sale offered thousands of pieces of property that included all those delinquencies that were not purchased at an annual tax sale. Often, these are slices of property that are in dispute or have unique problems connected with them. Speculators, however, find their own reasons for snatching these up. When I called Jack to tell him I had a "big" story, he warned me against use of that term unless it was genuinely a big story.

Well, it was. It was a front-page headline story in our paper the next day and in the *Chicago Daily News* the day after that. The *Daily News* story used the same examples that I had selected out of the thousands of properties that would be up for sale.

I was the only reporter or legman even attempting to cover the lives of the really poor of the city. I gave Jack an interview with a dumpster diver who explained what groceries he obtained from the receptacles behind local supermarkets along with a warning to those who might try to do it to watch out for broken glass. In his memoir, *Hales, Hef, the Beatles, and Me*, Jack quoted the dumpster diving interview and one I had with a poor woman from the west side, who addressed the question. "What ya cuts down on first when the money stops coming?" Jack went on to point out that my visiting such poor people helped inspire me to found the Neediest Children's Christmas Fund.

The project that I was most proud of working on under Jack was not the front-page stories, but The Forgotten Children's Fund, one that he had started and rallied his readers around for years. At a memorial held after Jack's death in 2006, I said, "It was beyond my conception that a newspaper columnist would devote himself as Jack had done to the most forgotten people in the United States—the mentally disabled in state institutions. I am still in awe of the man."

In his memoirs, he wrote of his efforts: "Nothing in my work meant more to me than my involvement with the mentally retarded, their families, and the men and women devoting their lives to helping them. I helped raise money and gifts for the retarded in the state institutions, lobbied for legislation to help them, and I have done volunteer work since leaving the *Tribune*."

That statement greatly understated what he had done year after year for the mentally disabled who were institutionalized. He wrote about them, personalizing them and using his column as a one-man band day after day for a month and a half before Christmas to collect money and gifts for them. He sent every donor a personal note of appreciation. Each day, after he went home from the paper, he was joined by his wife and children in counting the donations and sending out thank-you notes.

My assignment each November I worked for him was to visit the state institutions for the severely disabled in Dixon and Lincoln, Illinois and to put together stories that treated them as individuals with personalities who were in great need of society's attention.

When I began to see what the Neediest Children's Christmas Fund that I was starting was about to become, I asked Jack's blessing even though both he and I knew his efforts and mine would wind up competing for donations. Jack's response was an unequivocal, "Go with it." I was never more proud to be associated with him.

Once, when we were putting together a particularly nostalgic column about 1939 prices and customs, he explained to me, "I write these columns to keep the readers' interest and attention so they will stay with me for the more serious columns I do." Those were the words of a reflective and thoughtful human being.

The job of legman for Jack inevitably lasted two years and, if he considered you good, he helped you get hired as a regular reporter working for the paper's city desk. I was stunned when this happened. I think I felt more doubts about my being able to handle that position than he did.

It was another door gone through with me wondering how I could be so lucky. I would stay in this new position of city desk reporter for only three months and then a new, more propitious opportunity would be mine.

# 21

## Cherry Picking in Michigan
## With a Bunch of Guys Off Skid Row

*One of Blue's helpers was ready at the end of the day's work—for a price of 25 cents—to drive the men into a liquor emporium in town. The other was ready at the end of the day to operate the only entertainment available in camp: A craps table with a two-bit minimum.*

For a few months after leaving Jack's column as his assistant, I worked as a reporter on the city desk of *Chicago's American*. In doing the job, I never went into a war zone, walked among buildings still rumbling from an earthquake, covered a raging flood, or reported on any other major natural disaster. This does not mean that, in attempting to cover a story, my life was never at stake. It was.

A story with my byline appeared in the paper on August 23, 1965. It was datelined Traverse City, Michigan, and it stated that I had joined down-on-their-luck men of Chicago's West Madison Street who had jumped at the chance for jobs by getting on a skid row bus that would take them to the cherry orchards outside of Traverse City. The *Chicago's American* article told of my experience:

> ... I rode there on the bus with them. Having skipped shaving for several days and wearing the oldest, most-worn clothes I had, I got aboard it on Skid Row. When we arrived in the cherry orchard, the bus driver/crew leader brought the bus to a hard stop. He put his hand firmly on the lever for opening the door, but did not use it. His eyes scanned every face on the bus and then he smiled, pushing his coat aside to reveal a gleaming silver-handled pistol stuffed in his belt. Next, he laid out the rules and none of us dared ask a question or voice an objection.
>
> Our lives, I realized, were potentially at stake. And, because—despite my not having shaved and threadbare clothing—I was obviously the odd man out and no one could have traced where I was from or even who I was.

Two more weeks of brutalizing treatment confronted the men brought here by bus from Chicago's West Madison Street, filled with glowing promises of the big money to be earned while harvesting Michigan's cherry crop.

Two more weeks of dawn-to-dusk shinnying up narrow ladders into cherry trees, a bucket hanging from the belt and a 30-pound lug lying on the ground waiting to be filled, while a bullying boss barks:

"Now you get this straight. You start a tree you gonna finish it. You gonna pick the top and the center—and I'm going to make sure you do."

The professional pickers, the migrant workers who annually follow the crops, leave the fruit at the top and center of each tree. They find they need so much more time to harvest it that it takes them beyond the point of diminishing returns, as far as earnings go.

But the men from West Madison Street, mostly homeless derelicts are literally at the mercy of their field boss. They fear him physically, as I came to fear him. And they fear the lash of his tongue, his every statement beginning: "Now you get this straight!"

The men learned it was to be rugged their first night up here, four miles north of Sutton Bay and more than 350 miles northeast of Chicago. When the sun goes down there is a bone-chilling wind off Traverse bay. That wind whipped through the broken windows of the four bunkhouses.

There were no blankets. Only one of the bunkhouses had a pot-bellied stove, with cherry wood to burn. The men unable to sleep on cots with bare mattresses got up during the night to keep the fire in this stove burning. One groaned, "I thought Madison Street was bad. This is worse."

Their recruiter, the man who stood in front of the bus, parked daily in front of Chicago's Community Reading room, 921 Madison St., had made it sound attractive. He said: "They're paying $17 or $18 a day. You want to pick cherries?"

Not until they stepped out of the old school bus in the middle of a cherry orchard 27 miles north of Traverse City did they learn that:

The most an inexperienced picker can expect to earn at 60 cents a lug is $6 or $7. For most, the pay will be only $4 or $5.

Each would have to pay the field boss, an independent contractor, $5 for the trip from Chicago. It would come out of his pay.

The charge of 65 cents for breakfast, 65 cents for supper, and dinner in the field—at 35 cents a sandwich—came out of their daily pay.

The men found they are virtually servants of the field boss until the cherry season ends! Then the tomato season begins "around Toledo."

The 65-cent supper, sampled at 9 p.m. on the day of arrival, was a generous helping of steaming beans and ham-hocks with bread and coffee. The 65-cent breakfast next day consisted of thick slices of salt pork with bread and coffee.

The combination kitchen and eating cabin, screened on all sides, is separate from the bunkhouses and the privy, which make up the little colony in the middle of the orchard. There is no running water and no well. Water is brought by the bucket from a nearby spring.

Every time I saw those buses picking up farm and harvest workers on West Madison Street I used to wonder, "Where are they headed? What awaits the men who heed the recruiter's siren call?" Now I know.

When I entered the bus on the first morning, unshaven and wearing work clothes, I found that most of my fellow passengers had boarded the previous night. By sleeping in the bus they could save the cost of one night's lodging in a flophouse. The bus departed at 10:30 a.m.

Most of my companions were African-Americans. There was one Mexican and one Indian, as well as four or five white men who spoke with drawls familiar to the hill country. All were broke. None had eaten since the previous day, nor did any one eat until we reached our destination at 9 p.m.

No one, that is, except for our recruiter and field boss, the huge, intense man called "Blue," whom all of us came to fear. He was the contractor who owned the bus, made a deal with the Michigan farmer to pick the crop and had two assistants to help keep all of us sweating with fear.

When we got to Benton Harbor, where Blue lives, we made a half-hour rest stop at a filling station. Blue went home to eat. The rest of us filled up on filling-station drinking water.

One of our fellow passengers, a white man who said he was from Alabama, was drunk and belligerent when the bus left Chicago. Twice he sought to provoke Blacks into a fight. The bus driver put him off on the Indiana Tollway. This seemed the simplest way to get rid of the troublemaker.

A few of the men had "makings" for cigarettes. One had a bag of instant coffee grounds, which he mixed with cold water in a milk carton. He passed this mixture around for the others to drink. Nobody had any money visible, although I had sewn some bills in my trousers waistband.

These men seemed drawn together in camaraderie, seen in small acts of brotherhood.

When I gave one man a cigarette he smoked it halfway down and passed it along to the man across the aisle. When I gave another a caramel candy sucker he used a knife to cut it in two and pass a piece to the man behind him.

They talked of their hopes from this cherry harvest.

"I figure I can save enough to buy me one of them jobs at an employment agency," one said.

Several of the men said they thought the fresh air and hard work might counter-act the effect of Madison Street saloons. That was before they saw that fresh air, with the mercury dropping into the 30s, frosting the windows of the bus; before they felt the bone-weary hopelessness when they realized that the work was beyond their physical capacities.

One of Blue's helpers was ready at the end of the day's work—for a price of 25 cents—to drive the men into a liquor emporium in town. The other was ready at the end of the day to operate the only entertainment available in camp: A craps table with a two-bit minimum.

When I was ready to leave before breakfast one morning, I sought out one of Blue's aides and offered to pay him for driving me to town. He obviously was eager for my money, but he hesitated.

"Blue sure wouldn't like me helping someone get out of here," he said. "I'm afraid, really afraid, of what he might do."

Truth to tell, I was afraid too. I avoided the road, heading through the cherry orchard for Sutton Bay four miles away. Hitchhiking, I caught a ride into Traverse City and bought a bus ticket for Chicago.

By the time I had arrived back in Chicago after the long bus ride, I wound up in the hospital with a major blood clot in my leg.

Today, forty-nine years later, I can still picture the face of that man scanning mine as well as the glittering metal of his gun.

# 22

## A Personal Story
## of the Action Line Column

*The Action Line column was a unique form of journalism generously underwritten by the newspapers and of extraordinary benefit to readers in what has become an almost forgotten era.*

The Action Line column, which appeared in the pages of a succession of newspapers, *Chicago's American*, *Chicago Today*, and the *Chicago Tribune*, between 1965 and 1983, was a historic once-upon-a-time example of personal, advocacy journalism. The column's staff—of which I was the editor—handled an average of three hundred to four hundred letters a day, or between one and two million public service requests and consumer complaints over its seventeen years of existence. It was daunting. Its heavy day-by-day demands helped mature me. No one should confuse it with the present-day valuable, but highly understaffed daily attempts in the pages of a growing number of newspapers to solve people's problems.

Action Line was far more than that. We had as many as nine people on the staff and used the public relations departments of all the service agencies in town, passing on any number of requests every day to many of them. The newspapers today, with a staff of one, or at most two, attempts to resolve a reader's individual problem, the resolution of which then appears in print. The Action Line staff was exponentially different, as it attempted to handle every request or complaint we received. This is the inside story of that almost incalculable effort.

The Action Line was a unique form of journalism generously underwritten by the newspapers and of extraordinary benefit to individual readers in what has become an almost forgotten era. Credit for its success goes to the imaginative idea of a newspaper using its power to provide personal public service;

- the choice of a qualified and large staff to handle and report the effort;
- the ambitious intent to try to help so many;
- the resources the newspapers made available for its operation;
- the community helpful responses provided on an individual basis and in so many ways;
- and the reader support that told the editors of the paper that their investment was worth it.

A readership survey of the newspaper in 1968, three years after the column's initiation, showed that people read it more often than they did any other feature, article, or even headline in the paper except the baseball box score.

The original Action Line first appeared in the *Chicago's American* starting in August 1965. My former boss, Jack Mabley, who had a unique feel for what newspaper readers wanted, was the midwife of the column. Initially, it was principally a call-in service with a secretary transcribing a tape that recorded readers' complaints and problems. Two reporters were assigned to writing the new feature, but it quickly became evident to the editors of the paper that their hearts weren't in it and abilities were not up to it. Jack then recommended to the managing editor that I take over the column. When the latter, Luke Carroll, offered me the position, I replied, "No," but realized that a "no" was not a prudent answer to give one's boss. I quickly modified it to "I will do it until you get someone else."

I soon learned why the two reporters who had put together the Action Line through the first six weeks of its existence were taken off of it. They brought to my desk a large box of letters and transcripts of telephone inquiries that contained several thousand questions and problems that had hardly been read much less dealt with. I was horrified. Those were real problems. I had been reading the column and presumed the two staff writers were taking seriously its invitation to readers to phone or send in their problems, questions, and complaints. Every past request, except the few dozen that appeared in the paper, was there in the box, with no one having dealt with it.

In the first week of my writing the column, a reader sent in the question, "Why doesn't your newspaper print the results of the televised wrestling matches?" Not thinking my answer would actually make it into print, I cynically quipped, "Before or afterwards?" I could not believe the editors of the paper let my answer go into the paper. I was jubilant because it indicated I just might be given unexpected freedom and journalistic independence in editing the column.

I took every letter or recorded phone we received seriously, and my bosses not only liked this but also proved willing to expand the staff to meet the challenge.

In retrospect, I still find it difficult to believe that a major metropolitan newspaper would put someone in charge of such a venture who had never taken a course in journalism, did not own a house, was not married, had lived in Chicago for only four years, had a disability, and got his education behind the cloistered walls of a monastery.

They never did find someone else. Give or take a few weeks at the beginning and at the end, I served as its editor for all seventeen years of its existence. To a large extent, I was able to grow into the job surrounded at *Chicago's American* by individuals over those years who included Bernie and Annemarie Hanley, Milton Hansen, Chuck McWhinnie, Hildegard Ochtrup, Judith Birnbaum, Juanita Carlson, Julia Flores, and a long list of others meritorious short-term staff members.

They worked hard, and so did I. I began the policy of eating lunch at my desk and reading letters on the bus going back and forth to work. I learned how to read scribbling and to get to the heart of each of them quickly.

When a situation arose that we could not get through a secretary to talk to the person who could resolve a problem we would ask the secretary's name "so we might put it in the column." I cannot recall a single instance when this approach did not get us through to the person who could help.

The editors were pleased with the results in terms of the surveys showing a very high and sustained reader interest in the column. The column's initial focus was routine city, country, state, and federal government glitches in service ranging from persistent potholes to lost Social Security checks, with an occasional inquiry about Chicago or the newspaper itself.

When we happened to resolve two separate consumer problems in one column late in 1965, a window flew open to people that showed how else the column might serve them. Letters representing consumer problems quickly became more common than any other kind we handled.

At the time, a consumer movement was taking hold across the country. The problem was that it was meaningless to carry an article on what to watch for in buying an air conditioner, refrigerator, or range, for example. Very few would read such an article because most were not in the process of even thinking about buying that particular item at the moment.

An Action Line request, on the other hand, started with the immediate consumer issue that was here and now confronting an actual family or individual. We usually were able to resolve it by getting the manufacturer or retailer to replace it if it did not work or to show that the customer had not understood the instructions in trying to operate it.

We soon had to stop having people call us and so turned to a letters-only system. This approach proved far more effective as we developed a method of attaching an Action Line cover letter to the complaint and sending it to whomever we felt could or should help.

In the mid-1970s, I was quoted describing how Action Line worked for an in-house *Tribune* publication:

> The story of Action Line is not often dramatic. It is often tedious. It is a refund; a piece of mediation; a small and successful battle for justice; a referral; a re-evaluation in favor of a person who felt powerless; a good hard nudge to a small company that had refused to answer; or joining with an agency such as the Federal Trade Commission, to put a crooked company out of business.

Newspapers from around the country sent reporters and editors to study the Action Line and began columns of their own. I followed up with a number of them and asked whether they used our approach of attempting to follow through on every letter we received. Most of these journalists said, No, we found what you do would be too much work. The paper would never put the money out for it.

After my father, who lived in Detroit, died, I personally learned the disadvantage to the reader in their selective approach. My mother was having trouble collecting his veteran's benefits. I urged her to write the *Detroit Free Press'* Action Line. She did, but nothing happened. I then asked a reporter on our staff to handle her request but not to associate it with my name in contacting the Veterans Administration. He did, and the problem was easily resolved.

Our column remained interesting and well-read because we had qualified reporters writing about real successes the column experienced on the broad and deep level we provided community service.

The Action Line's help in finding missing people proved unexpectedly successful. For example, we received a letter from a woman who had not seen her daughter in eighteen years. Her husband had snatched the child out of her cradle and disappeared. With the help of someone working for Social Security, I reached the daughter working at a bank in Cleveland, Ohio. I suggested she be sitting down before I told her what I had to say.

I was glad I had. She had been told her mother had abandoned her. Her immediate concern was that her father might face prosecution. Her mother was so happy to be reconnected with her daughter that she had no interest in showing vindictiveness, and mother and daughter were reunited. For many years afterwards, the mother sent the Action Line staff a homemade cake on the anniversary of her being reunited with her daughter.

Not all worked out well. We located a young nursing student's mother who had skipped out many years before. The daughter called the day we gave her the address and phone number of her mother, "the happiest day in my life." But the reunion did not help her sustain that feeling as her mother and her mother's boyfriend attempted to get her to take drugs with them.

We were able to locate so many individuals that several times a year we would devote the whole column to it. Today, with the Internet, finding a person has become much easier. We had put considerable amount of work into following up leads and, of course, were successful only some of the time.

We also had more than a few complicated and bizarre requests. One man

THE ACTION LINE

The Action Line solves problems, gets answers, cuts red tape, investigates complaints, and stands up for your rights. The Action Line may be reached by writing to Chicago's American, 445 N. Michigan av., Chicago 60611, or by dialing 222-4444 from 10 a. m. to 9 p. m.

"How can a factory get away with not having any type of exhaust system for its soldering department? The girls on the line have to stand over soldering irons and inhale solder smoke all day long. This is an electronics factory on north California avenue. The bosses tell them they don't need fans, that the smoke doesn't hurt them. Yet they all have chest pains and a cough that comes from their heels. I used to work there some time ago, but these girls are my friends and I don't think they should have to suffer." —NELLIE TUMULTY

ACTION LINE: Exactly 100 violations of ventilation and safety ordinances were found by state factory inspectors after we received your complaint. These must be corrected within 30 days. The factory has 707 employes who have reason to thank you.

"Our sorority is planning to give a gift worth about $300 to a home for the aged. We've been thinking about perhaps a piece of equipment, such as a wheelchair." —M. A. J.

ACTION LINE: The director of a Chicago home for the aged was enlisted to reply to your question. She says wheelchairs are often useful to homes, as would be a hi-fi or stereo unit. No gift should be purchased, however, without first conferring with home officials, she says. "Someone bought us a wheelchair some time ago. We appreciated it, but could not use it. The thing would not fit thru the doors of our rooms."

THE ACTION LINE

"I have one of the 1958 Edsels of which there are very few left. Are there any clubs of Edsel owners? Is it considered a collector's item?"—BILL TIMMONS

ACTION LINE: National Markets Reports, Inc., which publishes the auto Red Book on price ranges, would not quote a price on the '58 Edsel. They say the car is obsolete and not accepted on the used car auction lot. However, an ad in the current issue of Automotive News, considered the industry "bible," lists a '58 Edsel for sale at $150. Ford's public relations office in Chicago says they never heard of an Edsel club and it is not a collector's item—yet.

*May 24, 1966*

mailed a certified check made out to the column for $10,000, which would be ours—he said—if we could clarify some language in a contract in which he felt he was being cheated over the ownership of a bakery. We handed the check over to the newspaper's legal department, which then helped him get his money back. Although the language of the contract did not help resolve the issue in his favor, we got a lawyer to explain to him the terms in the document.

Before the Neediest Children's Christmas Fund (not to be confused with Jack Mabley's Forgotten Children's Fund) came into existence, I would take letters from children and families who told us they were not going to have a Christmas. I would then hand them over to the reporters on the city desk who I felt might be willing to help out. It very often worked, according to the reports I got back.

Many of the requests we received came from people on welfare or trying to get on it. I presume few if any of them were subscribers to the paper, but that was never a requirement on our part. We got results for many because, like those of most agencies, the staff of the Welfare Department either really wanted to straighten out the problem or to avoid looking bad for not doing so.

One of the extraordinary things Action Line did over the years was to build up a long list of staff people in various agencies, utilities, companies, and city and county departments who were willing to go out of their way to cooperate in what we were attempting to do. More came to recognize that their concern for people in need was the principal motivating factor in their helping us.

*Chicago's American* became a tabloid, changed its name to *Chicago Today* in 1968, and retained both the Action Line and its staff. When *Chicago Today* (which the *Chicago Tribune* owned) folded in 1974, I was named editor of the column in the *Tribune* and found myself with a much larger staff, including five other reporters and two extraordinarily capable and caring secretaries, Lynne Manning and Lynn Bruder. The list of qualified and serious reporters was long and included John McCarron, Richard Bridis, Peter Fuller, Jerry Thornton, Emmett George, Mitchell Locin, Patricia Leeds, Monroe Anderson, Sheri Steinberg, and Joe Pete. For a while, we also had a version of the column in Spanish, which Ana Barrera handled.

In moving to the *Tribune*, I remained concerned about the rest of the *Chicago Today* Action Line staff, whom the *Tribune* did not hire. The *Sun-Times* offered two of them jobs to help begin a competing column and I was satisfied. But the editors subsequently changed their minds when they learned that the name Action Line was not available because the *Tribune*, which had called its column, Action Express, was going to use the name "Action Line" in its place.

Several months afterwards, I had occasion to be seated next to Emmett Dedmon, the publisher of the *Chicago Sun Times*, at a charity event and asked him about the incident. He told me he had not known about it. I gave the full details. Within a week, Chuck McWhinnie, who had been on the *Chicago Today* staff, was recontacted by the *Chicago Sun-Times* and hired to help initiate its column, Action Time.

In retrospect, I have to thank the Tribune Company, which owned the three newspapers on which I worked, for giving the column such an opportunity to be of help to people.

In 1983, I was taken off the column and named chief obituary writer for the *Tribune*. Sadly, the paper killed the Action Line several weeks later. Over the years, many former devotees of the column asked me what was the cause of the column's demise?

My answer to that question was that the mood of the people of this country had changed. The 1980s were becoming the so-called "Me Generation" that gave us the Reagan Administration and its deep welfare and War on Poverty program cuts. Alas, this nation seemed a lot less interested in seeing other people's problems solved. And Action Line became just one more of the victims of that attitude.

# 23

## Carol and I Get Married

The happiest, most meaningful moment of my life has lasted for forty-eight years. My heart knew it had made the right decision when I saw Carol in back of the church in her wedding gown, radiantly smiling and looking at me.

I lived oblivious of such a moment for eleven years, literally sequestered in an all-male seminary and then a cloister to keep me from realizing such an experience could await me. The payoff was supposed to be a special place for me in heaven anointed by one of His bishops in this life as a priest, a chosen man of God. Then, no longer having that available to me, I had inched toward the possibility of spending my life together with a woman.

Over a period of eight years I had moved away from my voluntary confinement and toward the bonding, falling in love, taking of vows, joy, missteps, right steps, sharing of life, and creating a family together. It took every bit of that time to move up to that point.

Our marriage took place on a breeze-kissed Saturday morning, April 16, 1966, with my brother, Father Bert, performing the ceremony with our families and friends in attendance. The years since then I have spent learning that there is little comparison between the two life choices. The goal, I learned, is not heaven or its rewards; but rather is persons, Carol, and the children that might entail.

She is a better person, smarter and kinder than I am. All her life—professionally, personally, and maternally—she has cared about others. People have been kind to me, but no one kinder than Carol. I have met nurturers, but no one who works at it more than she has.

In the monastery, I erected walls against intimacy. When I first started dating, I was confronted with them. I was afraid of hurting someone by starting and then unilaterally ending a relationship. I could not picture myself doing that. That became a quite a bit different than I thought it might be. I began by dating a very religious woman; but then she "dropped" me. Her comment, "You still have too much of the monastery in you." I asked what she meant by that. "Well," she said looking me straight in the eye, "at the door at night you say, 'God love you.'" That gave me something to think about, and I did that over the next several years.

Carol was special. She seemed as committed to caring about and understanding people as I had been to the religious life. Her father, because of mental illness, was absent from her home at times during her childhood. Her desire, which must have established roots at a young age, was to understand the cause and way to bring them back to the mainstream.. Immediately after high school, she studied to become a registered nurse, including months training in the very institution where he had spent some of those years.

Carol was working as a nurse at another state mental hospital when we met. We had once double-dated with other partners, but came to know each other better a year later through a mutual friend, Barbara Burns.

She had earned a bachelor's of science and later a master's degree in clinical psychology in order to teach psychiatric nursing. Of all of the jobs she has ever had, that one may be the one she loved the most. She understood the science and art of being a psychiatric nurse and how to imbue them in the students with whom she worked.

*Wedding Day, April 16, 1966*

When Carol learned about the mass genocide at the hands of the Pol Pot and the Khmer Rouge regime that resulted in the deaths of between one and three million people throughout Cambodia in the late 1970s, she knew she had to do something. She worked for the American Friends Service Committee to help generate a national response to the victims who survived the killings.

Carol then spent the next decade working for human rights that involved other countries in Southeast Asia, especially the Philippines.

She was appointed to the national board of the Women's International League for Peace and Freedom, and through it she was able to bring together women leaders of Vietnam, Cambodia, Laos, Japan, Thailand, Indonesia, and Sri Lanka to a 1983 international peace conference in

Gothenburg, Sweden. Some of these leaders—especially from Vietnam and Cambodia—had little contact with people outside their countries. This was a long way from her work at Elgin or Chicago state mental hospitals or teaching psychiatric nursing, but all of it entailed a profound understanding of humanity, human rights, and concern for the suffering of those whom society shunned or worse.

While I was working through Action Line to get someone's telephone bill straightened out, Carol was helping to free victims of human rights abuses throughout the Philippines during the reign of the brutal dictator, Ferdinand Marcos. Throughout the island nation, people who protested or even questioned the actions of Marcos "disappeared," were tortured, imprisoned, and often murdered. She learned that the Association of Major Religious Superiors in the Philippines was able to obtain documentation of the events involving the victims and then supply them to Amnesty International.

Carol received a grant from the J. Roderick MacArthur Foundation to help set up a network of people, churches and organizations in this and other countries willing to respond to these urgent action alerts when someone was believed to be tortured or had disappeared in the Philippines. The people in the network promptly flooded local police officials in that country demanding an accounting of what was happening to those individuals. It was effective. Many were released, torture in some instances was stopped, and the chances of being surreptitiously executed in their prison cells diminished.

In the midst of her teaching and human rights work, the City of Evanston hired Carol to help draft and upgrade regulations for the city's many nursing homes. The opportunity afforded her the channel to respond at a basic level to one her most urgent concerns. Working with two geriatric psychiatrists, Doctors Jerry Grunes and Jack Buffington, she formulated new rules that demanded higher and broader standards of care for nursing homes and make them more humane. After two long years, of hearings and advocating, these were adopted by the Evanston City Council and became landmark legislation. They were used as a template in states throughout the nation to upgrade regulations to make life more bearable and minimize suffering in nursing homes.

Meanwhile, I had long since learned to say, "I love you" instead of "God love you" to my soul mate. I thank fate for freeing me from the monastery so I could meet her and share her extraordinary life. I thank you, Carol. The ride continues to be wonderful and it is my pleasure to be told by you that it is the same with you. Our children? And what Carol did next? Subsequent chapters will tell the tale

# 24

## The Neediest Children's Christmas Fund: Chicagoans' Best Hour

*Acknowledgments to all.*

In 1969, Santa Clauses came to town for the poorest of the poor in the form of donors to the Neediest Children's Christmas Fund. The Santas were the generous people of Chicago, who came down the mythical chimneys of the poor magically bearing gifts. Over the next two decades, Chicagoans contributed more than $60 million for Chicago-area kids at Christmastime through The Neediest Children's Christmas Fund. It still exists as the WGN Neediest Kids' Fund and is handled through the McCormick Charitable Trust.

It was I who, in 1969, founded it. That sounds impressive and certainly would appear so in my or anyone else's obituary. It would also contradict the many published versions of how the Neediest Children's Christmas got started.

So let me put it straight: Thousands of people deserve higher praise and more thanks than I do for the self-sacrificing generosity and great effort that has gone into the fund. I early realized that any fund drive that was overly focused on its founding or founder was not and never would become effectively attentive to the city's neediest children. Therefore, as best I could, I intentionally diverted attention from my role in starting it. Others' overwhelming efforts and sacrifices on behalf of those children outshone anything I did. Their contributions will never get them write-ups about their roles in its success.

The fund as we came to know it started with a 1968 request to the Action Line. A reader asked if it were possible to make a donation that would go directly to a poor child at Christmas without any part of it being used to cover administrative costs.

I posed this question to Tobey Ostrow, who was then in charge of public relations for the Cook County Department of Public Aid. She answered that the department had a few thousand dollars leftover from the defunct Goodfellows' campaign. In that sense, the fund already existed, but it had no name, and no effort was being made to solicit donations to it. Until the cash ran out, she informed me, caseworkers were allowed to distribute five dollars per child to select poor families from the money that the public aid department still had left.

I thought the public aid's policy of letting the social workers do this afforded an opportunity if I could get together a number of other media people interested in building up the cash in the fund for the next year.

In February, I was going to invite several newspaper and television reporters to get together to discuss it. I didn't do it. Then in March I continued to postpone doing it. Then in April, the same. The time to do it was getting shorter and shorter. Finally, in May, I did. Seven showed up, with the real go-getter being *Tribune* columnist and WGN-TV show host, Bob Cromie. They all liked the idea, with each of them finding a way to promote the fund. Bob Cromie wrote a column about it and brought WGN the very enthusiastic morning drive radio host Wally Phillips into the effort.

One of the first organized efforts to support the fund came from the currency exchanges owners in Chicago. After reading Bob Cromie's October 1969 columns in the *Tribune*, they wanted to set out canisters and needed something to call the Christmas campaign. I glanced over Bob's column and selected a phrase he had used, "the neediest children" and crafted the title "The Neediest Children's Christmas Fund."

A year later, Arthur Allan became the public relations director for the Cook County Public Aid Department, and he became like the flaps on an airplane's wings in helping to get the fund well off the ground. His efforts along with those of Wally Phillips went beyond imaginative in getting newspapers, churches, bars, businesses, organizations, and radio and TV stations to promote the cause. None of these was too small for Arthur to approach or Wally to solicit over the radio. Arthur even managed to get an airplane to fly along Chicago beaches on the Fourth of July with an air trailer alerting people to The Neediest Children's Christmas Fund. He worked it out that he would write a story for his father's magazine about the pilot in exchange for a free in-air promotion of the fund.

To help promote it, Arthur and I wrote a book of interviews in 1971 about what Christmas was like for needy Chicago families and their children. We titled it *The Death of Christmas*. The paperback book sold thirty-seven thousand copies in the Chicago area that year. It was Arthur's idea that we donate all the proceeds from the book, down to the last penny, to the fund. Follett Publishing Company published the book and the Charles Levy Company distributed it. Both did so for free.

Norman Ross, a vice president of First National Bank and a long-time radio show host in Chicago, became the chairman of the fund and daily found ways to grease the wheels that kept it going. He also got the bank to handle the fund's money without charge. When something came up in conversation about getting the Charles Levy Company, the major distributor of magazines and paperback books in Chicago, to handle distribution of *The Death of Christmas*, the articulate and witty Ross asked Arthur and me, "Do you think it might be helpful that Charles Levy was my classmate in school?" It did so, of course, as did many of his contacts throughout the media in Chicago.

The interview approach used in the book also helped. Although, I was working for *Chicago Today* at the time, Arthur and I approached Clayton Kirkpatrick, who was editor of the *Chicago_Tribune* about the newspaper serializing our book. He looked across his desk at me, and said with a gentle smile, "We have our own interviewers."

True to his offer, he had *Tribune* reporters interview poor families throughout the Chicago area every day for a month and a half before Christmas to promote the fund. The paper continued to do this for years afterwards. It almost certainly represented one of the largest ongoing efforts by a newspaper in the city (or possibly elsewhere) to share with its

*A poignant cover, cartoon, and book of interviews*

readers the personal story of poverty in a major metropolitan area.

As the fund started to take off, I decided to remove myself from the picture and play down any part I had in it. Doing so would only help the fund and give the many others who were finding ways to promote it more elbowroom to do so. As a result, I promised myself to make a five-dollar contribution to the fund every time I told anyone that I had founded it. I think it, in the end, cost me somewhere around twenty-five or thirty-five dollars. It would have cost me more, but I became comfortable not telling people.

I was so successful in avoiding credit that Wally Phillips' obituary in my own newspaper, the *Tribune*, stated that he had founded it. So have other sources, including on the Internet. A 1988 article in the *Chicago Sun Times*_repeated a different version, one that claimed caseworkers had started The Neediest Children's Christmas Fund in the 1940s.

When I retired in 1998, Jack Mabley published the story of how I happened to found The Neediest Children's Christmas Fund in a column he wrote about me for the *Daily Herald*. He recalled that I had discussed it with him when I was getting it started. He called me the "unknown" founder. He also repeated the fact in his memoir, *Hales, Hef, the Beatles, and Me.*

It is, of course, in the long run insignificant who founded The Neediest Children's Christmas Fund other than that all who were connected with it starting from the very beginning believed that ordinary people are generous and willing to share what they have with those who have the greatest need.

If there is a lesson in all this, it is that sometimes small acts of kindness, with enough help and support from others, can explode into something much bigger. Some of the key people in making the fund such a success were Bob Cromie, Tobey Ostrow, Arthur Allan, TV reporter Sheri Blair, Clayton Kirkpatrick, Norman Ross, the staff of the First National Bank, the *Chicago Tribune*, the *Chicago Sun-Times*, WGN and, eventually, Oprah Winfrey, who helped promote it in the 1980s.

In the end, the real heart of The Neediest Children's Christmas Fund was radio station WGN's drive-time show host, Wally Phillips. With humor, imagination, perseverance, and total commitment, he tweaked every penny, nickel, dime, and dollar he could out of the pockets of his listeners. Even people who didn't listen to his show often heard about and responded to his pitches and promotion for The Neediest Children's Christmas Fund. To many Chicagoans, it was the very much Wally Phillips' Neediest Children's Christmas Fund.

Those who do not believe in the goodness of the many should have been in the offices of the Cook County Department of Welfare when the contributions, checks, coins, bills, and canisters came in at Christmas.

Wally contributed more than just fund raising to the campaign. He told not so much the stories of the poor, but the ones of the givers. He showed Chicago how generous its people could be. He was able to recruit thousands of offices and workplaces to take up collections for the fund. He named names—businesses, stores, factories, organizations, churches, schools, classes, sports teams, and ethnic groups. He got people to donate from jail cells, hospital beds, nursing homes, and kindergarten classes. His consistent message was that people are good and the more he preached it, the more they lived up to what he said about them.

The Neediest Children's Christmas Fund had its critics. Some of them who wrote for the newspapers felt the news media's job is to report the news rather than hype a cause. They also argued that, for whatever good it did achieve, the fund did not go to the roots of poverty.

These are valid points, but it is also fact that the fund-raising made many otherwise-disappointed kids a little happier, exposed the personal side of poverty, and made use of an often-dammed up reservoir of generosity in Chicago. It did not solve the problem of poverty in Chicago, but it did help mitigate and personalize it.

Gone are Bob Cromie, Norman Ross, Clayton Kirkpatrick, Wally Phillips, and tens of thousands of people who contributed to it. The fund has been renamed, but Chicagoans remain as generous as ever. Acknowledgments to all of you.

# 25

---

## Reporting the Unreported
## Lives of the Poor and Destitute

*A free press should ... never lack sympathy with the poor.*

JOSEPH PULITZER, ADDRESS TO THE STAFF OF HIS NEWSPAPER

**D**uring more than fifty years as a reporter and author, I interviewed or quoted thousands of individuals. They have included a former US President (Jimmy Carter), the daughter of one (Margaret Truman), Nobel Prize winners, US senators, Chicago mayors, Pulitzer Prize winners, comedians, and top athletes as well as famous actors and actresses. The ones whom I remember best have been those who were very poor. I could attempt to explain why, but I believe the best way to show it is by quoting what they had to say.

The following material is from a group interview with seven people who were on or had been on public aid. The first interviews appeared in the Tempo section of the *Chicago Tribune* in 1982. The subsequent ones in the chapter are from two books of interviews that I compiled: *They Speak for Themselves: Interviews with the Destitute of Chicago (YCW, 1965)* and *The Death of Christmas: Interviews with Forty-three Survivors* with Arthur Allan (Follett Publishing Company, 1971).

An excerpt from an interview for the *Chicago Tribune* following the 1981 President Reagan welfare cuts:

### "How bad it gets."

**Michael**: I'll tell you how bad it gets. I been down to where the only thing I had to eat was ice cubes.

**Wanda**: You can cut down on food. Especially, the last week of the month. You go in a lot of houses and you don't find any food whatever in the house. I know a man eats popcorn the last week of the month.

**Carl**: I am ulcer patent. I know what popcorn can do to you. And you pay the poor tax.

**Wanda**: Rice will fill you up. So will spaghetti. Anything with starch. For meat, you used to be able to serve kidneys and neck bones.

**Carl**: You know what neck bones cost in this neighborhood. Eighty cents a pound. I went into a store last week to buy chicken backs because I wanted some chicken and rice. They used to give away chicken backs. Now, they sold me these chicken backs for 59 cents a pound.

**Wanda**: And you pay the poor tax. All the prices are higher around here. The poorer the neighborhood, the higher the prices. If these cuts to people on welfare come, I don't know what.

**Carl**: People are becoming more concerned than I've ever seen them before.

**Wanda**: Last winter, I found out about an old couple who were only skin and bones. The woman had broken her hip and didn't even know it. She just knew it hurt. They had malnutrition so badly you wouldn't believe it. I went home and rounded up all the

*The voices of the very poor: 1965*

food I could. I called the ambulance. They didn't want to come at first because it had just snowed. I insisted. They were the skinniest people I ever saw in my life.

**Kay**: I was in a store last week. It was a Mexican store. And there was a little old man stuffing ears and tongue in his pockets. He even talked to me and asked me for a quarter. He knew I had seen him taking those things.

**Wanda**: You got to believe there are a lot of families around here that had no heat at all last winter. One I know, they got an electric heater and then it burned up. Then they had no heat. Some had an electric blanket. Others you just see the kids all dressed up like Eskimos. Not everybody has even clothes enough for that.

The following two interviews are from *They Speak for Themselves: Interviews with the Destitute of Chicago.*

### "You can't talk to them. You can't go see them."
—A Chicago mother

If I was on television, I'd tell them. I'd put things out so the big men could see them. I'd tell them that folks just can't make it the way things is. And you got these folks going around making big money and figuring out how people on welfare should spend their money. I'd tell them to try it and feed the food they're talking about to their kids.

But you can't talk to them. You can't go see them. I think talking face to face they would understand.

### "What ya can cuts down on first."
—A woman with five children

Don't ask me how you survive when the money stops coming in. That's what I wants to know. But I can tell ya what ya can cuts down on first.

We had this house full at Christmas time. Folks was good. Now it's all run out. But it gave the kids an uplift and they been smiling ever since. So we thanks God we got that left, their smiles.

The first things folks can cut down on are gas and lights. Ya puts on more clothes and I even saved $5 one month by using oil lamps.

"But ya really have to have one 40-watt bulb in the house to see and read by. The rest can be 25-watt light bulbs. And it's a sin to burn a light during the day. Most of the poor don't knows about this. I went in one house and theys had a 75-watt bulb and theys even had to use a shade.

And ya can turn yer refrigerator off at night if ya ain't got any perishable meats in it.

We uses gas and that's expensive. But the gas company is good. They shuts off the gas and I goes downstairs and turns it back on. They knows me.

I hear that one onion is worth a whole plate of anything else. So we cuts up an onion and puts it over rice or potatoes. Or ya can cut out the vegetable if ya got canned fruit. They counts the same.

Larry here, after you give him all the milk he wants, he goes back and steals the rest. When we got money, we gives 'em milk.

We gives 'em enough milk to fill up on. I think you should give 'em enough to wash 'em out with. Then you don't give 'em milk for a week or two. But I think that's the best way. Cuz if you can't give it to them regular, you should give 'em enough to wash 'em out with.

Mainly, we fill 'em up on potatoes or rice or spaghetti or corn bread. You don't feeds 'em potatoes or corn bread at the same meal like some people I know. And the rich people has salads and vegetables at the same meals. That ain't necessary for nobody.

We works all summer to beat the watermelon rap: we buys it from the grocery store instead of off the trucks.

Ain't none of these kids rights now got any underwear. I can get a undershirt for 20 cents at Goodwill.

Dresses are 57 cents to a dollar. A woman's dress is the best thing to buy for a child or a little girl cuz it's got the best materials in it. All you got to do is cut it down and ya got a real good dress.

It costs good money to get the TV fixed, but I think TV has caused more backsliding than whiskey.

You can get by, but you can't survive.

The welfare is really hard on the people what's can't spend money wisely and I don't blames 'em, but the childrens suffer.

For entertainment we all goes to church.

The following are from *The Death of Christmas.*

### "You Want to Listen to My Story?"

—Jesus, in a bar on Christmas Eve

It is Christmas Eve. We both here to have a drink in this bar. I tell you a Christmas story you not believe. You want to listen?

My mother lives in Puerto Rico. Before I born, she make the 'promisa.' That is like the oath. She promise to Virgin if she get her wish granted, she name the next baby after her or after her Son. My mother get her wish. Then, I born. She call me Jesus Maria for good measure.

Always, though, I not be satisfied with life. I try to kill myself, even in high school. I study encyclopedia of poisons. First, I try aspirins and get sick like you never see. Later, I try sleeping pills and I sleep for two days and two nights and they not think I live. Finally, I tried Veronal. But I started praying and I threw the pills under the bed.

You still want to hear my story? I tried drinking myself to death by becoming a drunkard. Never nobody loves me. I have been lonely all my life. One time, I get drunk and I put my head down on the railroad track and I pass out. I wake up in police station. A woman she sees me and she call police.

I am now 55 years old and I am ready to wait for death. I feel someone looks out for me. I feel it is God and He not let me kill myself. It is maybe because of the 'promisa' and because I have His name.

I'm glad you listen to my story. Maybe, you not see this is Christmas story. I do. My name is Jesus.

### "I'm an Old Woman and I Never Been Near a Jail Before."
—A woman wrinkled with age and worry

I'm 51 years old and this is the worst Christmas I ever had or dreamed of. I'm and old woman and I never been near a jail before. I'm used to a Christmas when you get all the kids together and the grandchildren and you put up the tree. Worst of all I'm in here for something I know nothing about. My brother got beat up and I had been to his apartment to wait for his wife who was missing, so I got accused of it.

Oh, this is the worst Christmas I ever had in all my 51 years.

I just hope someone in my family will make a Christmas for mother. She's 88 years old and I'm the only one to look out for her. Oh, I do hope they take care of her.

Other than that, I do know that I'm thankful to be alive and I know some folks got it even worse.

(Thanks to all those in such situations who spoke to me clearly and openly of their feelings and experiences. Their kindness in doing so helped me and my readers understand a little better the world in which we live and the people with whom we share it.)

* * *

Marion Street Press published my book *The Book of the Poor: What They Want and Their Right to Earn It*. It's about the poor, their plight, and their needs as well as the people and organizations who work in their behalf. More than a third of it consists of the words of the poor, who speak for themselves.

## 26

## "Neighborhood Dialogue" (1981–1983): Even the Voices of Garbagemen

*"When it's really hot though, you pay for your sins with the heat, the maggots, the sweat, and the smell. When it's 95 degrees out and you take off that lid, wow!"*

**M**odeled on my 1981 group interview piece with the very poor of Chicago, *Tribune* editor Jim Squires created a column, "Neighborhood Dialogue," in which I weekly interviewed the ordinary, the impoverished, or even the imprisoned people of Chicago. I did these columns in addition to my work as Action Line editor and later, as chief obituary writer.

The following Neighborhood Dialogue appeared in the *Tribune* June 4, 1982 under the headline: "To garbage collectors, their job is far from trashy"

**FRANK**: We are laborers for the Bureau of Sanitation, City of Chicago.

**WILLIAM**: More commonly referred to as garbagemen.

**FRANK**: I'd prefer to be known as a concerned city worker.

**GERARD**: This ward is pretty good.

**WILLIAM**: It's immaculate compared to others. When laborers come here on loan from other wards, they think they are in heaven.

**FRANK**: You have to be out there in the environment, though, to know what it's really like.

**GERARD**: It's a hard job. It really is, believe me.

**TOM**: People think you are overpaid.

**WILLIAM**: Some people say they would never do this job for anything. Others would gladly.

**TOM**: City garbagemen get $9.82 an hour, $78.72 a day.

**FRANK**: In this day and age, it's one of the best jobs to have. You don't hear of too many unemployed garbagemen. It doesn't have all the finesse of being a lawyer, but you're working every day.

**GERARD**: Eight or 10 years ago, we used to have a medical doctor come and work summers with us as a laborer. He was interning at the time. We have also had schoolteachers in the past.

**WILLIAM**: The job and the way people look at it, both have changed over the years. They used to say in the early '50s that the job on a garbage truck was "$10 a day and all you can eat."

**TOM**: There was a myth of garbagemen leaning on a truck and drinking a beer. You can't load a truck with 19,000 or 20,000 pounds two times a day by leaning on the truck.

**FRANK**: Our people are more alert than they were 10 or 13 years ago. They work together better behind the truck.

**GERARD**: We are more concerned about safety than we were years ago and about helping each other.

**FRANK**: Ours is supposed to be one of the most dangerous jobs in the country.

**GERARD**: You read articles and they put them up on the board showing that it's the most dangerous job. They tell about how many garbagemen injure their backs. In this city, our ward is either first or second in safety. Last year, we had only two or three accidents. One guy slipped on the ice and broke his ankle.

**TOM**: One of our men has been out over a year. When a truck backed up with its load, wood splinters hit him in the eye.

**RICHARD**: We are more alert to safety these days.

**GERARD**: And each truck is equipped with a winch. When a can is too heavy, we use our brains and use the winch. It may take an extra minute, but we do it.

**WILLIAM**: We had one this morning. Some people had loaded a 55-gallon drum with dirt. It rained and the can was too heavy to get on the winch. We dumped it over and shoveled the dirt onto the truck. You get an old rug and the rain hits it then it's triple the weight.

**TOM**: People put it out in the alley and we're going to take it.

**WILLIAM**: We emptied a can yesterday. It had nine bowling balls in it. When it's dear hunting season, you find the deer's head.

**TOM**: You do get used to the smell. You do become immune.

**WILLIAM**: When it's really hot, though, you pay for your sins, with the heat, the maggots, the sweat and the smell. When it's 95 degrees out and you take that lid off, wow!

**TOM**: Then, there's the wintertime when you have to dig in the snow to find the cans.

**GERARD**: It can be very, very bad in winter, especially with the ice. We work when it's 20 degrees below zero.

**WILLIAM**: And we work every day. The last day we didn't work was in 1976. I remember. It was my birthday.

**GERARD**: What you got to watch out for are aerosol cans. You get three or four in the truck's packer and they can blow up. Once a laborer pulls that handle, he never knows what's going to happen. That's one reason there isn't much conversation.

**WILLIAM**: Even worse is when someone puts in the garbage a portable barbecue that still has propane in it. It can blow up in the truck like an A-bomb.

**GERARD**: Another change these days is that there's a lot of junk pickers out there, many more than I have ever seen before.

**WILLIAM**: A lot more. The biggest problem for us is the aluminum can collectors. They see a bag, rip it open and leave the garbage strewn all over. We have to clean up. There are all kinds out there. You watch the market on paper. When the price is down, you notice stacks up and down the alley. When the price is up, you just don't see any. People are out there picking it up.

**FRANK**: You see husband and wife teams. Then, there's older people collecting bottles. You see many with grocery carts.

**GERARD**: People come along and take the brass off the bottoms of hot water tanks.

**WILLIAM**: Junk pickers find items and run garage sales. They get an old ashtray and will charge 25 cents for it at a garage sale. You see a lot more of them than ever before.

**RICHARD**: A lot of people are out of work. You can tell it because you see them in the yard and around the house.

**WILLIAM**: You can see it in how they shop. After I have picked up your garbage for some time I can tell you drink Michelob. You're laid off and you start buying whatever is on sale.

**TOM**: The people in this ward don't give you the cold shoulder. They'll give you a can of pop or whatever.

**WILLIAM**: You look at their property and you can tell a lot about them. If their yard is neat, you'll find their garbage bagged and neat. If the house looks like a mess, so will their garbage.

**RICHARD**: I once found $75 in somebody's garbage. It was an elderly lady's handbook along with all her papers. I gave it to her. She gave me $1.

**WILLIAM**: I found a nice set of false teeth yesterday.

**TOM**: Some senior citizens will present you with the neatest garbage you've ever seen.

**WILLIAM**: People have a sense of privacy about their garbage. Some of it is triple bagged and strapped and taped besides. Some people will stand in the alley and hand you their garbage and watch while you throw it in the truck and only then go back in the house.

**GERARD**: People know when you are supposed to be there. You get delayed or you are not there at the time they think you regularly are, and they will call the ward office.

**WILLIAM**: We can't work past 3:30 p.m. A person is partway down the alley after that time and they expect you to come down to where they are. You tell them you can't and they don't understand. You try to tell them you will be back tomorrow and their garbage won't spoil and no one will steal it. But people really treasure their garbage.

\* \* \*

The dialogue represents one of the oldest of literary forms. *Encyclopaeda Britannica* described the dialogue as "in the widest sense, a recorded conversation between two or more persons." Commenting on the fifth century Sicilian dialogues of Saphron of Syracuse, the encyclopedia said, "They depict brief realistic scenes of everyday life involving common character types." Plato's dialogues had immortalized the format.

After the feature had appeared weekly for two and a half years, *Chicago Tribune* Managing Editor Dick Ciccone thanked me and said that it had had its run and served its purpose. He added, "Your column has had an affect. We now use quotes in this paper a lot more as a result of it."

Curtis MacDougall, who was a long-time Chicago newspaperman, Northwestern University journalism professor, and author of the standard text on reporting, told me he did not recall any other newspaper before the *Tribune* having used group interviews or dialogues in an ongoing feature column.

# 27

## The Chicago Tribune Editor
## Chooses an Obituary Writer—Me

*I was, to put it charitably about myself,*
*an unorthodox newspaper person.*

Only one person on the staff of the *Chicago Tribune* in 1982 would have ever considered me the number one choice to become the newspaper's chief obituary writer. It was most definitely not I, nor any of the paper's rewrite staff, who saw writing obituaries as a job that required experience and an enormous respect for journalistic tradition. It was not any of us, but rather the person who would actually make the call, the editor of the *Chicago Tribune*, Jim Squires.

He not only selected me for the job but also opened the door to extraordinary leeway to change how obituaries are written and to make them more about people's lives than their deaths. He also permitted me to write about whom I chose, including ordinary people, rather than just those whom society or traditional news coverage had dubbed significant or important. It was clearly a change from tradition and, on his part, a gutsy decision.

Squires was young, new to the paper and willing to explore untrodden paths in journalism. I was, to put it charitably about myself, an unorthodox newspaper person. I had no journalism training and tended to draw outside the lines, not only because I did not always know where they were but also because my experiences were telling me that my way was working.

On the other hand, as I would discover, the rules for writing obituaries were set in stone, and there were any number of people on the newspaper committed to the traditional obituary style and willing to fight any way they could to keep the rules in place.

My basic premise was that obits could and should be far more personal. I feel to this day that almost every aspect of any newspaper could benefit from being more personal and less formatted. To readers,

I believe, the interesting kernel of any story is more often the "who" than it is the "what, where, when, and why." I also believe the "why" is too frequently ignored.

In my meeting with Squires, I had the advantage of

- having been told by an editor who was in the meeting that Squires had called my group interview with the poor "the best piece of journalism in the paper since I have been here" and

- his having given me considerable freedom in writing my new Neighborhood Dialogue column.

Nevertheless, I was horrified with this new assignment. I did not even want to read obituaries, much less write them. They were, to me, the most hidebound part of the newspaper. They were morbid and—with a few exceptions—generally uninteresting unless you knew the person. I had serious doubts about my ability to be creative in the straightjacket journalistic style in which they were traditionally written.

I had not taken Journalism 101, where I would have been taught how to write an obit. My seventeen years on the Action Line had consisted of using a question-and-answer approach, a sparse language, and a rhetorical construction that would never work in writing obituaries. I was not certain I was capable of writing readable and interesting obituaries in a traditional style.

I was willing to write about people's lives. But having to do so day-in and day-out about their deaths was something else.

"Can I make some changes?" I blurted out to Squires.

"Write a memo about what you want to do," he said. I was willing to, but was not optimistic that he would accept my proposals.

In the first place, a *Chicago Tribune* obit announced that someone had died by the very fact that the article about them was on the obituary pages. Then, "died" was in the headline of every one of them and it was repeated in the first sentence. Changing the headline and first sentence by getting rid of "died" as the verb in the lead was the first change I asked to make. I also wanted to be allowed to use quotes more and not just ones from prominent people. And why not make them stories instead of a resume of a person's life? And whom should we write about? Could I broaden it and include interesting as well as prominent people?

Did I always have to go into how the individual died? If it was gruesome, a murder or major accident, should that override how they lived? In many deaths, obits are written before there has been an autopsy, so listing the cause of death would in many cases represent only someone's guess.

Later, I would come up with a decided effort to include more women, members of minority groups, gays, children, people on the street and radicals, whose names had traditionally been banned from the pages of the *Tribune*. And how about ordinary people who are interesting, but never attained prominence?

I was concerned that most of the changes I was suggesting would not ever be approved. To me, the obituary page should not be a scorecard, where you scratch off those who have died and mention some of their accomplishments. Rather, it is a place in a newspaper where you use the deaths of people as a time to tell their stories. That was not what the readers of Col. Robert R. McCormick's paper in the past had expected on its obit page.

I wrote the memo with my wish list of changes. My day to start at the helm of the obit page was tomorrow, but I had not heard back from Squires. Which suggestions would he approve? So I asked.

"Yes," he said. I was startled. It was clear that he meant I was free to implement all my suggestions. I was being given enormous freedom to break the bonds of obituary writing at the up-until-then staid *Chicago Tribune*. It was exactly what I wanted, but it was also scary because I was headed into uncharted waters.

Three decades later many other major newspapers across the country have made at least some of the changes I proposed in that memo, with a few having gone even farther. It is difficult to estimate how much of it resulted, if any at all, from Jim Squires choosing someone who he knew would break the mold.

For me, trouble lay ahead. The changes would not come about just because first I wanted them to and second Squires had given them his stamp of approval. The powerful "last word" rewrite men were horrified with my innovations. Veteran journalists considered themselves the guardians of *Tribune* style and the unchangeable rules of obituary writing. Also, to be frank, my efforts at first exhibited a certain clumsiness that also often shocked their basic journalistic standards. This I also had to work through. I honestly believe that their resistance was also solidified, if not motivated, by their belief that each of them would have been a better choice than I did to be the paper's chief obituary writer.

They handled the situation simply each day by exercising their power to rewrite my obits and put them in the style in which *Tribune* obituaries had been written for generations. The word "died" went back into the first paragraph, the writing was more formal, the quotations were dropped, and the stories transformed into lists of facts.

And, in protesting what they were doing, I could not cite another newspaper in the United States that did not follow the rules they were advocating. Most certainly this included the style-setting *New York Times*, which followed the traditional way of writing obits and which had the unquestioned prestige to make precedent-setting changes and determine the level of significance, the race, and sex of the people about whom they chose to write.

Someone anonymously—presumably one of the rewrite men—put two unedited Kenan Heise-written obits on the bulletin board. One, I admit, was clumsily written and the other, to them, was irrelevant, being an obituary about a woman famous for wearing enormous hats.

Almost every morning over the first few months, I showed up at the door to the office of Dick Ciccone. In my hands would be the edited obituaries as they appeared in the paper and copies that showed how I had written them. "I will take care of it," he would promise.

The next day, I would get a reprieve. My obits would appear in the paper as I had written them; but, on the day afterwards, the style would revert back to the traditional format. One of my opponents so strongly objected to my changes that he requested of his fellow rewrite men that, should he die before me, I should not be the one to write his obit. When he did so, another rewrite man wrote it and mentioned in the obit the deceased's request that I not do it. I did not feel offended in any way. After years of writing them in that style, he truly felt the style of the traditional obit was better. Consequently, he got to die in the first paragraph, the way he wanted it.

The highlight of my efforts in those early days filled with the them-against-me battle was a comment Clayton Kirkpatrick, the esteemed former editor of the *Chicago Tribune*, made to me. He was taking a visitor through the city room and stopped by my desk. He introduced me to his guest and told him that I was doing a fine, innovative job of writing obituaries. I could not believe he had said it. Kirkpatrick was old school. He had been with the paper almost forty years and went back a long way into the time of Colonel McCormick. Nevertheless, in that short meeting, he gave my work his blessing and dispelled any last doubts I had about what I was trying to do.

The challenges to my obits slowly stopped, and I thought I had the won the battle. The paper then hired an eminent outside expert on journalistic style and assigned him the task of bringing conformity to the various parts of the newspaper. Another reporter told me the new style czar had commented, "No one on this staff should be allowed to write obituaries a different way simply because he wants to."

Obviously, I was that "one" and was not surprised to be called into an editorial meeting, which he conducted. I fully expected him to repeat his comment to my face. I came prepared with a short explanation that miraculously carried the day.

"I personally think," I told him, "that we can find a better verb for the first paragraph than 'died.' It can say what the person did in his or her life other than die." The eyebrows of the paper's style czar went up, and a smile appeared on his face in response to my argument.

"You are right," he said.

"What!" I said to myself. "He actually acknowledged my style and endorsed my independence." The battle for style in the obituaries was over. That was when I started attaching my byline to the obituaries that I wrote. That too made them more personal. Many years later, a staff member did a computer search of bylines in the Chicago Tribune. He informed me I was ahead of anyone else by at least one thousand.

Next came the bigger issue: who should get an obit in the *Chicago Tribune*? The understanding was that person had to be important, which was generally understood to be those whom the paper had being writing about for years: males, whites, conservatives, professors, politicians, doctors, priests, ministers, businessmen, musicians, artists, inventors, criminals, bankers, journalists (especially *Tribune* ones), and show business people as well as anyone controversial enough to have made the front page.

There was no actual list. Not even a verbal one. If there had been, I am not certain what I would have done with it. I knew what the understanding was, however, and only slowly moved away from it. I never received a single complaint from any editor for doing so.

I started publishing the obituaries of prominent Chicago African-Americans and members of various ethnic groups. Very few such persons in the past had ever made it to the obituary pages of the *Chicago Tribune*. I wrote about interesting people, whoever they were. Still, I missed paying adequate attention to the largest group of people being discriminated against on almost every newspaper in the country: women.

I did not really "get it" until I read a *Chicago Reader* column in the late 1980s complaining about women being excluded from obituaries.

All I needed was that nudge, and I was grateful to the *Reader* commentator for giving it to me. I immediately made the critic's sensitivity my own. Within weeks, the numbers of women receiving obituaries in the *Chicago Tribune* rose from about 15 or 20 percent to 35 or 40 percent. I was not attempting a quota system. I just wanted a marker that told me I was doing my job.

It was work, however, because people had long been skeptical that they could submit an obituary about a woman and have it published. Consequently, family members did not send them in. Another major reason for their omissions was the result of women being excluded from the boardroom and from many interesting jobs and professions. And the newspapers did not consider the providing of service to other people equal to handling their money or serving as their bosses.

I counted *The New York Times* obituaries two weeks in a row in the late 1980s. For the first seven days, the ratio was 28 to 1 and for the second, it was 32 to 2. Those ratios were men over women. I called the paper's obituary desk to register a complaint about it. The *Times* obit writer argued, "There are reasons for that."

"I know them all," I answered back. "I write obituaries for the *Chicago Tribune*. The reasons start with people not sending in ones about women because they don't think you or we would print them. But the second one is an unwillingness by people in our positions to solicit, choose, and research them."

The next time I called *The New York Times* obituary desk a woman was in charge.

Those reasons for excluding women from getting feature obituaries continued to bother me, and I never did get to anywhere near a 50-50 ratio myself. I got up to 40-some percent at best. The glass ceilings that women had faced was now excluding them from receiving obituaries. So I changed the rules for "newspaper material." I would as likely carry a nun's obit as a priest's, a nurse's as a doctor's and a social worker's as a businessman's. The material I wrote about was different but, with a little research, it could be every bit as interesting, and I could meet the various challenges to make it so.

One of the earliest problems I had encountered writing obituaries also concerned women. People, especially in pristine social circles, were often accustomed to want the obit to read "Mrs. Paul Jones" rather than "Martha Jones." In the name of the paper, I refused to do it. The fact that some wives had lived for their entire marriages in the shadow of their husbands did not justify the *Tribune* writing them up in death that way. Eventually, readers saw that the *Tribune* no longer wrote obits using "Mrs." and the husband's first name, and they stopped asking us to do so.

I loved to do the obits of aged radicals on the left whose names may or may not have appeared in the pages of the Colonel McCormick's *Chicago Tribune*. Of course, I also wrote about the ones on the right, who often had pages and pages of clippings with which to work.

I worked up an obituary on any interesting individual about whom someone provided me with enough information to tell the person's story. These included characters, offbeat personalities, street people, and even children. When I did one about a child, I worked hard to make certain it was about him or her and not about the parents, no matter how prominent they might be.

And contrary to the image many people have about obituary writing, I never in my fifteen years wrote obits ahead of time. If a person were so prominent that a prepared obit was essential, I left that to the expert reporters on the staff that had regularly covered him or her. I did write the first day obituary on Mayor Harold Washington, but several city hall and political reporters did the more formal and lengthy one the next day.

I believed that the best way to honor someone in an obituary was to get it right. I used quotations liberally, and never in my fifty years of journalism has anyone told me I misquoted him or her. I was, however, quite capable of making mistakes, especially omissions such as failing to put a spouse's name in an obit. Also, I was quite capable of making inadvertent mistakes. For example, I have a good memory for historical dates and a strong fascination with the history of World War II. Nevertheless, I wound up getting a chewing out from the city editor of the *Tribune* for absent-mindedly listing in an obituary the date 1943 instead of 1944 for the Invasion of Normandy. (I remember the date very well, I was eleven years old and in school. My classmates I very much anticipated it happening that day or the nest.)

By violating what many consider a journalistic canon, I eventually found a way to be extraordinarily accurate in the obits I wrote. I did this by reading them back to the family or friend. Journalists just did not do that. Although others eventually followed my lead, I initiated the practice very reluctantly and timidly, at first reading them to the family in a quiet voice.

My favorite challenge in writing obits was with the ones that came from the University of Chicago public relations staff. Its members were very good at their jobs and seemingly had unlimited resources. I took it as a personal opportunity to make obits I got from them more personal and better than competing newspapers, including *The New York Times*.

Any number of the University of Chicago professors and researchers about whom I wrote had been awarded the Nobel Prize or other prestigious honors. To me the key in writing about their lives and accomplishments was to tell in a clear and understandable way how such accomplishments affected the lives of others, especially the ordinary reader.

One such instance brings back a fascinating memory. I do not today remember the person's name, but in 1939 he had discovered a way to increase the octane level of gasoline. That was interesting, but "So what?" I asked.

"It made a great impact in the 1940 Battle for Britain," his associate explained. "The British Spitfires and Hurricanes were not really competitive with the latest German Messerschmitts in speed or maneuverability until they got the higher octane gas. It gave the British the advantage." The explanation clearly gave me a better verb and object in my lead than the word, "died."

I remember only a few of the names of the estimated ten thousand obits I wrote for the newspaper, but the facts have often stayed with me. I met a woman on a train to Minnesota who said her husband's obit had been in the *Tribune* a number of years before, but she did not think I had written it. He had been, she said, taken prisoner in the Battle of the Bulge. I did write it and was able to recite for her several details from his experience including a description of his long, freezing trudge to a prisoner of war camp deep in the heart of Germany.

Obits were always very personal to me and so were the people I interviewed in order to write them. They did not have to drop names of prominent people whom the deceased had known or give me quotes from his or her bosses. I preferred printing what those near and dear had to say.

The task of writing obituaries was not as heavy as some might imagine. I steadfastly maintained my belief that obits should tell about people's lives, more than about their deaths, no matter how unusual or bizarre their exit from this world might have been. Such facts belonged in news stories, not in the personal accounts of what they had done and why.

Certainly, one of those things that helped me the most in writing obituaries was the support I received from not only inside the paper, especially the staff of the reference room, but also the outside from family, colleagues, and friends. On rare occasions, relatives or friends were not forthcoming about a person who had died. I felt they had something to hide and I let them hide it. This approach may have disappointed a certain number of my readers, but it did not bother me. Because I received so much help and support, I was usually able to write quite interesting obituaries.

Here are the very kind and generous 1990 comments of a very articulate newspaper columnist and novelist, Bill Granger, about my obituary writing.

> Kenan specializes in obituaries, not as the dull, dreaded work assigned to someone on the nightshift because some momentary big shot shuffled off his coil between editions but as lovingly erected milestones marking the end of long and interesting journeys. There are some of us who read a Kenan Heise obit just because his name is bylined, even if we are unacquainted with the honoree. Invariably, we are glad we stopped to read the marker. His elegies, full of country churchyard simplicity, are more remarkable for being etched in a word processor in the hubbub of a big city newsroom.

# 28

## How Race and Gender
## Helped Transform the Tribune

*I insisted that we be right, that we be fair, that we tell it like it is, be honest and candid. And there were times in the past when I felt we were not as honest and candid as we should have been, that we did not always print both sides.*

HAROLD GRUMHAUS, WHO HAD BECOME PUBLISHER OF
THE *CHICAGO TRIBUNE* IN 1969

When they were young, two of my best friends—both African-American—lost their father because of cruel, racial prejudice. And no newspaper ever carried any story about either incident or, for that matter, the multitudes of parallel tragedies. Why? Because for much of the twentieth century the white news media had neither a presence in the black community nor any interest in covering what was going on there, even stories as dramatic as the deaths of these two men.

Charles Tyler—who has long been like a brother to me—was thirteen years old when his father, Eulie, went hunting in the woods in Virginia on the day after Christmas in 1953. His father attempted to climb over a fence, when his gun accidentally went off and he shot himself. His friends rushed him, hemorrhaging, to a hospital. But, simply because he was black, the emergency room to which he was taken refused to treat him. Every other hospital they took him to refused treatment. He bled to death as a result.

The father of Les Brownlee, another close friend and fellow reporter at *Chicago's American*, had suffered a similar fate. Les told of it in his autobiography (*Les Brownlee: The Autobiography of a Pioneering African-American Journalist*, Marion Street Press, 2007), which I helped edit:

> "The doctors at Cook County Hospital said they could have saved Reverend Brownlee's life if they had received him 15 minutes earlier," the family physician said.

Leonidas Brownlee's death of a burst appendix occurred Dec. 31, 1922 when he was 46 and I was seven years old.

Because of my father's skin color, Evanston Hospital was not open to him and no ambulance would transport him to another hospital. Dr. Penn had taken Daddy by Yellow Cab on a two-hour ride from our home at 1720 Emerson St. in Evanston's African-American ghetto to Cook County Hospital on Chicago's West Side.

In terms of health care and many other things, doors were still closed as if we were slaves.

In 1950, Les himself was hired by the *Chicago Daily News* and became the first African-American reporter for any of the city's downtown daily newspapers. Clem Lane, the paper's city editor asked him, "What can you bring to the paper that we do not already have?" Les answered, "A much better understanding of the South Side community than you have exhibited so far."

When I retired from the *Chicago Tribune* at the end of 1997, I wanted to remind my fellow reporters that the newspaper had come a long ways but not far enough and that an essential part of a reporter's responsibility was to stand on the ramparts, see what was happening, and tell the American public about it.

The traditional office send-off for a retiring reporter is a city room gathering of the editorial staff with cake, coffee, and comments. One of the top editors usually provides the latter. Often the individual's spouse attends. Coworkers add their good-byes with expressions such as, "It's been nice working with you" or "Boy, I can't wait until the day comes when I can retire."

Others, I am certain, have been tempted to speak their minds under such circumstances. I did it. Afterwards, several conservative staff members somewhat enigmatically told me, "That was some speech." Nine years later I ran into someone who heard it and brought it up. "People are still talking about it," he said.

"My wife, Carol," I started, "asked me to extend her regrets that she could not be here today and stand beside me. The reason is that she is in prison, not just in prison, but on death row. (*Gasps from some in the room.*) For those of you who do not know, Carol is an attorney and defends people condemned to death in the last stages of their appeals. Today, she is at Menard prison. She has visited clients on death rows in seven or eight states, and Menard Penitentiary in Southern Illinois, she tells me, is the worst she has encountered. Statesville is the second worst. She would rather be here, she assured me."

I next addressed the last three and a half decades of the *Tribune*, which I had witnessed.

"When I started working in this building," I said. "It was the middle of September 1963 and I had just returned from the Civil Rights March on Washington. It helped make me be aware that the *Tribune* did not have a single African-American working as a reporter, photographer, editor, copyboy, secretary, or even janitor. I was told there might have been a black janitor working in the second basement, but I was never able to confirm it.

"Chicago at the time had close to one million African-Americans, but this newspaper did not have even one of them on its staff."

My arm then swept across the collected *Tribune* staff, which then consisted of possibly one-quarter people of color.

"Times have changed," I said.

"When I started working in the building," I continued. "The *Tribune* paper had a number of woman working for it. With a few notable exceptions, most were doing soft news such as features, health, fashion, and society. A number of women working on news stories were assigned mainly as 'girl reporters' doing street interviews or tragedy sob stories."

Again, I swept my arm across the room and noted that my audience was 35 percent to 40 percent women, perhaps even higher.

"The managing editor," I added, "is now a woman. Times have changed," I repeated.

"When I started working in this building at *Chicago's American*, I was disabled. So I feel like I have had a special stake in this one. I had *gran mal* epilepsy. Jack Mabley, who hired me, knew it, but I don't think his bosses or the insurance company did. I doubt, if I still had epilepsy today, I could pass any physical to get a job here. I may be wrong.

"You know what? I have never seen a wheelchair in the city room of the *Chicago Tribune*," I said. "We do not hire the handicapped. Times haven't really changed.[1]

"This newspaper had gone through several generations of new technology at almost every level during the years I have worked in this building. It has been the shift in the racial and gender make-up of the staff, however, that to me was the most significant transformation the *Chicago Tribune* underwent during those years.

---

1   In the process of writing this chapter, I have learned that the *Chicago Tribune* city room does now have an employee who works from a wheelchair.

"Four years before I started at the paper, the United States Civil Rights Commission had said of the city: 'In terms of racial residential patterns, Chicago is the most segregated city of more than 500,000 in the country.'"

This lack of African-American staff members was notable in every area of its news coverage. It created a news blackout that helped Chicagoans tolerate all the evils that go with racial segregation: lack of opportunity, employment discrimination, unfair housing practices, every kind of police brutality against blacks as well as a genuine lack of basic fairness toward people of other races and ethnic groups.

In 1969, the *Tribune* changed. Harold Grumhaus became publisher of the paper and helped alter the thrust of the paper. In a later interview, he issued the following *mea culpa*: "I insisted that we be right, that we be fair, that we tell it like it is, be honest and candid. And there were times in the past when I felt we were not as honest and candid as we should have been, that we did not always print both sides."

According to Lloyd Wendt in his *Chicago Tribune: The Rise of a Great Newspaper*, both Grumhaus and his protégé, editor Clayton Kirkpatrick, referred to themselves as "open-minded conservatives."

The change in the news content of the paper was almost immediate. Kirkpatrick let loose the paper's very talented investigative reporting staff to do deep, analytical stories on racial discrimination, school segregation, police brutality, and hunger in Africa. The paper also began to hire more minority and women reporters, a lot more of them, and became far more objective in its reporting.

Other media in the city initially ridiculed the *Tribune* for "finally" discovering discrimination and police brutality. This change in the newspaper's coverage represented a dramatic and welcome new direction for the paper, which earned both respect and awards for what it had begun doing. But there was more to be done.

I had never before had met the late Cyrus Colter, a noted Chicago novelist and an African-American who wrote about black working-class people. I very much knew who he was and, apparently, he knew who I was and was reading my obits. When we did finally meet in the mid-1980s, he then introduced me to a black friend by saying I wrote the obituaries for the *Chicago Tribune* and added, "He writes about us."

I passed his comment on to *Tribune* city editor, Bernie Judge, who replied, "I'm proud of that," meaning that he accepted credit, and rightly so, for supporting and encouraging me in doing it. He was the one who hired reporters throughout the 1970s and 1980s bringing onto the staff

quite a few African-Americans as well as women and gave them responsible assignments.

As with so many other newspapers of the time, the *Tribune* did not
come to terms with the women's rights movement and the ramifications
of the Equal Rights Amendment. Newspapers have never presented the
history of women attaining their rights in the way that they have the civil
rights battle.

In writing the obituaries of older women, time and again I heard
complaints from their daughters and occasionally a son that their mothers
had been bitter in their last days over lost opportunity to be professionals
or an equal to men in receiving advancement. They realized they had
suffered as a result and so had their families. Among other things, they
were much poorer in their old age than if they would have been had they
been able to receive advancement or be paid at an equal level with their
male counterparts.

A glance at the employment record of the City of Chicago at the time
can today give us a glimpse of the stories the newspapers and consequently the reading public missed. Up until the early 1970s, the Chicago
City Council had never had a woman serve on it. The first two women
elected to it in its first 134 years were Anna Langford and Mary Lou Hed-
lund, both joining the council in 1971.

When a vacancy had arisen in the city council in December 1968, 5th
Ward Alderman Leon Despres urged Mayor Richard J. Daley to appoint
a qualified woman. In responding to the alderman's challenge, Mayor
Daley attempted to amuse the press corps by admonishing, "Let's not talk
about sex at Christmastime."

In 1972, Arlene Selvern and Margaret Hughes, under Alderman Despres' "direction," wrote "A Report on City of Chicago Employment Discrimination against Women." Among its findings were:

> "In the ten departments (of the city) we studied, we found strik-
> ing discrimination against women employees in terms of salary dis-
> crimination, concentration into low-paying clerical positions, and
> denial of advancement opportunities."

And:

> "Only three of the city's 41 departments are directed by women:
> namely, Consumer Sales with 67 employees, the Municipal Refer-
> ence Library with 14, and the Alcoholic Treatment Center with 53,

making a total of 134 employees, or less than 4 10ths of 1 percent of the city's 35,000 employees."

If the news media had adequately covered this story, change would unquestionably and justifiably have come sooner.

# 29

---

## What, Me Blog?

*I eventually found myself a regular on two different blogs: one, conservative; and the other, liberal.*

I have always needed to write, so blogging became inevitable, just as it has for so many others with the same need. As a result, I eventually found myself a regular on two different blogs: one, conservative; and the other, liberal. I quickly realized several carry-overs from my years as a newspaper journalist could ease me into it.

The first opportunity came when the late Thomas Roeser, a conservative columnist for the *Chicago Sun-Times*, invited me in 2008 to join an ambitious blog he had assembled called *The Chicago Daily Observer*. Its audience—principally, the city's conservatives—was somewhat different from any for which I had ever written. Yet it offered a distinct challenge to entice individuals to read my ideas no matter how much they might disagree with them. Tom gave me unlimited freedom and paid me well for my contributions.

It was on July 2, 2008, five months before the Presidential election, that he introduced me to the readers. He did so with great graciousness, especially considering how much we disagreed politically. He titled the introduction: "Why in Chicago? New Columnist Kenan Heise." It read in part:

> A note from Tom Roeser about a new addition, Kenan Heise.
>
> Barack Obama is carrying some of Chicago, its image and its reality on stage with him; but what is the image and what is the reality of Chicago?
>
> What is the image of Chicago and the reality, not just in terms of a Presidential candidate, but also ourselves and the world in which we live?
>
> What does Chicago mean, when we put it before such words as architecture, art, weather, politics, language, hot dog, sports, weather, culture, theater, or Presidential candidate?

I especially liked one word in Tom's summary about what my contribution was to be. The word was "why." Who and why go to the core of what I like to think journalism should be about. I figured the blog's readers might consistently disagree with my take on the "whys," but they could be forced to go along with me to the level of looking for causative issues, and that would be good. If I could challenge readers to discuss why, it was a good start. I did not feel I had to convert anyone.

One of my first blogs challenged the overuse of word "stupid" in criticizing anyone, including Paul Krugman's doing it in his column, even though I agreed with the rest of what he wrote. Another compared Senator Barack Obama with Chicago's 101-year-old liberal icon and my close friend, Leon Despres. Yet, another piece was titled: "Being Anti-Propaganda, Theirs and Ours."

To become a successful columnist, I believe, there are five individual disciplines we should incorporate in addition to being honest and relevant. I don't call them "rules," an overused and often-misunderstood term. Here are the disciplines:

First, be *interesting* and be so in the right away. You may want to startle or at least promise your readers substance up front. Second, make it *personal* to them. Third, get into the *whys*. Be *clear*. Tell your reader what you going to say and then say it. Finally, get an *editor* or perhaps, editors. I often ask the help of four—my wife, Carol; my brother, Joris; and friends. They care enough to do it and are tough and thoughtful, going over what I write before I submit it for publication. They are consistently helpful in my writing, but on occasion slightly painful to my ego.

Several years ago, a university press published a book on which I had worked. I told the editor that I did not mind substantial editing. As a newspaper reporter, I had been edited to some extent almost every workday. I had not always agreed with the edits, but I appreciated that, overall, they were doing a favor to my readers. The university press editor commented, "Good. Some professors do not even want us to put a period in when it is missing."

Balance is required along with a careful rereading by the writer. One editor of a column I wrote in the early 1970s for *Chicago Magazine* broke up a sentence; one, which he or she felt was too long. I asked to be called to go over the columns one last time, but on one case was not. The comment I was making was about Kenny Williams, a noted Chicago author/scholar—and a woman. In creating the change, the copyeditor made the pronoun in the newly created sentence "he" instead of "she." I had some apologizing to do to Kenny.

A more substantial blogging challenge arose for me when I invited two of my brothers and a nephew to write a blog together that we titled, *Lincoln Liberals.*

If you present an idea with intelligence, clarity and passion, it will be the passion that will have the impact.

One overriding core idea explains blogging's ability to get your and my continuing attention. Successful blogs are inevitably about people. They are about you, me, and them in that order.

When I was a reporter, the newspaper supplied me with a pool of readers. In writing a blog, you have to reach over the side of the boat and net them. The five disciplines apply more than ever, especially the one about being interesting right off the bat. I edit a retired economic professor's superb column on current events and constantly have to tell him the same thing, "Your lede is the third (or sometimes, fourth) paragraph. Move it up."

He needed to focus more on getting his readers' attention. You can achieve this more readily with sound bites or attention-getters than with sentences. So pull them into your material with quotes, words that tempt, phrases that can be remembered, and questions that need answers.

Mainly, focus your attention on the "how-to" of blogs, but even more on the "why-to-read-me" side of blogging. When you write a piece, put it down, pick it up and ask yourself why should someone want to read it? Don't ask, "What am I giving them?" but "What are they getting?"

And have fun.

# 30

## My Enduring Passions as a Bibliomaniac

*When we are collecting books, we are collecting happiness.*

VINCENT STARRETT

Forgive me, father, for I have sinned. I have owned and read far, far too many books. And I am not sorry in the least, not even a little bit. And if I had a chance to do it all over again, I would.

With a book before my eyes, I have sailed the Main, visited the Forbidden City, studied the Celts, tried to understand the mystics, objected to the Inquisition, toasted the Enlightenment, gotten excited about the Declaration of Independence, and the men and women who ever since have backed it up with their lives, their fortunes, and their sacred honor.

Through books, I have come to know Lincoln as my contemporary. In them, I discovered my adopted Chicago as an idea, with all its culture and quirks. And through them, I have tried to understand the present and project the future. I have walked into libraries and walked out a wiser, better educated and a more universal person. Books have given me poetry and a love for it; good architecture and a cheer for it; art and some comprehension of it.

Through books, I—like George Washington, Emily Dickinson, Mahatma Gandhi, and millions and millions of others—have experienced and come to recognize and make use of the light that has lit our way in the darkness. Books we have read, owned or just put our hands on have helped open our minds and cross-pollinate what we think and how we think it.

What is not to love about good books? "A good book will do at least one of three things," *Book Love* author John D. Snider penned. "It will give us an upward pulse to our ideals, yield food for thought, or add to our store of useful knowledge."

I have journeyed to the Lilly Library at the University of Indiana and the Harvard University Library to visit copies of the Gutenberg Bible out of appreciation and respect for the object, the first major book produced with moveable type that so changed and uplifted the world. My hands have held a first edition of Walt Whitman's *Leaves of Grass,* for which Whitman himself helped set the type. My eyes have read from beginning to end a Limited Edition Club copy of Darwin's *The Origin of Species.* Each of these tomes stunned me with its choice of words and expanded my thinking and knowledge. I could envision Whitman kneeling before a blade of grass or Darwin reviewing the records of pigeon lineage in his study while in exquisite pain from his illnesses.

I have read or perused the scriptures in multiple translations and formats, parts of the Koran and the Book of Tao, Aristotle and Plato, the writings of Thomas Aquinas, Dante, the catechism of Martin Luther, Thomas Jefferson, Benjamin Franklin, Thoreau, Emerson, Karl Marx, much of Abraham Lincoln's writings, Louis Sullivan, Frank Lloyd Wright, Emma Goldman, Clarence Darrow, books on Mormonism, Anis Anin, and biographies by the hundreds.

The power in books, their greatness, has been a battery that charged and recharged my brain cells, excited and re-excited my heart. My hands have held and my eyes perused the covers and contents of tens of thousands of books in bookstores, libraries, at book sales, in the collections of others, and in my own. From each I have gained at least a speck of knowledge—a title, a date, an author's name, a sense of craftsmanship, a feeling for the times when it was published, a designer's hand, an insight into its subject matter, and a small sense of a writer's or a publisher's goals and accomplishments. Each of these brief experiences has helped me grow—by some measure—in understanding and appreciating the worlds of reality and possibilities around me.

I have bought, sold, borrowed and loaned, written and edited, worn out and repaired, collected and given away, reviewed and criticized, organized and reorganized, understood and struggled to comprehend books as a key to life. My sermons on the care of books have been many, but I too have dropped or spilled liquid on them, been careless of them, thoughtless at times without a valid excuse.

I have collected and donated some six to eight thousand softcover science-fiction and mysteries to those incarcerated in several different prisons.

Haunting garage and house sales, I put together box after box of gothic and romance novels and mailed them to my mother. She devoured them often at the rate of two a day, and then in turn shipped them off to her eighty-year-old sister in the convent.

I have happily been a witness as poet Gwendolyn Brooks gave away copies of her books of poetry to toddlers who could not read but could have the poems read to them.

I have garnered works by and about Albert Einstein as well as books on science advanced beyond my ken and then shelved and fondled them in the optimistic belief that I would someday comprehend at least a little about the mysteries of the physical world and the universe.

With utter enjoyment and a reader's passion, I have consumed novels and historical books about civilizations, their rise, their falls, and the development of the modern out of the ancient world.

My model, if I actually have one, has been the Library of Alexandria, which by bringing books together and preserving them was the seedbed of our modern civilization.

I pass my bookshelves of various collected tomes and find myself smiling at memories from one or more, likely several of them.

Far too much money have I spent on books and then had to work doubly hard, without regret, to cover their costs.

Over a love of books, I have extended friendships with dealers, writers, and collectors into the hundreds.

I have been a bibliophile and yes—at times—a bibliomaniac.

These are all reasons I do not fear books will ever go away.

*My grandson, Julian, with his own collection*

What I do fear is that too many people in this and future generations will move away from books and never get to experience and develop the love of books that people in our generation and past ones have.

So, to hedge my bet, at least a little, I have given hundreds of books to my grandchildren—Dr. Seuss books by the dozens, pirate and dinosaur books, chapter and adventure books, Harry Potter, and books about music and musicians, history and science, humorous and imaginative ones, and just plain beautiful volumes.  .

Those who truly love the book know that it is more than the writing, words, and illustrations, but rather every detail of a book that can and does contribute to it being a thing of beauty. A book in the hand is an intrinsic reality akin to our own body and soul, a creation that was hammered out of the stardust atoms and given a spark in imitation of the union of spirit and flesh. We who live on this earth can no more disinherit the book than we can the stars in the sky or the animals and plants around us.

The cover is our way of protecting what is inside the book. The binding is that which brought to the pages a oneness. The dustjacket or paper cover is the promise as to what the book delivers. The flyleaf introduces the book. The colors, the tint of the pages, the touch of it, all are the balloons on the fence that proclaim it an "open house" wanting to woo us to buy it. The wear on the used book speaks of its history and use. And flipping the pages gives us a sense of its unfolding. The publisher's stamp, the listing of the edition, even the blank pages at the beginning are part of what we own or are borrowing. We speak of "my copy of the book," proclaiming its relationship to us. Even a library stamp makes it special because it says this is or has been community property.

The greatest adventure of the last five hundred years, I believe, has been the proliferation of books and the personal possession of them even by some of the poorest and most isolated of human beings. Books have imparted knowledge, expanded the imagination, consoled the human heart, opened minds, made people smile or enraged them about the ills of society, brought them closer to the spiritual, helped them make money, encouraged experimentation, supported laws, spread ideas, taught history and challenged the human spirit to evolve into something nobler and more far-reaching that it has ever been.

Hurrah for a good book, whatever it is about!

# Part V

# IN APPRECIATION OF
# SOME OF THE PEOPLE
# IN MY LIFE

# 31

## So This Guy Comes to My Door.
## I Had Forgiven But Not Forgotten Him

*I noticed he had a peg leg and red hair, wore a sports shirt,*
*and was balding. I had never met or seen him before, but*
*I well knew who he was.*

It was 1983.

So, this guy comes to my door. "I hear you have books for sale?" he asks.

Yes, I did have books in the basement, and they were for sale, but that was not what I said. I noticed he had a peg leg and red hair, wore a sports shirt, and was balding. I had never met or seen him before, but I well knew who he was. So I said:

"You think you can come in my house? You, who in 1952 traded Ned Garver from your St. Louis Browns to my Detroit Tigers for Vic Wertz, Dick Littlefield, Don Lenhardt, and others of my favorite Detroit Tigers?"

"Ahh," he said, about to counter; but I interrupted.

"You think people forget and forgive?" I challenged.

Another "Ahh," and again I interrupted.

"And then Ned Garver in his first game in Detroit fell off the mound and ..."

By now, standing solidly on his one foot, he took his turn at interrupting. "And broke his arm," he said.

"No," I protested. "It was his leg. He won exactly one game all year."

"I am certain it was his arm," he protested.

"Oh, come on in anyhow, Bill," I said.

It was Bill Veeck, the former owner of the Cleveland Indians, the St. Louis Browns and, two different times, the Chicago White Sox. He had won the World Series with his Indians in 1948 and, in 1959, brought the "Go-Go" White Sox to the World Series for the first time since the Black

171

Sox Scandal of 1919. Not surprisingly, I did manage to sell him some books, as he was noted for reading up to five of them a week.

Some years later, I had occasion to talk to his widow, Mary Frances, and brought up the incident that happened on my doorstep. This time, it was my turn to be interrupted. "I already heard about that," she said. "From the other side."

And years later, I once more showed that I really did not carry a grudge against him for that infamous 1952 trade. Almost twenty years after my encounter with Bill and six years after his death, *Chicago Magazine* asked several area residents and myself to name the two individuals we considered the most underrated and overrated persons in Chicago history.

My choice for underrated was clear and decisive. It was, of course, Bill Veeck. I described him in one of my books on Chicago as "a character with character." He uniquely brought the concept of democracy to baseball and sports, something that few people, especially in modern times, have attempted to do. He took the door off his office and sat in the bleachers so any paying fans who wanted to object about a trade he had made or pat him on the back for it could do so. In 1947, he had owned the Cleveland Indians and attempted to trade the very popular Lou Boudreau, the team's All Star shortstop. Fortunately for the team and himself, Bill failed to carry it off. The fans were upset and Veeck went around to the bars and personally apologized to any avid followers who were there. Throughout his career, he brought fans into the ballpark in record numbers and treated them with dignity, once sending a whole school to a movie when the game they had come for was rained out.

In the 1930s, he had worked under his father, who was the general manager of the Chicago Cubs. Bill then introduced the ivy on the walls of Wrigley Field and later, when he owned the Chicago White Sox, he initiated the fireworks displays at baseball games. He clearly understood baseball was basically entertainment and he was an original in making it more so.

But he also knew sports were not the most important thing in the world. At Cleveland, he signed Larry Doby as the first African-American player in the American league and later added to the Indians' roster possibly the top Negro National League player of all time, Satchel Paige. He walked on the civil rights March on Washington and the one to Selma and refused the aid of crutches in doing so.

I really have forgiven him, but I have not forgotten.

As for the most overrated individual in Chicago history, my vote went to Daniel Burnham. Burnham, as the chief architect for the World's Columbian Exposition, turned it from a reflection of a Chicago bursting with originality into a beachhead of New York's imitative culture on Chicago's shoreline.

He made it the "White City" in an era when white was the color of the wealthy, who alone had the means and the money to keep their homes, fences, and clothes white. And he selected for the fair a classical, architectural imitation of Rome and Greece rather than the more indigenous architectural American style blossoming in Chicago.

Classical architecture—with its out-of-touch temples, columns, and all-but-windowless buildings—was all New York. Chicago architects were at that very time creating a fresh and original style in which form followed the function of peoples' lives. Some of the same thinking on Burnham's part underlay his designs for *The Chicago Plan of 1909,* which fit Paris more than it ever could the city for which it was created. David Lowe elaborated on this in his excellent 1975 book, *Lost Chicago,* in which he forever indicted Burnham for The grandiose plan: "If giantism was Burnham's first sin, his second was an insensitivity to the importance of people....No wonder the cry went up that The Chicago Plan was in reality a scheme to tax the poor to pay for the improvements desired by the rich. No wonder one of Burnham's legacies to Chicago was a Loop almost deserted at night."

Of course, I forgive Bill Veeck; Daniel Burnham, not so easily.

# 32

## How Gwendolyn Brooks' Poetry Stirred Chicago's Spirit and Mine

*Her poems were so clearly of Chicago's Soul.*

**G**wendolyn Brooks was, for me, one of the kindest muses this nation will ever encounter in coming to terms with poetic beauty. I enjoyed her poems and experienced her in that role, as have tens of thousands of Chicagoans, especially the city's children, and most especially its very young ones.

I heartily recommend her short but truly profound poem, "of De Witt Williams on his way to Lincoln Cemetery." Her poems were so clearly of Chicago's soul. This poem's few words, its simple construction and bare-bones grammar compose the framework for what could be called an obituary for a dead nobody, who was in truth a somebody. This recognition of dignity in the most common of us all leaps out as the theme in this and in any number of her poems. The punchy words of the poem's refrain help us attain this perception:

> Bred in Illinois.
> Born in Alabama.
> He was nothing but a
> Plain black boy.
> Swing low swing low sweet sweet chariot.
> Nothing but a plain black boy.

What compression of an idea! What lack of pious sentiment! What an absence of ornate words! Gwendolyn, as a poet, was masterful and, as a maven, extraordinary. What highlighted many of her poetry readings were the moments prior to her performance that she spent with the preschool children, asking them questions, listening to their answers, and then repeating their quotes as part of her reading. Each child received a free copy of her small booklet, *Poems for Children.*

She—in so many ways—encouraged hundreds of aspiring poets

through poetry contests she sponsored, schools she visited, and even bars in which she read her poetry. I sent her a copy of a book of my poetry, *Our Dinosaurs are Dying*. She responded with a deeply encouraging letter calling my poetry:

> Big,
> cleverly conversational,
> appealing, indeed contemporary,
> and easy to read.

Nothing else anyone has said or done has so encouraged me in writing poetry.

Gwendolyn was the author of twenty books of poetry, my favorite being *In the Mecca*, a volume of poems about the people who lived in the Mecca, an extraordinary large and poverty-marred apartment complex on Chicago's South Side.

In starting off this chapter about her, I attempted to pick up her spirit and held back from shouting her credentials. I therefore did not begin with the recognition given to her and especially to her second book of poetry, *Annie Allen*. It was awarded the Pulitzer Prize for poetry, the first time it was given to an African-American woman. The book also earned her *Poetry Magazine's* prestigious Eunice Tietjens Prize.

The list of those who recognized her gift is long. She was Consultant in Poetry to the Library of Congress from 1985—'86. Among the honors Gwendolyn received were fellowships from The Academy of American Poets and the Guggenheim Foundation as well as the American Academy of Arts and Letters Award, the Frost Medal, a National Endowment for the Arts Award, and the Shelley Memorial Award. Gwendolyn was the State of Illinois poet laureate.

Still, none of her awards or titles impressed me as much as watching her reach out to little children as well as adults through her exquisite poems about nobodies who were somebodies.

She died December 3, 2000. I wrote a poem about her, and I will let it amplify on my feelings toward her:

### Gwendolyn Brooks

You, Gwendolyn,
were upon this earth,
in this city,
the tough/sweet voice of Chicago.

Your poems sang
the prosaic life
of the
old marrieds,
the kitchenette building,
the hunchback girl: she thinks of heaven,
Chocolate Mabbie
and the empty woman.

You made
each
conversationally poetic,
big,
and a vital, interesting,
part of America's life.

You took the white
into the ghetto
and
African-Americans
and other minorities
up above our city.

You shared
your word gifts
with the youngest of children,
free books of poems
they could scarcely read
so you recited for them
and they will be
hearing your voice
still
in the 22st Century,

a part of the music\sound
of this city:
a high note.

You,
Gwendolyn,
were
the delicate,
creative etcher
of reflections
in a city of chaos and creativity.

You enlivened
Chicago bars
and transformed forlorn classrooms
into sanctuaries
of words.

You turned
Sandburg's
City of Big Shoulders
feminine.

You made
Chicago
a black,
a woman
and a poet:
a town
proud
to be
Gwendolyn Brooks'
city.

And, I add with fun and pride, the poem that she wrote about me:

### The Life of Kenan Heise
by Gwendolyn Brooks

To dance around gypsy-like and eat junk and make things
go boom in the day-time,
To put forward a hand: to extend your hand that is speech
of redemptive Gift.
Isn't that part of what it is like to be you, Mr. Heise?
Does that sound like you?

October 27, 1998

# 33

## Henry Regnery:
## "Godfather of Modern Conservatism"
## and My Friend

*He was the conservative; and I, a liberal.*

**P**ublisher Henry Regnery's 1996 obituary in *The New York Times* deservedly called him "the godfather of modern conservatism." The obit told how his fledgling Chicago publishing company brought out William F. Buckley Jr.'s *God and Man at Yale*,

"… which threw down the conservative gauntlet at the feet of the liberal academic establishment and created a sensation in 1951 … Mr. Regnery created an even greater sensation within conservative circles two years later when he brought out Russell Kirk's *Conservative Mind* … which provided the underpinning for the later development of conservative thought."

Henry Regnery was all that and he was my friend; and I, his. He was the conservative; and I, a liberal. We met for lunch almost every week for six or seven years, visited each other's homes, and worked together on two (nonpolitical) books he wrote: *Creative Chicago* and *The History of the Cliff Dwellers Club*. I issued them through my small publishing company, Chicago Historical Bookworks, because he did not want the self-publishing image created by going through his own firm.

We found in one another thoughts to respect and to share as well as ones on which we thoroughly disagreed. I once told his wife, Eleanor, "I brag to my friends about our relationship and how it crosses political lines and goes up and over mountains." Her response was, "What do you think he does?"

Little things connected us. We shared an interest in Chicago's poetry, writers, and history. We discovered surprising common ground in our beliefs about fairness. And little things, we found, connected us and our spouses.

My wife's study partner in law school, Virginia Ertle, lived in Hinsdale, a western suburb of Chicago, where Henry and Eleanor had raised their family. We were amazed to realize that Virginia and her husband resided in the very same house in which Henry, Eleanor, and their family had spent almost twenty years. The Ertles invited the Regnerys, along with Carol and me, to revisit their home and gave a gracious and nostalgic tour to Henry and Eleanor.

The Regnerys had a summer home in Michigan and invited us there as the only guests for a recital by a member of the Chicago Symphony Orchestra. As Henry had for years, the performer played the cello. His solo performance was in gratitude to Henry for giving him his very extensive collection of cello music and arrangements. It was a special occasion not only for the music but also for witnessing the generosity and thoughtfulness that Henry had demonstrated.

The two of us argued firmly but gently about adding female writers' biographies alongside those of the dozen males in his manuscript of *Creative Chicago*. The work was about early twentieth century Chicago literary and cultural giants. I'm certain that he would have refused to add a single woman if I had made my argument on the basis of a quota or political correctness—both of which were sins to his conservative thinking. When I mentioned as one possibility Harriet Monroe, the founder of *Poetry* magazine, he readily agreed to add her. He continued to hold his ground on listing any more, however. "It was a man's era," he argued. "Yes it was," I agreed, adding, "but remember Abigail Adams' exhortation to her President husband, 'Don't forget the ladies.'"

We would get down to names and he would agree on a couple, but our next meeting would begin with him saying, "About that thing ..." We both knew what he meant.

Finally, I posed the question, "What if I were writing a book on the great political minds of the last half of the twentieth century and included only one conservative?" Henry seemed stunned. After considering the parallel between the two separate issues, he opened up and agreed to add four more women to the list.

He was conservative, but not so deeply committed to the Republican Party right or wrong that he was willing to support the Reagan Administration's war in Grenada or George Bush's in Iraq.

He once brought a very articulate friend of his to lunch, a man who had served as the speechwriter for Nixon's vice president, Spiro Agnew. The result was quite a lot of verbal jousting between his guest and myself. I think I did quite well, if I may say so; but when Henry suggested a return engagement of his friend to our lunch table, I turned it down.

"These lunches are personal," I said. "Let's keep them just for you and me." He agreed. We both liked telling stories (and sometimes retelling them) rather than expounding our contrasting ideas.

I was deeply impressed with the list of nonpolitical books his publishing firm had issued throughout the 1950s, 1960s, and 1970s. These represented quite a variety of titles and authors, including many non-conservatives whom other publishers would not have taken on. These included writers with a controversial message such as Frank London Brown (*Trumbull Park*), Mike Royko (with his first book, *Up Against It*), George Halas of the Chicago Bears (*Halas on Halas*), and reporter Patricia Bronte (with her gangster story-filled *Vittles and Vice*). I put together a collection of thirty to forty Chicago books that he had published during those decades and donated them in his name to a literary group in which he was active.

He and I would occasionally attempt to correct one another as to facts or offer a more apt description of our position on an issue, but it was always stated in a friendly, even if passionate, way. I am deeply proud that he, Eleanor, Carol, and I were friends and thoroughly pleased that Henry was open to adding those four women to *Creative Chicago*.

We learned from each other not only friendship but also sensitivity. In this era when too many people confuse political passion with meanness, I took hope and reassurance from the reality that "the godfather of modern conservatism," my friend, was not such a person. I miss him greatly, but will forever carry the imprint of his spirit on mine.

# 34

Connie Reuveni
I Saw Beauty—She Felt It.

*She lingered. I watched my clock.*
*I walked. She leaped.*
*I talked. She listened to the sounds of nature.*
*I wrote. She experienced.*
*And, then it all started coming together.*

*C*hicago: The Beautiful (Bonus Books, 2001) was an effort on my part to capture the vast and varied beauty of the Chicago region in words and pictures. It was, to understate the challenge, a daunting attempt. By pure accident and great, good fortune, I had an extra pair of eyes and an excited heart to help me with it. These belonged to Connie Reuveni, a long-time Evanston used book dealer, who was in the near-final stages of dying.

For most of the time I had known her, Connie was noted for never accepting an answer, straight or otherwise, without expressing some degree of challenge or measure of contention. Something abruptly changed that.

The cocoon that had fastened her wingspans cracked open one day as a result of her walking into my bookstore at the very time I was contemplating writing a book about Chicago and its beauty. She was, as far as I was concerned, a distraction. Even if only momentarily, she disrupted the plans I was in the midst of making to explore, as I had never done before, the natural beauty of Chicago.

I knew what I wanted to do, but I was questioning myself as to whether or not I had the eyes, the heart, and the voice with which to do it. Recently, I had begun more often stopping to smell the flowers, but nowhere near enough to turn me into a writer about nature. This book would be based in my doing this with freedom and abandon and not caring about the time it took or the deadlines, which would confront me.

Ultimately, this book would have to be less about my feelings and more about the surprises that waited me. Connie apparently had not noticed the small, frustrated shake of my head when she came into the store. Her focus was elsewhere. She had just received sad news, a tragic life sentence, and had no one with whom to share it.

"I have just come from my doctor," she said. "I have lung cancer." Her words were blunt and hit me in the chest. For whatever contention had separated us at times, Connie was someone real in my life. She was twenty years younger than I was and now facing death. I was the one with whom she was here and now first abruptly sharing that reality and fate.

I still do not know why I said it, but I did. I had just retired from the newspaper and had freedom with my time and schedule. Maybe, that was why.

"I will be with you on this, Connie," I said. I had no idea what a big commitment those words would entail or how much Carol and I would learn through Connie about life and death. And in no way did I realize how my pledge would open me up to the beauty I was hoping to find in the Chicago area.

Connie stood there silent. She did not grasp, nor necessarily believe my statement of future commitment. I think she wanted me to tell her the diagnosis was not true. I couldn't speak either. I had no further words with which to reassure her than my offer to be "with you on this." She acknowledged my offer and accepted my subsequent silence with just a slight nod of her head.

My agreement did not take much effort at first—an hour and a half several days a week to transport her back and forth to chemotherapy. I had, at the time, no particular schedule into which I had to squeeze that small favor. And besides, she was proving far less contentious than the Connie I had known for years.

Meanwhile, I was lining up bird-watching sites, forests, tallgrass prairies, dune landscapes, county parks, and special places along the river and the lakefront for my afternoons. How and why I started to take Connie along on my outdoor adventures, I do not remember. But what an experience it became!

> I saw beauty. She felt it.
> She lingered. I watched my clock.
> I walked. She leaped.
> I talked. She listened to the sounds of nature.

I wrote. She experienced.

And, then it all started coming together.

I was learning from her. Adjectives limped away as though they were no longer of use to me. My net chased verbs, strong ones that yipped action, happenings, life, hopes, and—above all—soul-filling beauty.

We visited the Hindu Temple of Greater Chicago, located in perhaps the most unusual natural setting in the area: the Illinois Historical Corridor. Carved out and forested, this region southwest of Chicago embraces the Des Plaines River Valley. What we saw was beauty, but what we experienced together was respect, the simple religious tribute of Hindu people who brought food and ate with their ancestors and divinity.

Connie and I dropped in at the Morton Arboretum. Our focus appropriated the trees and our goal changed from perusal to a desire to get to know and share them with the readers of the book I was writing. We chose ten individual trees to feature in the book:

1. White Oak
   *The individual selected as the Illinois Millennium Landmark Tree stands in the arboretum.*

2. Dawn-Redwood, once thought extinct
   *For years, naturalists were familiar only with its fossils until actual living ones were found in a remote part of China.*

3. Katsura Tree
   *Arguably the most beautiful or at least the most appreciated at the arboretum.*

4. Sugar Maple
   *October brings out spectacular leaf colors, brilliant yellow, burnt orange, and touches of red.*

5. Burr Oak
   *Bold, craggy, and majestic.*

6. Flowering dogwood
   *Connie's and my favorite.*

7. Shagbark Hickory
   *President Andrew Jackson was known as "Old Hickory" for being as rugged as the wood of this tree.*

8. Ginkgo or Maidenhair
*Awkward and angular when young, but beautifully sculptured, even "spiritual" as it matures.*

9. Accolade Elm
*Remarkably immune to Dutch Elm Disease.*

10. Eastern White Pine
*The tree of proliferation for the early white settlers.*

Connie, though tired, wanted to visit each of them. But the more exciting action for her turned out to be in the arboretum's Schulenberg Prairie, fifty-five acres on a modest hill that has remained prairie since having been restored in 1962. These acres have served as the template for most other prairie restorations in the area.

Tired and weakened though she was from illness, Connie slowly climbed the somewhat-steep prairie path, finally reaching its pinnacle. There, having lost her determined focus on attaining it, she stood and smiled defiantly at the world.

Perhaps Connie's greatest adventure was two days before she died. We went to the Peggy Notebaert Nature Museum in Lincoln Park to see the butterflies. The best way I can think to share my feelings about that experience is through a poem I wrote about it:

### Connie
### at the Butterfly Garden

Fluttering and zigzagging,
    gracious, imperturbable butterflies,
with energy quickly spent
    grasp how short their lives.

Focused and frenzied,
    they give little thought to rest
grasping warmth and procreating,
    they last but two weeks or less.

Connie Reuveni, clutched by cancer,
    cocooned and unable to fly,
curled and wheelchair-bound,
    has come to say a last goodbye.

Metamorphosed for the moment,
    her body gaunt and lean,
she stands to her feet
    and applauds the air with wings unseen.

Accepting of the magic—
    though of life's journey soon bereft—
which she now sees in the exquisite time
    for her and these playful friends left.

Connie leaves the nectared garden,
    abeam with fresh understanding and pride,
as a smile flutters from off her face
    toward the friend at her side.

    Connie's memory flutters still in my heart,
      whenever I visit that special place,
    for it was I who that day netted
      the butterfly smile from off her face.

Finally, Connie lived in a one-bedroom apartment overlooking a park. Carol and I helped her organize and clean it up as well as wash the nicotine-stained picture window overlooking the park outside. Now, during her last days, she could see the beauty that surrounded her.

After she died, we helped her family clean out her apartment and deal with her books. The thought occurred to me that this had been Connie's cocoon. What a butterfly she turned into! Whenever I reread *Chicago, the Beautiful*, she flits still through its pages.

# 36

## Some Kind and Generous Recognition
## by Allan Eckert

*His challenge and kindness inspire me.*

Throughout my life, kind support from others—especially in my writing endeavors—has provided me with extraordinary reinforcement in trying to accomplish improbable, if not impossible, goals.

I know many of my limitations as a writer because I encounter them every day in trying to write. I recognize myself as a driven and, very fortunately, supported writer. I have written for publication for more than fifty years because individuals have personally encouraged and helped me.

In my writing to this day, I am profoundly indebted to them. They have especially included Bill Ryan of *The Wage Earner*; Jack Mabley of *Chicago's American*; *Chicago Tribune* editors Clayton Kirkpatrick and Jim Squires; *Tribune* columnists Bob Cromie, Mary Schmich, Bill Granger, Rick Kogan and Bob Greene; Herman Kogan of the *Chicago Daily News*, Leon Despres, David Mamet and Gwendolyn Brooks; my publishers; my wife, Carol; my brother, Joris; any number of my friends and coworkers, as well as my sons, to name a few.

No one, however, has reached out to encourage my writing as eloquently and unexpectedly as the late nature writer and American historical novelist Allan Eckert. In 1981, he penned an unsolicited letter to *Chicago Magazine* so kind about my writing that I find it awkward for me to talk or write about it.

Before writing this, I had learned Allan had died. I had not found a way to get in touch over the last several years, but managed to do so a month before he died. In a phone conversation I was able to tell him how much kind words can do for a writer who has to struggle to be one.

In 1981, he sent a letter to *Chicago Magazine* about my book *The Journey of Silas P. Bigelow* (Collage, Inc. 1981). It was at this time that I had begun a new and different column in the *Tribune*, "Neighborhood Dialogue," and just months before I began writing obituaries for the paper. What he said in the letter renewed my limited faith in myself as a writer.

Allan won international recognition and acclaim as an historian, naturalist, novelist, poet, screenwriter, and playwright. He died July 7, 2011 at his home in Corona, California.

His book *The Infinite Dream* has been published posthumously and is in sequence to his great series on early America as peopled by Indians, frontiersmen, and pioneers. This last, his forty-first book, explores America's westward expansion beyond the Mississippi River, between 1834 to 1848.

He penned 225 scripts over fifteen years for the unique and popular television show *Wild Kingdom*, for which he won an Emmy. Books, which he wrote, were nominated on seven separate occasions for the Pulitzer Prize in literature.

Still, I believe, it is a person's writings far more than mere biographical facts that let us know what the individual has contributed to mankind. The following short description of a growing North American glacier from the prologue to his book, *Wild Season* (Little Brown, 1967), exemplifies this:

"Newly awakened from its eons-long slumber, the glacier had become a hungry monster ponderously grinding its way across a defenseless land. Its frosted teeth sank deeply into the earth in a hundred, a thousand, a hundred thousand bites. Its appetite was immense and in its gullet the ingested forests and fields, hills and dunes, were masticated by great ground granite boulders."

In 1981, although we had never met at the time, he wrote a letter to *Chicago Magazine*, which had reviewed my book:

> *The Journey of Silas P. Bigelow* is an absolute delight. It is prose poetry (or, more properly, poetic prose) in the truest sense of the word. In a career of having devoured virtually everything worthwhile that has been written about American Indians, I've never encountered anything that so deftly puts across the complex simplicity of our aboriginal societies; nor anything that so eloquently exhibits the love of the Indian for the land. Their love—and the author's—of nature literally surges out of every page. The grasp of Indian mentality is truthful and a delight to encounter. The simple philosophies of the principal Indian characters are beautifully and skillfully stated and far more meaningful than a cursory reading

reveals. One needs to treat this writing as if it were a fine rare wine, sipping and savoring rather than gulping. I think it altogether possible that in those pages there might well be as much to learn about love and sharing as in anything heretofore written. It embodies a joyously mystical quality and among the telling lines is the one which states: "... the greatest pain would be not to have love."

My what-if novel, *The Journey of Silas P. Bigelow,* takes place in a hypothetical Indian nation. This country is comprised of the territory between the Allegheny Mountains to the east, the Ohio River to the south, the Mississippi River to the west, and the Great Lakes to the north. The year is 1983, and the land had never been ceded to the United States. The following is chapter 1 of the novel.

# A Sanctuary on Lake Michiganin

I am in jail; a colorless cubicle that is trying to crowd me. "Protective custody," the United States Army is trying to call it. I am its hostage. I know too much.

Anger! Its rumblings are deep. They shoot pain into my heart and into my throat as I relive what has happened.

I also feel free. The bars on the window are not real. The walls are not winning their persistent battle against me. I am enveloped rather by the boundlessness of the tall-grass prairies of the Indian Nation.

I have been there. Birds, passenger pigeons, swirl over my head. These birds swoop and dart. They overwhelm my consciousness, sweeping away other memories of my tumultuous journey to Chicagou and the Indian nation.

I have been there. I became a part of Chicagou. I was at the vortex of its cataclysm. The storm has gone. I feel passive, subdued.

The birds insist on telling their story before I tell mine. I will let them.

The dominant Chicagou bird is the exquisite passenger pigeon. Here in the United States, east of the Allegheny Mountains, it is extinct. Not a solitary one can be found, not in zoo, aviary or game preserve. Yet the lands to the west, protected for and by the Indians, are home to flocks of tens of thousands of these pigeons, birds that survive only in a country where the natural bounty has been preserved.

Two hundred years are gone since 1783. The treaty of Paris ended the Revolutionary War and divided the United States and the Indian Nation.

The differences are accentuated by the fate in each land of the passenger pigeon. Man can exist without freedom. This bird, seemingly, cannot.

In Chicagou, I watched wild birds perform and dance in multitudes. They made a thunderous racket as they beat the air and yelled to proclaim their existence. Alighting by the thousands, they dominated the trees and the earth as they had the skies.

In their numbers they could blot out the sky. Yet, a single bird could catch your eye, an elegant and fascinating creature. I held a wild pigeon, an injured one, in my hand and felt it to be a piece of very fine china, though warm and alive as if from God's private collection. It cooed, almost purred with vitality, commanding attention and respect. I'm neither a bird lover nor watcher, just a person hypnotized by this minute item on the shelf of life's realities.

They fly low, skim and undulate over the landscape. No bird—except the eagle in its dive—is as fast. I saw passenger pigeons dart unerringly, quicker than a thought, through the woods. Nature has stored up in this bird special resources of exceptional speed, beauty, grace, and proliferation to help it survive the onslaughts of winter, hunter, and eclectic misfortune.

Until recent events, no passenger pigeon in the Indian Nation had ever heard the echoed thunder of a rifle or the clap of a pistol. No sportsman felt the easy squeeze of a trigger that could bag dozens of birds in one shotgun blast. Simply, the Indian Nation was successful in its 200-year struggle to become a haven for both Indian and wildlife.

In the 20 states that comprise the United States, a challenge solidified—oh so angrily—into the "American Fairness Doctrine." The central thrust argued that it was right and it was fair for the country to expand westward at the expense of the Indian nations, which produced a surplus of meat, grain, copper, and iron. The other nations of the world—since these commodities have been generously shared by the Indians—have been united in opposition to westward expansion by the United States.

Early this year I was given the assignment as a journalist to visit the Indian Nation. Specifically, I was to hypothesize in a series of articles about what the Indian Nation would be like if it had been part of the United States for the past 200 years. I do not claim to have been ideally suited for this role. Simply, my editor offered me the job, and I accepted enthusiastically. I was to be the first American reporter to journey to the Indian Nation in decades.

Speculators wrote and offered a thousand schemes for me to suggest to the Indian councils, ways to make more money and advance the cause of mankind simultaneously. "All" these writers asked was that they be allowed to offer their expertise to the Indians. One bizarre scheme was to turn a stretch of the Lake Michigan shore into a cemetery so that Americans who wanted to migrate to the Indian Nation could at least do so after death. This presumably would save room in U.S. cities, and the Indians certainly would not have to fear being overrun with the dead. The footnote on the letter was an urgent: "I await your promise that you will propose this idea to them."

Business people were not the only ones to approach me. Unofficial representatives of the U.S. government also sought to "brief" me. The issue constantly was referred to as "sensitive." The honest description was "explosive." Pressure for expansion westward had not subsided for 200 years. Politicians came up with tactics and new arguments constantly. Each new generation had to deal with it, and about once every 20 years the situation became ugly.

Signs indicated it was headed in that direction again on the two hundredth anniversary of the 1783 Treaty. The United States was crouched—the word cannot be too strong—for attack as I blithely set off for Chicagou.

Only later would I learn that an out-of-uniform intelligence officer, Major Dick Thoreau, whom I met briefly, proposed sending into the Indian Nation an American citizen "cloaked in innocence and ignorant."

A century before, hunters used a similar tactic to capture and kill thousands of passenger pigeons, blinding one by lacing its eyelids shut, then attaching it to a long pole, or "stool," to lure other birds into its large net.

I was to be my country's "stool pigeon," part of a very sophisticated and deadly trap.

# 36

## Mike Royko:
## The Nice Side of the Guy

*The handwritten inscription on a copy of the book's cover reads: "Youse*
*better watch out, Heise. I'm gunning for youse. Al." Not until that*
*minute did I realize that Al Capone, though long dead, could still write*
*and that he and Mike Royko had the exact same handwriting.*

Journalists had a short, simple word for the talent of their fellow
reporter/columnist Mike Royko. That word was "good," as in "he's
good." The expression of it was encased with a tone of respect for
his journalist talents that others could never replicate.

But what about Mike Royko, the man?

He was without question the most popular as well as the most loved
and hated Chicago journalist of the last one hundred years. His career
spanned a third of that century as the city's top newspaper columnist,
writing with a biting wit and a one-of-a-kind insight for the *Chicago Daily
News*, the *Chicago Sun-Times*, and finally, the *Chicago Tribune*.

In 1972, he won the Pulitzer Prize and throughout his career, dozens
of other top journalism awards. By the 1980s, his daily column was ap-
pearing in 615 newspapers across the country. Royko died in 1997 but
lives on in the books he authored and in the ones written about him.

He did not try to pass himself off as an especially nice guy; as a matter
of fact he often seemed to try to want to give the opposite image. Still, it
was my personal experience that he could prove deeply sensitive to many
who were getting, to use a street cliché, "the short end of the stick." His
sensitivity did not extend to his cigarette smoking, however, as people
with offices next to him could testify. Nor did it cover some of his heavier
drinking bouts.

Mike could be as brilliantly sarcastic as anyone whom you will ever
meet and often was. Chicago politicians and aldermen in particular were
regular targets of it. Of them he wrote: "I've always enjoyed Chicago

aldermen, and I believe that if they went away the city would be a much poorer place for their absence. Just how much poorer I don't know, because it would depend on how much you can stuff in a suitcase."

About their obsequiousness to Mayor Richard J. Daley, he commented: "When the mayor says, 'Sit,' most of them not only sit, they bark and roll over."

He relished putting down the self-important, the cheats, and "smart-alecks" both in person and through his column. Local politicians, he maintained, fell into all three categories. A sign in his corner Tribune Tower office read: THE EAGLE DOES NOT HUNT FLIES. It epitomized his disdain for the petty and narrow-minded of this world. And many of these were individuals whose sole accomplishments to him were to get themselves elected to the Chicago City Council or other Chicago and Illinois political offices.

Extraordinarily quick, Mike brandished his wit like a master fencing champion with a rapier. He could be friendly as well as intimidating, sometimes both at the same time. Even on those occasions when he seemed distracted, he was often aloof and always interesting. And interesting is what his columns and writings were, which was often true of even the ones with which you disagreed.

Mike was a storyteller, by far the best one I ever met in my life. My relationship with him consisted for the most part of stopping in his office every once in a while and exchanging stories about the city's characters and their way of expressing themselves, his third most favorite subject after Chicago politics and the Cubs. He could be acerbic about Chicago language and its usage if he was talking to someone local, but highly protective of it against outsiders, especially New Yorkers.

Here is an example from a late 1960s column, when he was with the *Chicago Daily News*. In it, he was trying to explain (or perhaps a better verb might be "hammer home") a clarification to an editor at *Vogue* in New York. He argued with emphatic emphasis that the magazine's inclusion of "clout" as an "in" word was a theft by New Yorkers of "an old Chicago word and a distortion of its meaning." He proceeded to inform her of its Chicago usage:

> Clout means influence—usually political—with somebody who can do you some good.
>
> In simple English, a bailiff might say, "Somebody beefed me that I was kinky and I almost got viced, but I saw my Chinaman and he clouted for me at City Hall."

As everybody know, that means, "A citizen complained that I did something dishonest and I was almost fired, but I contacted my political sponsor and he interceded in my behalf with my department head."

He then added: "She stuttered...I'll bet nobody has told her she was wrong since she left Iowa or Nebraska, and went to New York to become a career woman and ruin her complexion."

It might, I acknowledge, be difficult for her or others whom Mike similarly skewered to accept that he had a soft side. His acerbic sword was seldom in its scabbard. I once invited Mike to do a signing of his book *Dr. Kookie, You're Right* at my bookshop in Evanston. During a lull, he took a pen and scratched a message on the cover of a book I was trying to sell. It was a copy of a drama that I had written—*Alphonse: A One Man Play in the Words of Al Capone*. He wrote: "Youse better watch out, Heise. I'm gunning for youse. Al."

Not until that minute did I realize that Al Capone, though long dead, could still write and that he and Mike Royko had the exact same handwriting. I treasure this personal iconic example of Royko's wit as Chicagoans do his biography of Richard J. Daley, *Boss*, and the six books of his columns that were published. His niceness, like his humor, was close to the edge and unique.

His columns were like morality plays written backwards and, as such, made him a good and thoughtful entertainer. His basic message—scrambled up in his wit, sarcasm, and at times, mockery—was for people to break whatever prejudices or political ambitions prevented them from being decent to one another.

Mike was not always sweet to people, preferring instead to call individuals and their motives as he saw them. He would answer his phone gruffly and often growl when people wanted him to expose those who were their enemies. He was never happier than when snapping at the self-righteousness of those who pretended to be above the fray. These were the flies and he soared around them not like an eagle on the wing but like a threatening vulture about to attack rotten carrion.

And yet he could pull back and be soft. He told me the following story with a decided twinkle in his eye and pride in his voice. It was about an overnight piece on a pathetic Chicago sad sack, who became the target of a lesser eagle, who would have thought it sport to hunt him. I will not name the target, but he was once the batboy for the Chicago Cubs, and went on to become vice president of the Metropolitan Sanitary District of

Cook County, an agency that arguably housed one of the highest percentage of jobs obtained through patronage in the county.

The man's unique penchant was for gaining publicity by muscling his way into almost every front-page picture of someone famous visiting the city. At this, he was uncannily successful. He also was the board president of a local UHF TV station, one that ran on a shoestring along with a great deal of ignored incompetence.

On a slow news day in 1965, I was working on the city desk and was assigned to cover a press conference the man had called to announce a new general manager of the TV station after the last one had resigned after two weeks. Along with a handful of other reporters, I waited and waited in the station's outer office to be called into the press conference. Staff arguments were loud and could be heard through the thin walls. The place was a highly unprofessional mess. Here are several paragraphs I wrote in an article about the experience:

> There are hooks on the wall, but no pictures hang from them. The phones have been disconnected except for a pay phone on the wall next to the director's desk.
>
> The board president announced, "I am appointing Andy Muldoon acting general manager without pay until Friday, at which time he too, can resign."
>
> The appointed general manager objected to the reference that the job is payless.
>
> "Don't tell me what to do," the board president said. "I'm running this station."

My editors liked this flat, factual reporting and felt it would make a quirky front-page story. The board president—character that he was willing to be—surprised the people on our paper's desk by calling to ask, "Was that a good story or not?"

In times past Mike had been more than willing to report the man's bumbling, but eventually alcoholism made him so pathetic that Royko, then lead columnist at the *Chicago Daily News*, no longer consider him fair game. He had become, in Mike's description, "just one more of the city's sad, unemployed drunks."

When the paper's night editor ran across a ha-ha incident about the man, no sympathy held him back. The story was that the woman with whom the man was living had locked him out. He stumbled off to a locksmith to help him get back in. As the locksmith was working on the lock, an indignant female voice from inside asked, "What in hell are you doing?" This led to a fight outside the door in which the locksmith hit his would-be customer in the nose.

When Royko heard the paper was going to run the story, he felt neither eagles nor newspapers should hunt flies. He went to the city editor and asked him to kill the article. The night editor was furious and protested, but Mike prevailed. He bragged to me, "It was the only time in my career I ever used my power on the paper to kill a story."

It might have not mattered much one way or the other to the sad sack in the story if it had run. He might have asked whether it was good publicity or not. Still, it played to something in the good side of Mike Royko.

Like many, if not most of his readers, I did not always agree with Mike's columns. I recall one occasion when his good friend, Studs Terkel, and I were standing in front of the *Tribune* trying to point out to him the errors of his ways in that day's column. It was a not a fair fight. It was just the two of us against Mike Royko.

Royko was an inveterate Chicago Cubs fan, its most famous. In his last column, he had written about the supposed curse that Billy Goat Tavern owner, William Sianis, put on the Chicago Cubs for their not allowing him to take his goat into the stadium. The only curse with which the Cubs were burdened, he wrote, was from an ownership that for too many years proved reluctant to acquire any black athletes to play for the team.

He got no argument from Studs or myself on that.

# 37

## Leon Despres:
## My North Star

*To Studs, Len had helped take his fellow Chicagoans to a greater free-dom through making their world more human, just and civil.*

**L**eon Despres ("Len" to just about everybody) was my hero. We hung out, spending an afternoon or two together at least once a week over the last ten of his 101 years. I worked with him on a book he wrote titled *Challenging the Daley Machine: A Chicago Alderman's Memoir* (Northwestern University Press, 2005).

He was my close friend, but he was more than that. I learned exactly how to describe him from our mutual friend, Studs Terkel. Studs said that Len was his "North Star." And I realized that is what he was for me as well. Studs looked at his friend of almost seventy years and said, "You are the one. You have pointed me north. You have been persistent and reassuring."

"Follow the drinking gourd," Studs then chanted.

To slaves, the Big Dipper in the sky above them had appeared like the hollowed-out gourds used as drinking ladles on plantations throughout the South. Using it, they could locate off its tip the one clearly fixed star, Polaris, the North Star. It could lead those trying to escape slavery, they had been told, to the North, to the land of freedom.

According to Studs, Len had helped take his fellow Chicagoans to a greater freedom through making their world more human, just, and civil. To him, the phrase showed how Len had guided him and others ever forward, ever heading in the direction of greater freedom from the repression they had to accept in the past. Len embraced Studs' metaphor with equal fervor and repeated the words, "Follow the drinking gourd" to mark the journey the two of them had made and still were making. He called the historic words "an established truth such as Einstein's mathematical $E = mc^2$" or Louis Sullivan's architectural credo, "Form follows function."

It takes symbolic language, a metaphor, to describe Len Despres and the love and fairness that he sought for both Chicago and its people. He was, as Studs said, "persistent and reassuring." Over his last decade, I served as Len's Boswell, his tag-along scribe.

He was best known for his role as the vocal independent alderman of the Fifth Ward from 1955 to 1975 and later as the Chicago City Council parliamentarian (under three mayors), but even more as the city's full-time sentinel and unswerving conscience. Both over his long career and in his final years, his aspirations for the city and concern for its possibilities were profound. He was a man of enormous hope, persistent action and constant kindness to Chicago's diverse people, especially its disenfranchised poor. His concerns and effectiveness had a distinct impact on Chicago's race relations, music, culture, unions, law, architecture, art, books, and history.

Marian, his wife of seventy-five years, died several days short of his ninety-ninth birthday. In the emotion of the situation, he told me he was no longer as interested as he had been in reaching one hundred years of age. Instead of succumbing to this tempting discouragement, he did an about face, and the two of us spent at least one afternoon each week getting re-involved with the city. I recorded these efforts in a book, *Chicago Afternoons with Leon: 99 Years Old and Looking Forward* (AuthorHouse, 2007).

Len's last major public speech—given at the age of 100 at the Chicago Historical Museum's Fourth of July celebration in 2008—called to the city's attention the injustices it had perpetrated in the 1830s toward the Pottawatomie, Chippewa, and Ottawa Indians, who were cheated out of the land on which he and his audience stood.

It was not just his heroic civil rights battles in the Chicago City Council, nor his rescue of the city's great architecture, nor even a combination of all the causes for which he fought that were the measure of this man. Rather, it was how intensely he loved the small as well as the big things in life and the little people as well as the more successful. I saw it in him in

- the few extra moments he always lingered in visiting a public park— almost any one in the city;
- the meticulousness with which he had followed through on the 20,000 requests for help he received as an alderman between 1955 and 1975;
- the three-year battle he initiated against lead paint poisoning after a child in his ward had died from it;

- the stacks and stacks of postcards he mailed out to encourage and support others in their various efforts to contribute to the city;
- and the literally thousands of rallies he attended and speeches he made to support human rights causes in Chicago and civil rights in the South.

My friendship with Len Despres—as he approached and turned 100 and then 101—was for me akin to discovering a treasure chest full not of gold and jewelry, but rather of shared values and rare generosity. I cannot believe it really happened, or that he is now gone. He was so personal and so special as a part of my life.

Perhaps my most vivid memory was of his unwavering opposition to the death penalty. Specifically there was the time, when thousands upon thousands throughout the state opposed the death penalty, but he was the only member of the public who stood up in support of a last-minute effort to block the last execution in the state's history.

He alone, other than the man's lawyers (including my wife, Carol), showed up before the Illinois State Clemency Board in Springfield in 1999 to make a final plea on behalf of Andrew Kokorales, the last person whom the State of Illinois put to death. Governor George Ryan often said he himself was so troubled by the execution of Kokorales that it led to his decision to impose a moratorium on the death penalty in the state and subsequently to commute the death sentences of 167 Illinois death row inmates. Although in his nineties, Len traveled to Springfield and testified before the clemency board, which was holding the final, determining hearing on Kokorales' fate.

It was not the only time he stood alone in behalf of what he believed. Especially during the first of his four terms as Fifth Ward alderman in the Chicago City Council, he frequently lost crucial votes 49 to 1 to Richard J. Daley's patronage-enriched aldermen. At council meetings, Len often had his microphone turned off or lost the floor to a scurrilous "point of order" call by an opponent. In the end, however, he saw many of his civil rights issues and much of the socially concerned agenda for which he had fought ultimately prevail.

It was unvarnished joy for me in the last years of his life to feel as though I were strapped aside him in a rocket ship heading toward the stars. I think over the years a lot of people have enjoyed that same experience with Len.

Len was big in life, but it was the little things that also surprised and delighted. He had a warm sense of humor, a real wit and a love of parks that was like a child's. One of the most rewarding experiences I had with him was to take Marian and him, in their wheelchairs, to Washington Park on the border of the Hyde Park neighborhood. Once there, they wheeled themselves to a special place on the edge of the pond where they went on dates in the late 1920s.

For his ninety-seventh birthday, several generations of a family of his friends held a party at their house in his honor. Marian was not feeling well enough to attend. Ironically, the party was being held on her ninety-sixth birthday, which was two days after his. His speech before cutting the cake was simple. "Today," he said and then repeated the word in saying, "Today is the happiest day of my life." No one missed the point. Marian's birthday, not his, was the happiest day of his life. He was incredibly appreciative that they were still together. Later at their apartment, I had the pleasure of sharing the comment that Len had made about "the happiest day of my life" with Marian. After hearing it, she turned to look in his direction and smiled.

He loved Jackson Park, which he could see out his window; but he also seemed to love every inch of every park in Chicago. In the late 1960s, he had one of his most famous battles with the Mayor Richard J. Daley, when the latter took part of Washington Park away to build a school and parking lot. In 2006, the Friends of the Parks gave him their Lifetime Commitment to the Parks Award.

At the age of ninety-nine in 2007—as Chicago bid for the 2016 Olympics—he threatened to boycott the event if Chicago won its bid and went through with its plans to build a stadium in Washington Park. He could not stand to picture any of its grassy areas turned into a cement parking lot. Had Chicago held the Olympics, he would have—on the occasion— been 108 years old. He did not live long enough to see Chicago lose its bid and learn that Washington Park would continue to be, as he called all of the parks, "the lungs of the city."

It was his commitment to fairness and equality that most led him to battle on the floor of the Chicago City Council. He sought in the 1960s to break the patterns of segregation in Chicago that caused the United States Civil Rights Commission to call it "the most segregated city with a population of more than 500,000 in the country."

At ninety-nine, he was back into the battle, offering the sole voice excoriating the Chicago Housing Authority and its commercial developer allies for "human cleansing" the Near South and West sides. He condemned the policy of rooting out and sending to an unnoted and

*Studs Terkel (left) and my wife, Carol, with Leon Despres*

unsoftened fate between fifty thousand and one hundred thousand CHA residents. He equated this conscienceless dispersal of residents helter-skelter into the poorest and already the most congested neighborhoods with that of the removal of the Indians in 1835.

In another effort on behalf of Chicago, Len paid a visit to the administrative offices of the Chicago Public Library and looked at the original records from the days when his father, Samuel, served on the library board. Ironically, he found in them support for his own call for the library to provide services in homeless and abuse shelters, nursing homes, jails, and juvenile detention centers. In checking the records, he learned that 105 years earlier his own father had chaired a committee in charge of a similar project that used stores and ethnic centers as neighborhood "delivery stations."

For the foreword to his memoirs book we used a speech that the late Mike Royko had given in introducing him as the main speaker at a 1971 fund raising dinner. In it, the famed newspaper columnist with a sharp eye for what went on in the City Council said of Len: "So I am introducing Alderman Despres. Throughout his career he has been in the forefront of just about every decent, worthwhile effort made to improve life in this city. Being in the forefront, he is usually the first to be hit on the head with the mayor's gavel."

It was my privilege to see Len Despres staying in the forefront of just about every decent, worthwhile effort made to improve life in this city until he died on May 6, 2009 at the age of 101.

# 38

## Studs Terkel:
## An Explosion of "Curiosity"

*Studs' eyes opened. He looked around to measure his audience and then bellowed one word from his cushioned armchair. His voice cracked as he uttered his answer as to the stimulus that had driven him all his life, "Curiosity."*

Allow me the pleasure of recalling Studs Terkel's response when I asked him the question that caused him to jump up out of his seat. Len Despres, then ninety-nine years old, and I were visiting our then ninety-four-year-old mutual friend in the living room of his North Side Chicago home. The inimitable Studs—former actor, radio host, and Pulitzer Prize winning author of *The Good War: An Oral History of World War Two*—was tired and slumped in his favorite easy chair.

If he were not dying, his occasional cryptic comments were making it clear that he truly wanted to do so. The veteran battler for the disenfranchised and forgotten people in our society was weary, very weary and repeatedly fell asleep in the middle of the discussion going on around him. His contributions to the conversation had dragged it down. They had consisted of Studs asking us what we had for lunch, complaining about the various ailments that were afflicting him, and saying he wanted to die. Len and I were near to falling asleep ourselves and about to leave when I asked the nodding Chicago icon who was our host, "Studs, what's motivated you to do all the things that you have done over the years?"

Studs' eyes opened. He looked around to measure his audience and then bellowed one word from his cushioned armchair. His voice cracked as he uttered his answer as to the stimulus that had driven him all his life, "Curiosity."

His voice had a deep-seated energy that over the years since the 1930s had enthralled radio, TV, and even movie audiences as well as at many hundreds of cause-driven rallies. Then, startling us even more, Studs jumped to his feet like a killed-off actor taking back the stage. His hands gestured excitedly and his booming voice filled the room for almost an hour with his words echoing throughout his plant and book-filled living room. He shared with us a panorama of razor-sharp memories and wise eyebrow-raising insights about life. He was magnetic. And what he was saying, as so often in the past, proved well worth our attending to every word as we would for the greatest of dramatic performers.

A few moments before he may have wanted to die, but in each of the moments he was filling with his fulsome response to my question, he was as alive as anyone I could ever remember. The contrast in the man was like an oil well uncapping. This muscle-creaking ninety-four-year-old put aside his cane and actually broke into a slightly jerky two-step dance. His gyrations punctuated the excited memories that poured out of him.

"I have been curious about everything," he said in a voice that used the fullness of his diaphragm to project his words. A case full of various books he had written stood behind him and confirmed his assertion. It held copies of the curiosity-driven, best-selling interview books he had authored about Chicago, working, music, the Depression, jazz, old age, approaching death, and his classic *The Good War*.

In overriding his prior morose physical condition, Studs' explosion was providing his small audience with a micro model of what the Big Bang must have been like. It was not the living room floor, which he had claimed as his stage, but a stage upon which to release his reenergized expression of the rights of his fellow human beings and his renewed happy interest in life.

He talked and reminisced about many people and things, but his main focus was on his friend of more than seventy years who was present in the room, Len Despres. He recalled with vivid and accurate memory their first encounter on June 8, 1937.

Len was then a young labor lawyer speaking at a workers' rally to protest the Memorial Day Massacre ten days earlier at the Republic Steel Corporation in Southeast Chicago. Just days before Studs gave us his recollections, I had happened to have read a lengthy account of the massacre and the protests that had followed. The man standing before me so full of passion was relying on his memory of events that had occurred seven decades before and his reminiscences were unbelievably accurate. Studs recalled the simple, direct words that the then twenty-nine-year-old Despres had uttered with intensity on the occasion, "Workers should have the right to organize."

"You spoke from your heart," Studs reminded him. Studs, then a young law school graduate and would-be actor, had never met nor heard of Len before that day; but now he could sill recall Len's speech and describe his demeanor on the occasion. The two had subsequently become close friends and shared formal and informal platforms time and again to speak on civil rights, human rights, labor, and political issues. The Pulitzer Prize winning oral history recorder took this occasion to recall with wonderful detail his own verbal account of what happened seventy years before. He spoke with continued vigorous gesture and animated expression as he recounted:

> It was ten days after the 1937 Memorial Day Massacre. It had been a massacre, a real one. The Chicago police shot and killed ten steel company strikers and billy-clubbed and gassed dozens of strikers and members of their families outside the gates of the Republic Steel Corporation factory in Southeast Chicago.

> The steelworkers had marched in protest in an effort to get the Southeast Side firm to recognize their union. At the company's request, Chicago's mayor, Ed Kelly, had sent the police there. It was supposedly to keep order, but in reality was a way to intimidate the strikers.

> The workers' wives and children had joined them on the picket line so they could picnic and celebrate Memorial Day with them.

> Allegedly, somebody threw a rock and the police began shooting, using teargas and their billy-clubs. They shot and killed ten workers and seriously wounded 35 others as photographers and news cameramen took pictures of it. A government commission later published these images and shocked the nation.

> The strikers and their families ran toward Sam's Bar, a local tavern that had been serving as their headquarters. Right afterwards, I was there at Sam's and saw injured people lying all over the place. Harry Harper, I remember, had lost an eye.

> Ten days later there was a bitter protest meeting at the Chicago Opera House. One of the speakers was Carl Sandburg, the poet. He droned on and on in a slow, monotonous voice. "The score," he said, "was ten to nothing."

> And then there was a young labor lawyer who got right to the point. His name was Leon Despres. There was no showoff stuff, no tempestuous display, only an outburst of genuine indignation. He spoke from his heart. That is what made his comments so powerful.

It was an experience I had any number of times before with Studs. His mind was in charge of the facts and quotations filed in his prodigious memory under ideals and convictions. Studs and his deeply considerate, activist wife, Ida, have been special persons in my life as well as in my wife's for a long time. He immensely admired both Carol's work as a human rights activist and then as a death penalty lawyer. Whenever we met, Studs never failed to grill me—whether on the street, in a poker game, or now in his home—immediately on what she was doing.

His and my personal relationship went back to 1965, when I wrote a book of oral interviews with the poor in Chicago, *They Speak for Themselves: Interviews with the Destitute of Chicago*. I sent him a copy.

Ida, a mutual friend later told me, had insisted Studs interview me on his WFMT radio show. I considered it at the time and still do, the best conducted and most thorough interview of my life. Studs had done his homework, underlining the sentences on more than half the pages of his copy and often quoting from my interviews without having to look at them.

Over the years, I have entertained the thought that my volume might have helped serve as a template for the great interview books he contributed to America's historical record.

*Studs Terkel making a point with Leon Despres*

He brought out his first, *Division Street: America*, 1967—two years after *They Speak for Themselves*. If nothing else, reading my work showed him that real voices of ordinary people in uninterpreted interviews can come together to produce a coherent and, I believe, readable and interesting book. Insofar as it was so, I am humbled by the possibility and ever thankful he gave us all the oral history record he did—each and every book of it.

He interviewed me on his show any number of times, invited me to his birthday parties, spoke at my bookstore, visited me at the *Tribune*, and told other poker players that I sometimes bluffed. He contributed the foreword to a book, which I wrote with Mark Frazel, titled *Hands on Chicago*. In it he honored me by stating, "When it comes to finding out all sorts of things about this town's past and much of its present, Kenan Heise is my man."

And when it came to showing me the power for good that one person can pack into one notion, curiosity for one's fellow human beings, Studs Terkel was my man and a lot of people's.

Studs lived another year and a half and had a wonderful, friend-filled ninety-fifth birthday Party at the Chicago Historical Museum. He died at the age of ninety-six on Halloween 2008.

# Part 6

# FAMILY AND THOUGHTS

# 39

## My Family Heroes
## at Their Best

*We all come across situations in which a family member or friend
gives of his or herself beyond measure for another: a disabled child, a
mentally disabled brother, a family member in prison, a relative with
Alzheimer's, an individual parent, aunt, uncle, grandparent or even
child dying from cancer, a severely wounded veteran, an alcoholic or
someone with a drug addiction.*

*Millions of such people inhabit our world and I, for one, am
comforted that I live in the same universe as they do.*

On August 16, 1956, I lay prostrate on the sanctuary floor of Duns
Scotus College chapel in Southfield, Michigan. I was face down,
participating in a ceremony in which my Franciscan classmates
and I were taking solemn, lifelong vows of poverty, obedience, and chastity. Through the latter vow to God I foreswore among other choices in
life ever getting married, having a wife or family, or fathering any children. I was taking these vows out of what I felt was the noblest of intentions, pleasing God by giving up what others treasured dearly.

Until then, however, I had never seriously considered the idea of marrying or having a family. To the best of my memory, I don't recall ever
having dreamed or fantasized about it. I had never experienced the passion or afterglow of a kiss or a hug or the ecstasy of romantic feelings.
Consequently, it was not with a painful ache or feeling of loss that I took
that vow of chastity. Fate would deal me a different hand than the one
that I had laid down on that floor to swear to hold onto.

Two and a half years after taking those vows—when I seemed useless
to my religious superiors because of their perception of my epilepsy—I
petitioned the reigning pontiff, Pope Pius XII, for release from my vows.
He, or rather his minions, in the name of God and the Church, dispensed
me from having to keep them.

Nine years and any number of attempted relationships later, Carol and I got married on April 16, 1966. Now—more than almost five decades into that marriage—we share three sons, two-daughters-in-law, four grandchildren and a dear "inherited" granddaughter. The latter, Justine Ritchie, was given the title, when Carol's and our once-upon-a-time foster daughter, her mother, Ruth Ritchie, died.

If I can look back on my life as interesting and in a number of ways meaningful, I now realize it has been because—free of those vows—I have had a family and life that afforded me extraordinary opportunities and encouragement. My family has represented an exciting and challenging upward-spiraling arc on the journey of my life. One incident stands out.

In January 2010, my youngest son, Ben—then thirty-eight years old and unmarried—had a serious, life-threatening stroke while visiting in California. There followed almost immediately a second one. He was placed in the intensive care unit of a hospital in Thousand Oaks, California and subsequently moved to a rehabilitation hospital in Long Beach, California.

Because of a recent, serious blood clot in my upper thigh, I could not travel the distance, even by train, to be there with him. Carol also had a serious health condition, trigeminal neuralgia, that made it problematic for her to fly there. Travel by train would take days and put her out of communication with Ben's caregivers.

Our eldest son, Tiger, was raising three children, working in a mental hospital, and in a full-time, extremely challenging master's degree program in nursing. Nevertheless, he left immediately from his home, work, and studies in Minnesota to spend a week in California at his brother's bedside. His return home flight across the United States passed a plane carrying our middle son, Dan, to do the same bedside sitting. The work interruption was not convenient in the least for him either. His sales job's compensation was tightly tied to quotas and required a strong push at the end of the month to meet quota if not keep his job. He, nevertheless, left for California before the month was over and spent days with his younger brother until he stabilized and carol arrived.

Eleven years earlier Ben himself had left a West Coast job to return to Evanston, where Tiger and his wife, Jill, were expecting twins. His sole reason for giving up his job and returning to Chicago was to be part of his nephews' lives and assist in any way he might in raising them. Responding to Ben's strokes and plight, Carol stayed with him for nine weeks as he recuperated. It was an intense experience and required every bit of support she was able to give.

In the meantime, our dear friends of forty-eight years, Charles and Janice Tyler, who lived in Huntington Beach, California visited Ben in the hospital and stayed with him there before Tiger arrived. They then graciously welcomed our family one by one—including eight weeks of hospitality to Carol and Ben when he was finally released from the hospital—to stay with them. Finally, when Ben still could not travel for another week and Carol had to return home, my niece, Claudea Heise, gave up a week of her vacation as a supervisor at the EPA and went to his support. Another niece, Monica Smith, also flew to California form New Jersey to spend some time with him, as did her brother, Cliff.

Ben needed all this attention as his right side was paralyzed and his voice all but gone. He underwent daily intense physical, occupational, and voice therapy to restore him successfully to his former ability and agility. Did it help?

*(Left to right) Tiger, Dan, Carol and Ben in the Vatican*

Ben, when he finally arrived back home in Chicago, immediately started working and performing in his job at the highest level. Each of those who went to California provided the encouragement, attention, and necessary chauffeuring for him to receive the therapy so necessary in the early and critical stages of recovery. Carol's therapeutic support worked wonders for our son even before she ever arrived in California. According to a nurse in his intensive care unit, her supportive voice during an hour-long phone call was able to lower his blood pressure by twenty points. Ben appreciated the consideration he was getting and his focus continued to be on getting better and finding ways to show his gratitude toward all who helped him.

Such crises are not all that rare in families, nor is the stepping forward of other family members in coming to rescue when someone is ill.

Still, those who went to Ben's aid are my special heroes, individuals with whom I have had the opportunity to share family for four decades in a multitude of situations. Often I was the one suffering an affliction and receiving such care and concern. When I had a kidney removed because of cancer, it was Ben who stayed with me through the first night.

We all come across situations in which a family member or friend gives of his or herself beyond measure for another: a disabled child, a mentally disabled brother, a family member in prison, a relative with Alzheimer's, an individual parent, aunt, uncle, grandparent or even child dying from cancer, a severely wounded veteran, an alcoholic or someone with a drug addiction. Millions of such people inhabit our world and I, for one, am comforted that I live in the same universe as they do.

As I wrote this, I happened to be in the Chicago Rehabilitation Institute witnessing the very kind of professional and personal concern of which I was writing. In front of me, a therapist and a mother were working to calm down a multiply handicapped young boy, employing a dozen forms of tenderness to reach him with the message, "You are going to be all right." Finally, the professional succeeded by telling him, "Us rocketeers can do it."

In another recent example, Carol and I recently met a woman whose teenage son was severely mentally and physically handicapped. At a large Christmas dinner we watched her help her son with an aplomb that was astounding as he glided his way through interactions with others. The mother later told Carol that that when he was young and first in school, her son would come home and beat her up every day. She persevered through that and we were witnesses to her success with him.

For the most part, these individuals' greatness and goodness are hidden behind the walls of their homes, on the next block or among a group we might be tempted to look down upon or ignore. They proliferate especially among the very poor of the world, where personal concern has to make up for much that we who live in various degrees of comfort take for granted.

I was deeply pleased and privileged to see my family's response to our son's misfortune. And seeing it, I certainly am deeply thankful I got out of that vow never to marry or have children—especially considering the spirit my wife and children have.

# 40

---

## Carol with Her Law Partner, Alan Freedman, Defend People on Death Row

*The headline reads: "Gov. Ryan Erases Death Row." The banner below it states: "Demon of Error Haunts System." The latter phrase was from the message in which the governor commuted the sentences of (or, in some instances, pardoned) 167 prisoners facing execution in Illinois. The rest of the front page personalized these individuals by printing the names of each in capital red letters. On my framed copy, thirteen of the names are circled in blue ink.*

**T**he spiritual books I absorbed in the monastery presented the world as at best a morally neutral place where everyone held values decidedly inferior to those that we in the "religious life" embraced. No one argued the point—it was a given. When I left that life, I had a lot of relearning to do and a considerable bit of pride based on my former calling to reevaluate. The process of doing either did not prove easy.

Carol provided a unique prism for me to see this and work it out. It was through her that I have gained a new appreciation of the goodness that exists in the world and slowly surrendered a lingering pride about having aspired to the priesthood.

Just as I trained to serve God, she did so to serve mankind. She earned four professional degrees in her efforts to be an effective force in helping others, especially those to whom the words "the least of my brothers (and sisters)" could apply. Over those years, Carol has been a wife, a mother, a registered nurse, a clinical psychologist, a teacher, an international human rights activist, and an attorney. For the past twenty years, she worked in seven states as a lawyer, representing persons on death row in the last stages of their appeals.

The years that she spent studying to become a professional caregiver and counselor more than doubled those during which I prepared to become a priest. Many professionals—who see the world's need and its complexity—put in the years of training she has. Doctors, nurses, teachers, economists, and scientists earn their basic degrees, get into specialties and then in many cases do extensive good for humanity. This writing effort started off a thank-you book to acknowledge how much goodness I found to exist in the world. Carol's work, her attitude, and the commitment showed me that she did what she did not merely to earn money or acknowledgment, but rather to practice her honed skills in focused, effective endeavors.

It was neither exciting nor comforting for her as a lawyer and a woman to enter a visitor's prison cage to meet with a death row inmate. I could not do it. Nor could I have worked on a locked psychiatric ward as a nurse as she had done for years. I do not have the courage or the unmitigated determination she and her law partner, Alan Freedman, showed. I use Carol as an example, not because I think she is the only person with a vision of helping others, but because she has done it so well and is the person closest to me who is doing it.

I especially appreciate her as a parent of our children. With them and our grandchildren, she is kind, generous, intelligent, and imaginative. It is difficult for others to conceive how little training I personally had much less handling an infant or raising a child, considering the fact that I spent the ages of thirteen to twenty-four in a seminary and monastery. I feel Carol has more than made up for my lack of training and set the standard for both of us.

After almost a decade involved in human rights advocacy in Cambodia and the Philippines, Carol was determined not to diminish her efforts on behalf of justice. As a result, she enrolled at John Marshall Law School in Chicago and in 1992 at the age of fifty graduated from honors.

Through our son, Tiger, who was working at our bookstore, she met Alan Freedman that same year. He was a seasoned civil rights lawyer and looking for someone to help him in an appeal on behalf of a client on death row in Michigan City, Indiana. Carol was able to assist in communicating with the truculent client, ultimately helping him to be ruled mentally retarded and ultimately being resentenced to a lengthy prison term, shortened by his efforts to make remarkable strides toward rehabilitation.

Alan and Carol—both dedicated to the work and to the clients whom they represented—subsequently formed the Midwest Center for Justice, which handles almost exclusively last stage appeals in death penalty cases. These two capital appeals lawyers work with several others including

Larry Komp, Marie Donnelly, Gary Prichard and John Magrisso, who work with them on individual cases. They do not represent their clients at trial but as their counsel in the very complex final stages of the state and federal capital appeals process.

Alan had started as a lawyer for the Legal Assistance Foundation. His masterful understanding of the law saw him early in his career build two cases that went to the United States Supreme Court. After decades of litigating civil rights cases, he eventually began representing persons facing execution. They now represent death row clients in Indiana, Ohio, Kentucky, Mississippi, Alabama, and Louisiana. They no longer have cases in Illinois because the death penalty has been abolished here.

One of my proudest possessions is a framed copy of the front page of the *Chicago Sun-Times* dated January 12, 2003. The headline reads: "Gov. Ryan Erases Death Row." The banner below it states: "Demon of Error Haunts System." The latter phrase was from the message in which the governor commuted the sentences of (or, in some instances, pardoned) 167 prisoners facing execution in Illinois. The rest of the front page personalized these individuals by printing the names of each in capital red letters. On my framed copy, thirteen of the names are circled in blue ink. They are James Ashford, Peter Burton, Paul S. Erickson, Jonathan Haynes, Demetrius Henderson, Tuhran A. Lear, Jerry Mahaffey, Johnny Neal Jr., John Pecoraro, John L. Szabo, Drew Terrell, Walter Thomas and Patrick Wright.

Attorneys Alan Freedman, his former partner, Bruce Bornstein, and later Carol represented these thirteen. Alan and Carol's firm—Midwest Center for Justice—practiced one of the most complex and emotionally challenging areas of law. A life is at stake in each case, and justice in such situations can hide in the most tangled sections of the laws that govern men and nations. Alan and Carol spoke on their clients' behalf at hearings that Illinois Gov. George Ryan held before making his final determination. While focused and eloquent on behalf of their clients, they remained sensitive to the families of the victims, many members of whom were present in the room. They respectfully acknowledged their presence and apologized for the suffering they had undergone and still were enduring.

On one occasion afterwards, one of the prosecuting attorneys—who presented the case against her clients—acknowledged his respect for the concern they demonstrated in the hearings for victims' survivors. While virtually every death row case was presented at the scores of hearings, they were the only defense attorneys who reached out to the survivors.

I framed copies of that front page of the *Sun-Times* for each of our three sons as well as myself so we could treasure and be inspired by her efforts.

Alan and Carol have been unusually successful death penalty attorneys. In the cases they accept, simple innocence—"He or she didn't do it"—is not their criteria for accepting a case, although they sometimes do not discover the full truth until after digging deep into the trial and outside records. Often, they find that glaring mistakes and daunting prejudice occurred in the proceedings, errors so serious that they offended the United States Constitution and tainted the results.

In more than half the forty-some cases they have litigated, they obtained some relief for their clients, whether it was a new hearing, a resentencing to life in prison without the possibility of parole, or a lesser sentence. It is the fate of the client, not praise and recognition for their own accomplishments that is important to them. They have a poster in their office that reads, "Those who seek publicity are not worthy of receiving it."

In many cases, lawyers attend the executions. In one instance when a condemned client asked if they were going to be present at his, Alan told him that doing so on their part could make it more difficult to accept the next case. His response was: "Don't come. I would rather have you fight for the next guy."

Despite such exchanges, Alan and Carol do not want their clients to see them as their heroes or buddies, but rather that they desire to establish a sufficiently meaningful rapport with them to research the case and defend them as best they can.

Carol is my friend because of who she is, and my hero because she is deeply concerned about "the other."

Why are Carol and I so against the death penalty? One reason is found in the words of Clarence Darrow: "There is just one thing in all this question. It is question of how you feel, that is all. If you love the idea of somebody being killed, why, you are for it. If you hate the thought of somebody being killed, you are against it."

# 41

## My Grandchildren's
## Spoiled Rotten Day

*And this special one-day focus on my grandchildren's specialness works. I know it does because it has communicated exactly what it was intended to and secondly, because my grandchildren—by the time they were five or six years old—brought it back to me on their own and wanted to spread it to others.*

**E**volution has a special and unique way of bonding first and third generation humans—grandparents and grandchildren. It is an effective and affectionate means to communicate care, concern, traits, and memory. We could call it "spoiling." I wonder whether it exists elsewhere in the animal kingdom.

To Carol and me—and probably to most, but not to all—grandparents, spoiling comes naturally. Perhaps because I cannot recall my own grandparents bonding with me, I looked for and found a way to personalize and institutionalize this means of connection so my own spoiling would be more meaningful. My grandchildren and I created what we call: Spoiled Rotten Day.

And this one unique day focuses on their specialness works. I know because it communicated exactly what it was intended to and secondly, because my grandchildren—by the time they were five or six years old— brought it back to me on their own and wanted to spread it to others. This is its story, the history, and the outline of my grandchildren's and my Spoiled Rotten Days.

My maternal grandmother and my paternal grandfather died before I was born. When I was little, realizing I did have one grandmother and one grandfather (albeit on different sides of my family), I asked, "Why don't grandma and grandpa get married?" I thought it was a good idea. My parents considered it so "cute" that they told their friends about it. Other than that it was not an ingenious idea, I recall no affectionate incident that bonded myself with either living grandparent.

When our oldest son, Tiger, and his wife, Jill Schwendeman, announced they were going to have not one child, but twins, I was happy for them but a little challenged. I have deep vein thrombosis in both legs—I had had blood clots several times. Would I ever be able to pick up my twin grandchildren, much less carry them up and down from their third-floor apartment? How would my not being able to walk with them in my arms hinder the relationship I might so easily otherwise have with them?

I worried in vain. My legs were not as much of a problem in lifting or carrying them as I had projected. I was able to pick the babies up and tote them short distances. And we developed a relationship, affectionate and unique. For one thing, I retired from the *Chicago Tribune* about the time they were born. For a second reason, both of them proved to be easy and extraordinarily sweet babies. And, thirdly, their being twins obviously meant that their parents could use the time and help I was willing to give in the form of babysitting or just playing with them.

By going to work selling flowers door to door when I was five years old, I had missed a vital element in my childhood. My focus and pleasure derived too much at that age from succeeding and providing a part of my family's earnings rather than from playing. My twin grandsons, Skyler and Soren, helped me fill in a part of my development, which had been missing. They taught me how to play and enjoy doing so.

Then when they were four years old came the bombshell. My son, his wife, and my grandchildren were going to move to Stillwater, Minnesota, four hundred miles away. It was news that was especially painful to me because I do not fly and the distance would represent an extra challenge on my part in being able to visit them. We have worked out a solution: I, by taking Amtrak; and they, by readily and often driving the distance back and forth.

But the separation—the profound reality of it and the extra burden it would entail—was at the time like a serious limp in my walking into a future I had envisioned. I loved the relationship that the two four-year-old boys and I had developed, and I wanted it to grow and blossom—not to be curtailed in any way—as both they and I grew older. Then came the idea: Spoiled Rotten Day.

Spoiled Rotten Day is not simply about treats and gifts, although it is about those also. Usually, the day is the first full one after they or I arrive for a visit. It has an elaborate set of traditions that represent one-day rights for them to be free of certain constraints. The list, over the years, has grown.

First of all, they (and, over time, all or any of my grandchildren) do not have to say "please" or "thank you" to me on that day. They do to others as usual, but the requirement—as far as it involves me—is suspended for the one designated day.

The day always begins with the same ritual. I make pancakes and give them a strict and stern lecture about limiting the amount of syrup they put on their pancakes to a mere drop. I even attempt to hold the bottle as they pour the brown liquid, but somehow every single time we have done it, each of them has managed to create a lake of syrup rather than a droplet of it on their pancakes. I grumble about their behavior. They giggle.

In addition, there is a list of rules that are suspended for the day. It started with the boys being allowed at the age of four to go into the refrigerator on their own, releasing a restriction that otherwise was not stated, but nevertheless understood.

Next our attic! They were never to go into our attic, which was restrict-

*Skyler, Grandpa Kenan, and Soren.*
*Who is "spoiling" whom?*

ed because the chaotic arrangement of boxes, contraptions could be a danger or at least a hazard for small children and an unsecured window out of which they could fall. In addition, next to the front window, was a large papier-mâché tiger that looked out on passing small children (and adults.) On Spoiled Rotten Day, with supervision, the boys could go up to the attic, look around and say "hello" to the tiger.

There next is the now obligatory visit not only to the nearby toy store (or, at their house, the local Target department store), but also to a second hand shop. And creative thinking has added special treats such as my pulling them in the backyard on a toboggan even though there was no snow.

Julian, who came along five and a half years later, now has his own list. He loves the train with consuming passion. So, since stops for both the METRA and the "L" are only blocks away, I am able to take him one way on a short METRA ride and we then can return on the "L." And, of course, we visited the toystore (now defunct) and nearby "Dave's Rock Shop, which he loves no less than the train.

Adeline, the four-year-old daughter of my son Dan and his wife, Amanda Jones, has also started enjoying the honored customs of Spoiled Rotten Day. She loves the train ride every bit as much as Julian does.

And, before going to bed, each of them gets a story of their choosing told or read to them by me or their grandmother (who, in their opinion, is better at it).

What happened very quickly in the history of Spoiled Rotten Day was that Soren and Skyler came up with the idea that I too should have one myself, and it should come the day after theirs. On my Spoiled Rotten Day, each of them made a special card or a gift for me and, if they happened to be arguing or fussing, I had the right to remind them and they do stop immediately.

Julian, at the age of six, had a different approach. He shared it with Grandma before he generously gave it to me—he would take me for a ride on the train and a visit to Dave's Rock Shop, as I had done for him the day before.

And, I don't remember whether it was Skyler or Soren who said it—but it does not matter—"Every kid should have a Spoiled Rotten Day."

I may be eighty years old and no longer what the world calls young, but we each and every one of us has fun and, based on the results, some worthwhile and meaningful experiences. And we all have come to the conclusion that "spoiled is good" and the children and grandparents of this world could stand to have a lot more of it.

We have had our experiences with Spoiled Rotten Day photographed by portrait photographer Carol Mosolygo. She and our four spoiled-rotten grandchildren and Carol Mosolygo and I have self-published them as a book titled *Spoiled Rotten Day* (AuthorHouse, 2011).

While for the twins, Spoiled Rotten Day is no longer as special as it once was, it remains a treasured memory of our youth together. And their younger brother and cousin anticipate it as much as they did.

I have started extending Spoiled Rotten Day to other neighborhood children. I love it. And they tend to like it, too.

# 42

## If You Were King or Queen
## of the United States of America?

*Americans have always assumed, subconsciously, that all problems
can be solved; that every story has a happy ending; that the application
of energy and good will can make everything come out right.*

ADLAI E. STEVENSON, *CALL TO GREATNESS*, 1954

A friend who loves thought-provoking questions challenged me,
"What would you do if you were king of the United States of
America?" My answer:

Hold an election tomorrow or as soon as possible to dethrone me.

Do everything I could to get everyone I could to participate in it.

As a citizen, take personal responsibility for our nation, its morality,
and its future.

Down deep, to me this is what being an American means. We do not
need a king or queen—not even should one be able to solve this country's problems, or even if you or I were that king or queen. We are a
democracy, and problems—we have tons of them—but as Al Smith, the
1928 Democratic candidate for President, said, "The cure for the ills of
democracy is more democracy."

We are a nation of kings and queens. Every voter in this country is
one. Since our nation's earliest days, we have been committed to a political system that relies on us as citizens rather than either tyrannical or
even benevolent monarchs to govern ourselves. No matter what the situation is, we basically need to rely on the simple decency of the people and
what Thomas Jefferson called their (and our) "latent wisdom."

It all comes down to you, to me—to us—and to our willingness to
take personal responsibility and to believe it can matter. Ultimately, it
depends on respect for one another and each person's rights and even
their feelings.

The Tea Party members and conservative radio hosts, no matter how right or wrong they might be on issues, often fail to realize that friendship and cooperation trump meanness and competitiveness. The opposite of democracy is the feeling that the people (including ourselves) cannot make things better, so we should let those who promise that they supposedly share our ideas, our values, our convictions, and backgrounds do it.

All of democracy—I believe—comes down to whether we believe in and trust one another and ourselves. We may be tempted to complain continuously about how stupid almost everyone else but us is, how red-state people might be stunted by religious righteousness, or the blue-state ones by secularism. In the end, our mission is to come together and make certain that the government of the people, by the people, and for the people shall not perish from this earth.

The best way to learn to believe this more ourselves is to teach others. It is neither civil war nor an angry mob action but the open democratic process through which respect is maintained and our deepest values preserved.

# 43

## A Great Adventure

*Be kind, for everyone you meet is fighting a great battle.*

PHILO OF ALEXANDRIA

*Each of us has cause to think with deep gratitude of those who have lighted the flame within us.*

ALBERT SCHWEITZER

Like any autobiography, this book is about me. But it is also about you and them—the interesting and fascinating individuals who have helped me and all of us become happier, more meaningful human beings. My life had hurdles, but people who were close to me and ones whom I had never met assisted me in getting over them. I thank them.

And this is about you, because it is about kindness and all who helped any of us in any way to be who we are. We live in the land of the free among good and considerate people. And this, for me, is what has been and is a blessing on my days on this earth. For this kind of help and support—the kind I could pass along—I am doubly thankful.

I had once wanted to be a priest, which I thought to be the most giving of professions. I studied years toward being ordained. Because, however, I developed epilepsy, the Catholic Church's canon law stopped me. My life went on, but in a very different direction.

I earned my living first as a door-to-door salesman and then for more than fifty years as a journalist and author, despite the fact that writing for me has been more of a challenge than a natural talent.

My training as a journalist was limited, consisting principally of studying thirteenth and fourteenth century scholastic philosophy in Latin. Furthermore, because I am an almost hopeless idealist, I readily tend to overreach whatever talents I do have.

Yet the alternate life I found to the priesthood and monastery has been good. The paths I have gone down have proved fascinating and rewarding. And I have accomplished my hopes and dreams beyond what I ever thought I would. My moments of meditation are on how much I owe this to the concern, generosity, and help of others.

I write this book not only because the kindnesses I have received have resulted in a great adventure but also because any of its rewards are shared, reciprocal ones. I borrowed the title of this chapter from the words of Louis Sullivan:

> Kindness, seemingly so weak, is in fact the name of a great adventure which mankind thus far has lacked the courage, the intelligence, the grit to undertake.
>
> It is the quiet, the serene forces of nature that are the most powerful; and the force we call democracy, lying inexpressibly deepdown in the heart and the spirit of man, is seeking, ever seeking its expression.

He was speaking not of patronizing acts of benevolence that some would substitute for justice, but rather of genuine expressions of friendship and inclusion. In providing heartfelt help to others or accepting it, we prove ourselves not their betters nor their servants but one with them as their democratic equals.

Moments of concern, efforts to help, deeds of care and beauty—both great and small—go back millions of years. They each reach back even before our ancestors were fully human, and number at this point more than all the stars in the sky and leaves on the trees. Those who showered them on others and on me, we need—I need—to thank.

I have at times perceived myself as insignificant and invisible, but the caring of others assured me I was not. I have wondered at times whether people did care, but learned and relearned that they can and they do.

A "thank you" is big, not so much when our parents tell us to say it or when we mouth it inattentively; but when it is a deliberate token of gratitude and appreciation between equals, it is ennobling for both.

In this book, I have acknowledged and thanked a number of individuals, to reciprocate and mentioned names in doing so. But I have at best done this with a comparative few rather than the many to whom I am in debt, the scattered stars rather than the universe of them.

These pages point to some of the concerns and acts of fairness I have experienced, the people who have been just and good to me and to others. Even starting to add them up takes me back to the better moments of my life. My gratitude is not toward concern itself, but rather to the people up and down the line, as they say, who showed it.

A "thank you" is rarely equivalent to the deed, the smile, the help, and the concern shown. So let it be in this case. Yet writing this book has brought back so much of the excitement, richness, and magic of other people's personas that I am compelled to express it.

The story of those to whom I owe thanks goes back a long way, through evolution to every creature and character in my lineage who fought for survival for itself, its species and its young. It touches back through eons to those who stretched themselves to become more than they were, to crawl up out of the water, stand on their two feet and migrate toward a better life.

I thank them. I do so emphatically. They lived their days and their shortened years in behalf of that to which their best instincts, if not fully understood the challenge of humans to be "better angels," led them—life itself and its perpetuation.

And I was—as were you too—the beneficiary of each individual who reached to give what was good to those who would arrive in the future. These daring, caring individuals invented hope and made it the North Star of the aspiring individuals on this earth. They fashioned love out of the clay of instinct and helped evolve the muscles of their face to create approving and encouraging smiles. Their ingenuities, adaptations and experimentation worked to expand their brains and ours, adapt their hands and ours, and grow the size of their hearts and ours.

I thank also the people of history who survived hunger, war, and pestilence at prices beyond my imagination to perpetuate our species and return it to its task of continuing its existence, living, and loving.

I thank Lucy of Africa, whose bones we have from a million years ago, the unnamed mothers, midwives, and vulnerable female children who were the glue of the families that bravely migrated forth from Africa to almost every unknown sector of the world.

I thank the males for their resourcefulness, hunting and gathering instincts, their courage as well as their protection of the less strong, sometimes with their lives.

My gratitude goes out to those human beings who first grasped individual consciousness as an expansion of their existence and turned it into communication, concern, culture, art, philosophy, caring, and sharing.

I thank the great heroes of history: Buddha, Hatshepsut, Abraham and Sarah, Moses, Homer and Plato, Sappho, Euripides, Aristotle, Eratosthenes, and every woman who worked to earn the good name of mother, daughter, or sister.

I thank the prophets, wise men, Jesus of Nazareth, and the good people of religious hope and concern.

I am grateful to the many who suffered so much want, hurt, hatred and disdain, all the time keeping alive the spark of humanity.

I thank the rebellious and the questioners who cut paths through the dense forests of blind obedience, obsequies and righteousness.

I thank the writers, scribes, bookmakers, librarians, newspaper staff, and booksellers who joined together to catch the lightening of enlightenment in a bottle and send it on a journey that washed up on my shore.

I offer thanks to the migrants of history who, adjusting to the need for room and sustenance, populated the earth and expanded its possibilities.

I do not express any of these "thanks" without emotion and genuine appreciation, and I apologize if it is in any way self-serving. My gratitude goes to those who sustained life itself in the worst of disasters and most impossible of situations.

I appreciate the Arabs who protected the ancient world wisdom through the Dark Ages, the scribes who copied the documents, the scholars who transcribed and translated them and the librarians who preserved them.

I am grateful to Dante for writing *The Divine Comedy* and allegorically stretching the literary tools of man to describe human nature.

I thank the millions who died from the Black Death from 1347 to 1350 because many of them tended to others and consequently became afflicted themselves, leaving behind a memory greater than the culture, art, and writing that was almost destroyed along with human life.

Thank you, Johannes Gutenberg, for changing the world in which we live by inventing a process for mass-producing movable type, the use of oil-based ink, and the wooden printing press.

I thank those who opened the world's mind to the scientific method, to inductive reasoning, to the benefits of curiosity over absolute certainty, to the idea of fact and inquiry over hammered faith and closed-minded certainty.

I thank those who discovered experience as a steady and true road to knowledge.

My thanks is humbling when I extend it to Michelangelo, Leonardo DaVinci, and other fifteenth, sixteenth, and seventeenth century artists, sculptors, writers, and architects who created a new world of the beautiful, lasting and inspiring.

I thank William Shakespeare for every line his characters uttered.

I thank the men and women of the Renaissance, who in so many ways cracked open the doors to the modern world and its possibilities.

I thank those who dared to esteem tolerance, acceptance, and common concern over the heavily rewarded "virtues" of obedience and loyalty first and foremost.

I thank for their forbearance those people unjustly or unnecessarily imprisoned.

I thank Thomas Jefferson for focusing this nation on human rights by writing the Declaration of Independence with the words and ideas he used.

I thank Abraham Lincoln for reminding us that we are a "nation, conceived in Liberty, and dedicated to the proposition that all men are created equal."

I thank Franklin Delano Roosevelt for showing us that we as a nation in need an economic bill of rights as well as a political one.

I thank Dr. Martin Luther King for challenging Americans to have a dream for this country, a very big and generous one.

Yet, more than anything, I am thankful to all the people who in a dark, scattered-site, resourceless world worked alone or together to keep alive and bright the grand sparks of life, will, and intellect.

I want to thank also nineteen-year-old Confederate Sergeant Richard Kirkland of the 2nd South Carolina Volunteers for his inspiring act of kindness. The young soldier, unable to bear the moans of the wounded and dying Union troops left from behind a stonewall during the Battle of Fredericksburg to offer them succor. Although refused permission by a Confederate general to help them under the protection of a white flag, he loaded himself with canteens, crossed the wall and spent an hour and a half reliving their suffering, both sides gave him a rousing cheer for doing so. He died a year later during the Battle of Chickamauga and is buried in the Quaker cemetery in Camden, South Carolina.

I personally want to thank every one of my friends for being a friend.

And to the kind as well as the imaginative and heroic individuals who went before us, I say with appreciation, "By God, they did it."